Professional Communication Skills in Social Work

D0073732

Professional Communication Skills in Social Work

Nancy Sidell
Mansfield University

Denise Smiley
Lackawanna College

Boston   New York   San Francisco
Mexico City   Montreal   Toronto   London   Madrid   Munich   Paris
Hong Kong   Singapore   Tokyo   Cape Town   Sydney

Senior Series Editor: Patricia Quinlin
Series Editorial Assistant: Nakeesha Warner
Marketing Manager: Laura Lee Manley
Production Editor: Pat Torelli
Editorial Production Service: GGS Book Services
Composition Buyer: Linda Cox
Manufacturing Buyer: Debbie Rossi
Electronic Composition: GGS Book Services
Cover Administrator: Elena Sidorova

For related titles and support materials, visit our online catalog at www.ablongman.com.

Copyright © 2008 Pearson Education, Inc.

All rights reserved. No part of the material protected by this copyright notice may be reproduced or utilized in any form or by any means, electronic or mechanical, including photocopying, recording, or by any information storage and retrieval system, without written permission from the copyright owner.

To obtain permission(s) to use material from this work, please submit a written request to Allyn and Bacon, Permissions Department, 75 Arlington Street, Boston, MA 02116 or fax your request to 617-848-7320.

Between the time website information is gathered and then published. it is not unusual for some sites to have closed. Also, the transcription of URLs can result in typographical errors. The publisher would appreciate notification where these errors occur so that they may be corrected in subsequent editions.

ISBN-13: 978-0-205-52421-1
ISBN-10: 0-205-52421-4

Library of Congress Cataloging-in-Publication Data

Sidell, Nancy.
    Professional communication skills in social work/Nancy Sidell, Denise Smiley.
        p. cm.
    Includes bibliographical references and index.
    ISBN 978-0-205-52421-1 (alk. paper)
    1. Communication in social work. 2. Social work education. 3. Social work administration. I. Smiley, Denise. II. Title.
    HV29.7.S53 2008
    361.301′4–dc22   2007016515

Printed in the United States of America

10 9 8 7 6 5 4 3 2 1   11 10 09 08 07

To Michael Sidell who always supports me
—NLS

To my children, Brandon and Jonathan, and my best friend, Clifford:
Many thanks for your support and encouragement
—DLS

CONTENTS

PART THREE Professional Verbal
and Nonverbal Communication

4 What Are Verbal and Nonverbal
Communication Skills?   64

PART FIVE   Communicating with Clients

8   What Is Cultural Diversity?   123

PREFACE

Welcome to the Social Work profession. As future members of the profession, it is important to understand how social workers communicate with one another and their clients. The purpose of this book is to introduce you to professional communication. The goals include:

1. Enhancing your understanding of written, verbal, and nonverbal communication concepts.
2. Providing references and direction for conducting social work research.
3. Learning important terms used in the social work profession.
4. Preparing for practice courses and field education experiences.
5. Ultimately, preparing you for professional social work practice.

In the field of social work, professional communication skills are necessary when working with clients, social agencies, and communities. Each chapter in this book reiterates the need for social workers to possess proficient communication skills in work and social settings.

Chapter One provides historical details about the formation of social work and the various past and present contributors to the field. Understanding the social work environment and context serves to increase your communication skills, resulting in a successful social work practicum.

Chapter Two discusses the expectations and practice of social work. Exploring various social work settings, fields, and demographics of rural and urban areas will assist you in deciding the type of social work that you would like to do in your geographic area of interest. Recent activity and competition relating to various social work fields and education are also included. This chapter will assist you in developing a professional and impressive resumé and cover letter, along with preparing you for an interview. The professional communication tools implemented throughout the chapter will assist you in the "self-promotion" process, and capturing the attention of a prospective employer.

As you move to Chapter Three, the process of carrying out social work research is presented in great detail. You will be exposed to available literature and the steps to take in order to access and use up-to-date and current resources in both the library and on the Internet. Peer-reviewed journal article components are broken down and explained to assist you in understanding the process of scholarly research conducted in the social work field. Also provided are the tools to aid you in developing your own professional social work research for publication.

Chapter Four discusses the value in being acutely aware of the significance of nonverbal language and behavior displayed in various contexts. A large percentage of communication is nonverbal, thus it is essential for you to be familiar with the PERCEIVE concept so that you can successfully decode your client's nonverbal language and behavior. Numerous concepts and terms pertinent to establishing and maintaining effective communication with your client are presented in the chapter.

Chapter Five begins to link your classroom learning and experiential education together. Classroom learning and experience work together in preparing you for a successful career in social work. This chapter prepares you for supervision by providing various scenarios you can practice with classmates to increase your professional communication skills. It also provides you with the necessary tools to resolve supervision issues. By understanding your role, the role of your supervisor, and increasing your professional communication skills, you will be able to get the most out of your practicum or internship.

Chapter Six stresses that your primary mission as a social worker is to enhance human well-being and assist in meeting the basic human needs of all people in a community. You can do this by earning the trust of your clients and the community you serve. *Right to privacy, confidentiality, and privileged communications* that provide the link to building client trust are discussed. Justifications for privilege, exceptions to the rule, and threats to confidentiality are also presented in this chapter. By understanding all these components of confidentiality, you can establish client trust, and increase your ability to communicate in a professional manner with your clients.

Chapter Seven discusses the importance of proper documentation in social work. To ensure the client's situation is correctly assessed and understood, and appropriate planning and intervention are implemented, proper service documentation is critical. It is essential that the content in client files is accurate, and that you use the proper type of case note recordings in your practicum. The chapter contains scenarios and hands-on documentation exercises to enhance your written professional communication skills necessary for preparing social work documentation.

Chapter Eight focuses on the importance of cultural competence, or being able to relate to, and understand, various cultures. With cultural competence, you will gain a personal awareness of your own culture, while equipping you with the tools to understand various client cultures. Remaining open-minded and empathetic to various client cultures will enable you to serve clients in the most effective and positive manner. The chapter provides hands-on exercises that reinforce the various concepts surrounding culture competence. With this, you are able to enter the social work field equipped with skills that can be used in a culturally diverse society.

The importance and controversial issues of spirituality, religion and secularism in the social work field are discussed in Chapter Nine. Spirituality, religion and secularism are defined and contrasted in order to assist you in understanding the tenets of social work. Maintaining client diversity acceptance and sensitivity in relation to the concepts is emphasized. Also discussed is client empowerment because it is the central theme to professional social work. Client empowerment emphasizes the client's strengths, resiliency, coping style, and ability to succeed. All these elements are pertinent to accentuating your client's success. Various strategies to assist you in facilitating the empowerment process are highlighted in the chapter. Spirituality and empowerment work together in the team-oriented process you will have with your client.

Chapter Ten exposes you to the diversity that exists in the social work field. It is pertinent that you consider each client's cultural and gender aspects when developing client interview questions. Examples of open- and closed-ended questions and hands-on client interviewing exercises are included in the chapter. The examples and exercises will assist you in gaining a thorough understanding of how social workers professionally communicate with their clients during the interview process.

Chapter Eleven defines the reflection process that is used with clients in the social work field. Successful client reflection requires empathy, understanding and professional verbal and nonverbal communication skills. The three types of reflection include content, feeling and thinking or meaning reflection, and these concepts and applications are highlighted for you in the chapter. You and your classmates should take advantage of the individual and group reflection practice exercises in the chapter so that you learn to properly use the reflection process with your clients. These exercises will also aid you in further developing various professional communication skills needed in social work.

Chapter Twelve will assist you in perfecting the art of positive confrontation skills so that you can communicate with your clients in a constructive and direct manner. Positive confrontation skills are used in social work so that communication between the worker and client remains honest and encouraging. The chapter contains a *Do's* and *Don'ts* of positive client confrontation section so that you can see the negative consequences of this technique if it is not used properly. Information giving is discussed due to the important role it plays in providing the proper and professional services your client needs and deserves. It is intended that this chapter will help you increase your professional communication skills relating to both positive client confrontation and information giving.

Chapter Thirteen focuses on cultural characteristics of the rural community due to social work increasing in this specific geographic area. It is essential that you understand the diverse cultural characteristics of a rural community. Being aware of the fact that each rural area is unique is especially important if you choose this geographical location to practice social work. Being equipped with accurate information and facts, along with having a thorough understanding of your clients' various lifestyles and behaviors, will assist you in the communication process with your clients. It is essential that you become familiar with ethical issues that exist in a rural community so that you are able to communicate with those you serve in a professional and successful manner.

Chapter Fourteen ties all the components of the book together for you in an all-embracing manner. Various professional communication skills pertinent to the social work profession are briefly reviewed, with concepts and procedures pertaining to social work duties and responsibilities highlighted. The chapter reiterates the need for you, as a social worker, to acquire various professional communication skills and tools that are necessary in your contribution to continuing the success of the social work profession.

This entire textbook is laid out in a user-friendly way. Important terms, concepts, and skill-building communication tools are highlighted throughout the chapters, along with being listed in the *Key Words and Concepts* section at the end of each chapter. Simple, easy-to-understand charts and tables listing permanent and interesting information can be found throughout the textbook. Thus, this book provides a concise picture of the social work field, and the significance of having professional communication skills. It is a practical addition to every social worker's professional library.

ACKNOWLEDGMENTS

The authors' appreciation goes to the following persons for their assistance and support: Gayle Kreitzer, Dr. Timothy Madigan, Dr. Thomas Caulwell, Amelia Van Tol, Dr. John Mansfield, and Dr. Janice Purk.

We would also like to thank the following reviewers: Arturo Acosta, El Paso Community College; Margaret Elbow, Texas Tech University; and Larry Livingston, University of Illinois-Springfield.

Professional Communication Skills in Social Work

1

History of Social Work

In order to understand the importance of possessing professional communication skills when working in social work, you must have historical details about the discipline. Also, understanding the social work environment and context is pertinent to your professional social work practicum. So, before you begin your communication skills-building journey, let's look at some very important historical events surrounding the development of social work, and at various past and present contributors who have been diligent in making the field of social work a successful practice.

Section One: Formation of Social Work in England

Elizabethan Poor Laws

Organized charity began in England in 1601 under the direction of Henry VIII. Under his direction, the government took over the Church's human services functions and developed a program known as the Elizabethan Poor Laws. This particular program provided shelter and care for the disadvantaged (Colby & Dziegielewski, 2001; Johnson et al., 1998; Schmolling, Youkeles, & Burger, 1993). Under the Elizabethan Poor Laws system, the disadvantaged were grouped into three categories:

1. The poor who were capable of working
2. The poor who could not work due to age, disability, or motherhood responsibilities
3. Orphaned and/or abandoned children (become wards of the state)

(*Disadvantaged group source*: Schmolling et al., 1993)

Unfortunately, the citizens who were considered "work-able" under the Elizabethan Poor Laws spent their days laboring in state-operated workhouses. Life in the workhouses was barely tolerable, characterized by immense overcrowding, filth, and inadequate food and sanitary conditions. Those who were considered incapable of working were placed in *almshouses* (poorhouses) so they could receive food and shelter. Conditions in the almshouses mirrored those in the workhouses (Schmolling et al., 1993).

Thomas Bernard

Eventually, citizens such as Thomas Bernard, a social reformist in the late 1790's, were aroused to anger by the increase in the number of poor living in destitute conditions and being abused by the government's policies and laws. Adding to this anger were ill-managed relief programs and misuse of funds. Many citizens knew something needed to be done to help the poor and impoverished citizens of London (Huff, 2002; Strode, 1940).

With support and assistance from the Bishop of Durham, Thomas Bernard founded *The Society for Bettering the Condition and Increasing the Comforts of the Poor* in 1796. With this program, the problems of the poor and impoverished were assessed, and the goal was to "work intelligently for their happiness" (Strode, 1940, p. 16). The care and concern for the poor and impoverished started with Bernard but did not stop there. Some of the English leaders who became prominent spokesmen on poverty and the organizations that were established for the poor in England after 1796 are presented in Table 1.1.

Octavia Hill

Octavia Hill (1838–1912) is best known as the "Pioneer Social Worker." Hill purchased condemned houses in the slum sections of London in 1865. Through hard work and persistence, the houses were remodeled, rebuilt, and rented to the poor for a fee they could afford (Barker, 1995; Ramsay, 1991; Strode, 1940).

Hill believed in "helping the poor to better their own condition rather than provide them with funds that lacked sympathy and counsel." Hill states, they should provide "not

TABLE 1.1   England's Historical Organizations and Leaders in Social Work

Name of Organization	Year of Formation	Purpose
London Mendicancy Society	1805	To assess the problems of the poor and to provide charity and compassion.
London Charity Organization Society	1870	"The diminution of poverty and pauperism by cooperation of benevolent forces and the diffusion of knowledge touching charity and benevolence" (Strode, 1940, p. 16).
English leaders from the universities of Cambridge, Oxford, and London		
Charles Kingsley John Ruskin Dr. Thomas Arnold Charles Bosanquet Cardinal Newman William E. Gladstone	1870's–1900	They all played an important role in the charity organization movement, along with having an important bearing on the character of the movement.

(*Table 1.1 content sources:* Barker, 1995; Colby & Dziegielewski, 2001; Strode, 1940)

alms but a friend," and "It is not enough that what we do is benevolent, we must ascertain that it is really beneficent too," (Strode, 1940, p. 17). Through her philosophy and ground-work, Hill, among other contributors to the social work field in England, also provided the foundation for social welfare programs in America (Barker, 1995; Huff, 2002; Ramsay, 1991; Schmolling et al., 1993).

Section Two: Formation of Social Work in America

America's Social Welfare Programs

The early organized charities in America were based on the five principles laid down by the *Early London Charity Organization Society*. The principles included:

- The **coordination** of relief-giving agencies to prevent duplication of effort and over-lapping of services.
- The **substitution** of friendly counsel, assistance in securing employment, medical aid, and other services for monetary relief.
- The **individualization** of causes of poverty.
- **Continuation** of the principles of less *eligibility;* nothing should be done for the poor that would make their lot better than that of the poorest laborer who provided for his own needs.
- **Persistence** of the belief that the righteous prospered and that the poor were some-how to blame for their own poverty.

(*Early London Charity Organization Society source*: Strode, 1940, p. 17)

Social Welfare during the Industrial Revolution Era

The late nineteenth and early twentieth centuries were periods when America underwent many societal changes. With the beginning of the Industrial Revolution, immigration and urbanization were all in full swing. Society was changing rapidly, and one consequence of the United States' transformation was an increase in the number of poor and impoverished. Severe poverty and despicable living conditions became the lot—at least initially—for most European immigrants who came to America seeking a better life. Many of the established citizens residing in the eastern part of the United States, especially New York, Pennsylvania, and Massachusetts, strongly felt something needed to be done to aid America's newcomers and improve their living conditions (Colby & Dziegielewski, 2001; Huff, 2002; Morales & Sheafor, 1998; Schmolling et al., 1993; Strode, 1940).

Indeed, the living conditions for the immigrants arriving on the eastern shores of New York, Philadelphia, and Boston were appalling. With no inland facilities to house the newcomers, the immigrants met with employment and assimilation barriers and they had to take residence on nearby shores. Starvation, illness, crowded living conditions, poor sanitation, blatant begging, and depravity could be seen everywhere. Government relief was not sufficient, nor could private charities eliminate the horrific living conditions of the newcomers (Schmolling et al., 1993; Strode, 1940).

Boston's Charity Organizations.   Reverend Joseph Tuckerman's organization, the *Boston Society for the Prevention of Pauperism* (1835), which provided services to poor families, influenced the development of the Charity Organization societies in the 1870s (Barker, 1995). Also formed in Boston, much later, in 1875, was the *Cooperative Society of Visitors Among the Poor*, an organization that offered a program comparable to the one Octavia Hill established in London (Strode, 1940).

New York's Charity Organization Society.   The first ***Charity Organization Society*** in the United States was established in Buffalo in 1877. The obligations of these societies surrounding the administering of relief included the following:

- ***Registration:*** The agencies participating in the organization were required to fill out a card for each case they were working on. All the cards were filed in the society's central office in order to prevent overlapping of services and fraud. Eventually, confidentially became a concern, and the central file only included objective facts. The confidential information remained with the individual agency servicing the family.
- ***Investigation:*** The investigation proceedings were carried out by paid agents who were believed to be well informed about methods. They were also responsible for instructing and training the social workers, or "friendly visitors," all of whom were volunteers at this time.
- ***Recording:*** When the organization first began, the recorded information was kept in public files at the registration office. However, due to confidentiality, the *National Conference of Charities and Correction* recommended that the data be secured.
- ***District Plans:*** Cities were divided into districts, with a paid superintendent or secretary assigned to each district. Through this system, neighborhood offices were opened to provide easier access of services to the needy. The secretary and/or superintendent and the social workers were able to provide better assistance to the clients because they were familiar with the area and its demographics. Eventually, social workers were able to maintain a friendly and neighborly attitude toward the applicants and their problems. Cooperation also increased between fellow workers and community resources. Meetings between staff and agencies were also held.
- ***Referral:*** According to Strode (1940), "An accepted function of the charity organization societies was acting as a clearinghouse of welfare information" (p. 21). Social workers were responsible for knowledge of all the social resources and the specific aid each one provided. They also had the duty of referring clients to hospitals, clinics, recreation centers, day nurseries, soup kitchens, and various other services that the client needed.
- ***Provident Schemes:*** To maintain the organization's philosophy of "rendering services rather than giving relief," the societies developed *provident schemes*. Provident-loan funds, lodging for homeless men, wood-yards providing employment, nurseries and kindergartens for mothers with children, legal-aid, and working-girl associations were set up through the social workers. Social work committees were

also formed to investigate societal problems such as tuberculosis and juvenile delin-quency. These committees laid the legislative foundation for various social services.

■ *Relief Giving:* Eventually, most of the charity organizations operated for social work turned to the practice of providing relief rather than services. This change occurred because various agencies labeled social workers "uncharitable," and numerous clients were resistant to character-building and just wanted instant "relief" to take care of their situation.

■ *Friendly Visiting:* The roots of social work lay in the philosophy of "friendly visit-ing." The 1878 proceedings of the *National Conference of Charities and Corrections* stated that "visitors of the poor" were to be voluntary positions. Some of New York's leading citizens, including Theodore Roosevelt, assisted in establishing an organized system of voluntary visiting to check on clients and report their status. The system was also established to ensure that intelligent sympathy and proper aid were given to those who needed it and to "weed out" those who were abusing the system. The con-cept of "friendly visiting" had an official definition to go with the organized system that was established earlier. According to Strode (1940), the 1887 proceedings of the *National Conference of Charities and Corrections* defined friendly visiting as "an agency of social reform, to which we look for the elevation of the poor and ignorant" (Putnam, M., 1887, p. 149 as cited by Strode, 1940, p. 23).

(*Organization Society's obligations sources*: Colby & Dziegielewski, 2001; Huff, 2002; Johnson et al., 1998; Putnam, M., 1887; Strode, 1940)

Section Three: Important Contributors to Social Work

Jane Addams and Ellen Gates Starr

Jane Addams and Ellen Gates Starr pooled their efforts and established the most famous nineteenth-century settlement house, *Hull House*, in 1889. The house was opened in a poor west-side Chicago neighborhood and helped forge a strong bond between the immi-grants and social workers, along with "bridging the gap" between rich and poor. By the twentieth century, the United States had over one hundred settlement houses. In 1931, Jane Addams was the first American woman to win the Nobel Peace Prize (Colby & Dziegielewski, 2001; Henslin, 2005; Huff, 2002; Johnson et al., 1998; Morales & Sheafor, 1998; Schmolling et al., 1993).

Mary E. Richmond

Mary E. Richmond, America's social work pioneer/leader, is known for her writings sur-rounding the philosophy of *scientific charity*. Richmond's works include the following:

1. **"The Need of a Training School in Applied Philanthropy,"** a paper presented at the 1897 *National Conference of Charities and Correction.* The next year, the

society held a summer course entitled "A Class on Philanthropic Work" in New York. By 1907, the course was held for a nine-month period at an institute now known as the New York School of Social Work.

2. **"Friendly Visiting,"** a paper presented at the 1907 *National Conference of Charities and Correction.*
3. *Social Diagnosis*, the first published textbook in social work (1917), marked the first recognition of social work as a profession.

(*M. E. Richmond sources*: Barker, 1995; Colby & Dziegielewski, 2001; Huff, 2002; Strode, 1940)

By the early 1900s, social work was widely considered to be a profession. Organizations supporting the social work profession were forming in the United States and worked together to provide a definition of what constituted social work. The duties and expectations of the social worker were also becoming clearer.

President Franklin Delano Roosevelt's New Deal Plan

The 1929 stock market crash and the *Great Depression* of the 1930s brought much change to how Americans lived and to the social welfare system. President Herbert Hoover began the tremendous job of implementing programs that would stabilize the economy, but was soon replaced by President Franklin Delano Roosevelt (Colby & Dziegielewski, 2001; Johnson et al., 1998; Morales & Sheafor, 1998; Schmolling et al., 1993).

President Roosevelt was unwavering in his goal to reduce the rampant unemployment and poverty of the depression years, and to resuscitate the American economy. In 1933, he therefore established a series of government aid programs under his *New Deal* plan. Unfortunately, several programs were trial-and-error and short-lived. Among the short-lived programs were:

1. **FERA**, the Federal Emergency Relief Administration
2. **CWA**, the Civil Works Administration
3. **WPA**, the Works Progress Administration
4. **CCC**, the Civilian Conservation Corps
5. **NYA**, the National Youth Administration

(*New Deal Plan sources*: Colby & Dziegielewski, 2001; Johnson et al., 1998; Morales & Sheafor, 1998; Schmolling et al., 1993)

One of President Roosevelt's *New Deal* programs, the social security system, was very successful, playing an important role in bringing the social welfare system under the funding and supervision of the federal government. The **Economic Security Act of 1935** established the social security system, which provided cash assistance to retired workers. The act also established Assistance to Families of Dependent Children (AFDC), unemployment insurance, cash assistance, health benefits, and services for the disabled, families, children, and seniors (Colby & Dziegielewski, 2001).

Section Four: Definition and Characteristics of Social Work

Defining Social Work

Milford Conference. Because the field is so vast and diverse, many steps have been taken in order to find, and agree on, a definition of social work. Representatives from the *American Association of Social Workers* met in Milford, Pennsylvania, in the 1920s to create a concise definition of social work. The members could not agree on one definition, but the agency executives at the Milford Conference did find that similarities in social work practices outweighed differences. Because of this finding, efforts to develop an acceptable definition of social work continued (Johnson et al., 1998; Morales & Sheafor, 1998).

NASW. The 1950s was a time of unity, change, and a new interest in defining social work. The following list of organizations pooled their resources and came together to form the **National Association of Social Workers (NASW)** in 1955:

- American Association of Medical Social Workers
- American Association of Hospital Social Workers
- National Association of School Social Workers
- National Association of Visiting Teachers
- American Association of Psychiatric Social Workers
- American Association of Social Workers
- American Association of Group Workers
- Association for the Study of Community Organization
- Social Work Research Group

*In 1955, NASW developed the first professionalized code of ethics for social workers.

(*NASW sources:* Colby & Dziegielewski, 2001; Greenwood, 1957; Johnson et al., 1998; LuSove, 1965; Morales & Sheafor, 1998)

Harriet M. Bartlett. Through the formation of the NASW, social workers were beginning to feel some unity among themselves, and a working definition of social work began to form. Harriet Bartlett, who chaired the committee to form the NASW, wrote an essay, published in *Social Work* in 1958, entitled "Working Definition of Social Work Practice," which outlined the common goals of social work practice, along with distinguishing it from other professions. Three of the major goals were:

1. To **assist** individuals and groups in identifying and resolving or minimizing problems arising out of the disequilibrium between themselves and their environment.
2. To **identify** potential areas of disequilibrium between individuals or groups and the environment in order to prevent the occurrence of disequilibrium.
3. To **seek out**, **identify**, **and strengthen** the maximum potential of individuals, groups, and communities.

(*Harriet M. Bartlett sources:* Bartlett, 1958, p. 268; Morales & Sheafor, 1998, p. 35; NASW, 1999)

By the 1970s and 1980s, the NASW had published several editions of the major journal, *Social Work*, which enhanced the understanding of the social worker's role. However, a comprehensive and acceptable definition of social work still had not been established. Eventually, through recommendations from a parallel task force that was working on a job classification system for social workers, the NASW Board of Directors was able to develop a concise definition of social work that eventually received widespread acceptance. According to the NASW's definition, *"Social work is the professional activity of helping individuals, groups, or communities enhance or restore their capacity for social functioning and creating societal conditions favorable to that goal"* (Morales & Sheafor, 1998, p. 35; NASW, 1999).

Characteristics of Social Work.   Several key characteristics are associated with social work. As you read and think about the following material, it will become clear why the social work field is considered vast and diverse, as well as having various definitions applied to it.

1. *People helping people:* Continuous interaction is the key to helping those in need. The social worker focuses on the interactions between the client (s) and the social environment. Individuals, families, groups, communities, and organizations benefit in their day-to-day life situations when social workers provide support, information, and links to various programs and intervention services.

2. *Addressing the needs of at-risk populations:* According to Colby and Dziegielewski (2001), "At-risk populations comprise those people who, for any number of reasons, are vulnerable to societal threats: Children, the elderly, and those who have been victimized by a person or group, and now are vulnerable to unwarranted pain and resulting problems" (p. 8).

3. *People need to be helped:* With this philosophy, services provided are considered important to the community good. *Sanction*, or community consent, comes in many forms: state licensing, professional certification, and funding support. This ensures that services are provided and that the public is being lawfully served.

4. *Activity and services are agency-based:* Many social workers practice within social welfare agencies. These agencies are either public, with funding from federal, state, or local tax dollars, or private, with funding resources coming from donations or foundations. A small percentage of social workers practice independently, and most who do are educated at the master's level or beyond.

5. *Social work as a profession:* Professional education starts in the classroom through baccalaureate and graduate-level programs. Professional training through internships expands students' knowledge and skills. Professional social workers are expected to follow the code of ethics that has been established through the NASW.

   (*Social Work Characteristics sources*: Colby & Dziegielewski, 2001; Compton & Galaway, 1999; Johnson et al., 1998; Miley et al., 1998; NASW, 1999; Schmolling et al., 1993)

Dimensions of Social Work.   Nancy Carroll (1977) described social work practice as "diverse and multidimensional" (pp. 430–432) and stated that the three dimensions were social technology, social units of concern, and social problems. For more details on Carroll's view of social work, see Table 1.2.

TABLE 1.2   Nancy Carroll's Diverse and Multidimensional View of Social Work Practice

Social Technologies	Social Units of Concern	Social Problems
Social Planning	Individuals	Drug Abuse
Community Organization	Families	Alcoholism
Research	Small Groups	Adult Criminality
Supervision	Formal Organizations	Juvenile Delinquency
Consultation	Communities	Mental Retardation
Administration	Regions	Mental Illness
Group Work	Societies	Child Abuse and Neglect
Family Therapy		Racial Discrimination
Casework		Poverty
		Illness

(*Table 1.2 content source:* Nancy Carroll, Associate Professor, School of Social Work and Community Planning, University of Maryland at Baltimore, 1977)

Section Five: The Social Work Milieu and Context

What Is Social Work?

As previously noted, the National Association of Social Workers (NASW) defines social work as *"the professional activity of helping individuals, groups, or communities enhance or restore their capacity for social functioning and creating societal conditions favorable to that goal"* (Barker, 2003, p. 408; Morales & Sheafor, 1998, p. 35; NASW, 1999). Social work is an applied science that focuses on helping people reach an effective level of psychosocial functioning, along with implementing societal changes that will enhance the well-being of all people (Barker, 2003).

What Does a Social Worker Do?

As a social work major, you may have encountered the following question at a party or holiday get-together, "What does a social worker do?" Well, this is a very complicated question that cannot be answered before the party is over! However, we can say with certainty that social workers practice professional social work values, principles, and techniques when:

1. Helping people obtain tangible services
2. Providing individual, family, and group counseling and psychotherapy
3. Assisting communities or groups in providing or improving social and health services
4. Participating in relevant policy processes working toward legislative programs that will benefit a large segment of society

(Barker, 2003, p. 408; NASW, 1973, pp. 4–5)

The July 2000 *General Meeting* of the International Federation of Social Workers in Montreal, Canada, established that "The social work profession promotes social change, problem solving in human relationships, and the empowerment and liberation of people to enhance well being. Utilizing theories of human behavior and social systems, social work intervenes at the points where people interact with their environments. Principles of human rights and social justice are fundamental to social work" (Barker, 2003, p. 408).

Professional social workers have knowledge of human development and behavior, as well as social, economic, and cultural institutions, along with an understanding of the interaction that takes place between these factors (NASW, 1973). The social workers' attributes, knowledge, and skills are filtered into their practice through professional communication skills.

Why Are Professional Communication Skills Pertinent to the Profession?

Social work is a very diverse occupation that continues to expand in roles and services. Social workers today can be found in various settings that include, but are not limited to, private practice, mental health, health, schools, community agencies, public welfare, agency administration, policy and planning, and areas that have been devastated by large-scale disasters. The social worker intervenes and works with individuals, couples, families, groups, and communities. Their task is to assist the population-at-risk in overcoming social and health problems (NASW, 1999; Schmolling, Youkeles, & Burger, 1993).

In order for the social worker to understand and assist the populations-at-risk, empathy and a sense of diversity are necessary characteristics. Social workers who possess and retain professional knowledge and communication skills are able to provide successful services in the remediation, restoration, and prevention process.

Hence, we welcome you on an excursion that will certainly enhance your professional communication skills and prepare you for a career in social work. Thus, the present volume will help you expand your knowledge of social work roles and duties, introduce you to professional communication, and prepare you for a successful career in professional social work practice.

REFERENCES

Barker, R. L. (1995). *The social work dictionary*. Washington, DC: NASW Press. Retrieved September 30, 2005 from the Web: http://www.naswdc.org

Bartlett, H. M. (1958). Working definition of social work practice. *Social Work, 3*(2), 5–8.

Carroll, N. K. (1977). Three-dimensional model of social work practice. *Social Work.* Washington, DC: NASW.

Colby, I., & Dziegielewski, S. (2001). *Introduction to social work: The people's profession.* Chicago: Lyceum Books.

Compton, B. R. & Galaway, B. (1999). *Social work processes*, 6th ed. Pacific Grove: Brooks/Cole Publishing Company.

Greenwood, E. (1957). Liaison report to the American Sociological Society on the National Association of Social Workers. *American Sociological Review, 22*(6), 750.

Henslin, J. M. (2005). *Sociology: A down-to-earth approach.* Boston, MA: Allyn & Bacon.

Huff, D. (2002). *Progress & reform: A cyberhistory of social work's formative years.* Boise State University. Retrieved October 5, 2005 from the Web: http://www.idbsu.edu/socwork/dhuff/history/central/core.htm

Johnson, H. W., et al. (1998). *The social services: An introduction.* Itasca, IL: F.E. Peacock Publishers.

LuSove, R. (1965). *The professional altruist: The emergence of social work as a career, 1880–1930.* Cambridge, MA: Harvard University Press.

Morales, A. T., & Sheafor, B. W. (1998). *Social work: A profession of many faces.* Needham Heights, MA: Allyn & Bacon.

National Association of Social Workers. (1999). *NASW Code of Ethics.* Retrieved September 21, 2005 from the Web: http://www.naswdc.org

Putnam, M. C. (1887). *Proceedings of the National Conference of Charities and Correction.* p. 149, in Strode, J. (1940). *Introduction to social case work.* New York: Harper & Brothers Publishers.

Ramsay, R. F. (1991). Transforming the working definition of social work into the 21st century. *Research on Social Work Practice, 13*(3), 324–338.

Schmolling, P., Youkeles, M., & Burger, W. R. (1993). *Human services in contemporary America.* Pacific Grove, CA: Brooks/Cole Publishing Company.

Standards for social service manpower. (1973). Washington, DC: National Association of Social Workers.

Strode, J. (1940). *Introduction to social case work.* New York: Harper & Brothers Publishers.

2 Communicating About Yourself

Section One will assist you in exploring your "goodness of fit," and the expectations and practice of social work. In *Section Two*, you will be exposed to various social work settings, fields, and demographics of the rural and urban areas. Recent activity and competition relating to various social work fields and education are included.

In order to launch your career, you must develop a professional and impressive resumé and cover letter that speaks "self-promotion." *Section Three* discusses the traditional format of a resumé, brings you into the contemporary world of the e-resumé, and walks you through the development of a professional cover letter. *Section Four* will help you prepare for the interview. Both sections provide detailed information and examples to assist you in grabbing the prospective employer's attention through the use of professional communication skills.

Section One: Exploration

Understanding the expectations and practice of social work is the first step in the exploration process. The second step is being aware of your personal goals and values, and deciding whether the field of social work fits your career interests.

Expectations and Practice Exploration

Expectations and Practice. To start the exploration process, let's consider expectations and practice within the field of social work. Although social work is immensely diversified in relation to the fields of interest and the populations served, two aspects remain constant: social work expectations and practice.

According to NASW (2006), "Social work practice consists of the professional application of social work values, principles, and techniques to one or more of the following ends:

1. helping people obtain tangible services,
2. counseling and psychotherapy with individuals, families, and groups,

Applying what you have learned . . .

Expectations and Practice

2.1. You are going to develop two lists in which to complete a compare/contrast exercise.

 a. Make a list of your personal attributes that you feel enables you to fulfill the social work expectations and practice discussed.

 b. Have a friend or classmate make a list of your personal attributes he/she feels will enable you to fulfill the social work expectations and practice discussed.

2.2. Compare your two lists. Make note of the similarities and differences. Save your lists.

2.3. Develop a list of your goals in social work. Consider the social work duties listed above.

 a. Do you believe your goals match those of the social work profession? How do they differ?

2.4. Take time to reflect on, and develop, a list of your personal values.

2.5. Refer to the lists you developed in *Exercise 2.1*

 a. Do you feel your personal attributes provide the motivation to meet and exceed the expectations and demands of social work?

2.6. Overall, how would you rate your social work "goodness of fit"?

Once you consider the social work standards and expectations, and conduct your personal exploration, you are ready to look at the social work job market.

---

3. helping communities or groups provide or improve social and health services,
4. and participating in legislative processes working towards legislative programs that will benefit a large segment of society." (NASW Website, 2006)

NASW (2006) also stresses that "the practice of social work requires knowledge of human development and behavior; of social and economic, and cultural institutions; and of the interaction of all these factors."

Internal Exploration. According to Towle (1954), "Social work exists because the community has had a conscience about the disadvantaged and an altruistic impulse to protect those who need help for survival" (p. 13). Social workers fulfill this duty by helping people:

1. Function the best way they can in their environment
2. Deal with their relationships
3. Solve personal and family problems
4. Face a life-threatening disease
5. Deal with and solve a social problem such as inadequate housing, unemployment, a serious illness, disability, or substance abuse
6. Assist families with serious domestic conflicts (child and/or spousal abuse)

(NASW, 2006; Towle, 1954; U.S. Department of Labor, 2006)

The first step in your internal exploration is to consider Towle's explanation for the existence of social work. Second, establishing your **"goodness of fit"** can be done by asking yourself the following questions:

1. Is my goal as a social worker consistent with the traditional mission of the profession?
2. Do my values match the values of the social work profession?
3. Am I motivated enough to meet, and exceed, the expectations and demands of the social work profession?

(*Goodness of Fit sources:* D'Aprix, Dunlap, Abel, & Edwards, 2004)

Section Two: The Job Search

Social work is a very diverse field whose roles and services continue to expand. The key to finding a position that fits your specific area of interest is your awareness of these unlimited career opportunities in the social work field.

With the information provided in this section, you will be able to grasp the diversity of the social work arena, while gaining a focus of interest and direction toward a specific branch of the field. With focus and direction, you will feel more secure in applying for a position with an organization. Launching your professional and successful social work career in your field of interest will become viable.

Today's Job Market

Today's job market has changed, and social work is not exempt from this change. Social workers can still be found practicing in the public sector, assisting the disadvantaged population. Recently, however, there has been a trend toward the private sector in which the social worker provides an array of services to clients from various social class populations (D'Aprix, Dunlap, Abel, & Edwards, 2004).

Fields of Interest.   Social workers today can be found in various settings that include private practice, mental health, health, schools, community agencies, public welfare, agency administration, policy and planning, and areas that have been devastated by large-scale disasters.

The characteristics and demands of the population that social workers assist have changed and increased, and the areas of practice have expanded to meet these changes. Whether you decide to enter the public or private sector, you can expect to find a number of fields of interest available to you (see Table 2.1).

Activity and Competition.   The U.S. Department of Labor's Bureau of Labor Statistics (BLS) shows that social work is one of the fastest growing careers in the United States. Social workers held approximately 562,000 jobs in 2004. According to the BLS (2006), "Employment of social workers is expected to increase faster than the average for all occupations through 2014" (U.S. Department of Labor, 2006).

TABLE 2.1   Social Work Fields of Interest

Addictions, Prevention, & Treatment	Dementia	Housing Assistance
Adolescent Health	Disaster Relief	Institutional Care
Adoption & Foster Care	Diversity & Equity	International Social Work
Advocacy, Consulting, & Planning	Domestic Violence	Mental Health Therapy
Alzheimer's	Eating Disorders	Military Social Work
Behavioral Health	Employment Services	Outpatient Treatment
Child Abuse and Neglect	Family Preservation Services	Parent Education
Community-Based Services	Genetics	Peace/Social Justice
Community Mental Health	Gerontology Services	Political Development
Criminal Justice	Health	Public Welfare
Crisis Intervention	HIV/AIDS	School Social Work
Chronic Pain	Hospice & Palliative Care	Veterans Services
Depression		

(*Table 2.1 content sources*: NASW, 2006; U.S. Department of Labor, 2006)

Employment.   In 2004, approximately 9 out of 10 social work positions were in health care, social assistance industries, and state and local government agencies (health/human services). Although most social workers practice in cities or suburbs, the field is consistently growing in rural areas (U.S. Department of Labor, 2006). Table 2.2 breaks down the employment of social workers in 2004 (most recent data).

1. *Children and Families.* Strengthening families has always been a key priority of social workers. Family lifestyles and structures are changing; thus the NASW advocates prevention and rehabilitation changes that will meet the needs of contemporary American families.

2. *School Social Work.* School social workers assess the social, behavioral, emotional, or economic problems that prevent a student from learning. Through professional judgment, the social worker refers the family and student to appropriate professional or community services. Follow-ups continue to ensure that services are provided and conditions monitored.

TABLE 2.2   Social Work Employment

Employment	Number of Social Workers
Child, family, & school	272,000
Mental health & substance abuse	116,000
Medical & public health	110,000
All other positions	64,000

(*Table 2.2 content source:* U.S. Department of Labor's Bureau of Labor Statistics, 2006)

3. ***Mental Health Therapy.*** Clinical social workers provide assessment, diagnosis, and treatment of various emotional problems, mental disorders, and substance abuse/chemical dependency. The Substance Abuse and Mental Health Services Administration (SAMHSA) reported that professional social workers were the nation's largest group of mental health services providers in 1998. Social workers are recognized as one of five core mental health professions by the Federal Law and the National Institutes of Health (NASW, 2006; U.S. Department of Labor's Bureau of Labor Statistics, 2006).

4. ***Medical Social Work.*** Social work in the medical field includes helping patients and families cope with problems that accompany illness or that inhibit recovery and rehabilitation. Problems include economic issues, disability, and lack of resources such as personal support systems after discharge to home. The social worker also provides supportive counseling to the patient and family members. Ongoing monitoring and assessing are required so that services can be modified to meet the changing needs of the patient and family.

5. ***Gerontology Services.*** The United States is experiencing a demographic transformation in relation to the aging population. The number of people age 65 and older is expected to reach 70 million by 2030. According to the NASW (2006), "This growing population of older adults will create an unprecedented demand for aging related programs, policies and services" (NASW Website). NASW has established an *Aging Initiative* program in order to raise awareness about geriatric social work practice, as well as to increase the number of professionally trained and credentialed social workers to serve this population.

6. ***Disaster Relief.*** According to the U.S. Department of Labor (2006), over 40 percent of the trained American Red Cross volunteers in 2004 were professional social workers.

7. ***Elected Offices.*** Over 170 social workers held national, state, and local elected offices in 2004 (U.S. Department of Labor, 2006).

(*Social Work Employment sources:* NASW, 2006; U.S. Department of Labor's Bureau of Labor Statistics, 2006)

Education

At the present time, 600,000 people have social work degrees, and a 30 percent increase is expected by 2010 (NASW, 2006; Bureau of Labor Statistics, 2006).

- ***Bachelor's Degree.*** The most common degree held by social workers is the Bachelor's Degree in Social Work (BSW). The BSW is still sufficient for some social work positions. However, an *advanced degree is becoming* the standard requirement for many positions.
- ***Advanced degree.*** A Master's Degree in Social Work (MSW) is usually a requirement if your interest is practicing in health and clinical settings. Various public and private agencies may also require an advanced degree. These positions include supervisory, administrative, and staff training. In order to teach in colleges and universities, a Doctorate in Social Work (DSW or Ph.D.) is typically required.

TABLE 2.3   Social Work Education

Bachelor's Degree (BSW)	Advanced Degree (MSW, DSW, Ph.D.)
Accredited programs = 442 (2004)	*Accredited programs = 248 (2004)*
Prepares you for direct service casework.	Prepares you for work in your chosen field of concentration.
Course work includes: 1. Social work values & ethics 2. Dealing with culturally diverse clientele & at-risk populations 3. Promotion of social & economic justice 4. Human behavior & the social environment social welfare policy & services 5. Social work practice 6. Social research methods 7. Field education	**Course work includes:** Programs that continue to develop your skills required to: 1. Perform clinical assessments 2. Manage large caseloads 3. Take on supervisory roles 4. Expand your knowledge and use of social services necessary to meet client needs
Supervised field experience = minimum of 400 hours	Supervised field instruction = minimum of 900 hours

(*Table 2.3 content source:* U.S. Department of Labor's Bureau of Labor Statistics, 2006)

■ *Licensing.*   All states and the District of Columbia require licensing, certification, or registration in order for a social worker to practice and use professional titles in the social work field. Licensing standards vary from state to state, and you should research the requirements needed in the state in which you plan to practice. The Association of Social Work Boards (ASWB), the National Association of Social Workers (NASW), and the U.S. Department of Labor's Bureau of Labor Statistics (BLS) are resources you can use for beginning your search. See Table 2.3 for Social Work Educational Requirements.

(*Social Work Education sources:* NASW, 2006; U.S. Department of Labor, 2006)

Demographics of Interest

Social workers assist those in need in several geographical areas, with the two extremes being rural and urban. While each community is unique, often geographic areas share common social problems such as poverty, domestic conflicts, illness, and substance abuse. The demographics for each are discussed next.

Rural.   An objective definition of "rural" in which all academic concentrations agree does not exist. Thus, we will describe "rural" as sparsely populated country areas (less than 2,500 citizens). Rural areas also contain housing units *not* classified as urban (Henslin, 2005; Martinez-Brawley, 1980; Pugh, 2000; U.S. Census Bureau, 2006). See Table 2.4 for further details on rural demographics.

TABLE 2.4   **Rural Demographics**

Description	Percentage of Rural Population
Poverty households	14.2%
Children in poverty	20%
Households w/inadequate food supply	11.6%
Unemployment	5.8%
Physicians' practices	9% of nation's total practices
Families w/member(s) who have a disability	30%
Young (25–39), single, not college educated	60%
Young (25–39), married, not college educated	55%
Older population	*25% (of U.S. population)*
Elderly: age 65 and over	*12% (of U.S. population)*
Population growth	0.4% (between April 2000 & July 2003)
Federal, state, local funding	$233 billion ($4,747 per resident)

* *Italics indicate the percentage of the United States' total population.*

(*Table 2.4 content sources*: Krout & Dwyer, 1991; Mather, 2004; U.S. Department of Agriculture, 2004; U.S. Census Bureau, 2006)

Urban.   According to the U.S. Census Bureau (2006), an urban area consists of a densely populated, large central place with at least 50,000 citizens. Surrounding clusters with populations of at least 2,500 citizens in each cluster are also considered urban. See Table 2.5 for details pertaining to urban demographics.

TABLE 2.5   **Urban Demographics**

Description	Percentage of Urban Population
Poverty households	12%
Children in poverty	17%
Households w/inadequate food supply	11%
Unemployment	6%
Physicians' practices	91% of nation's total practices
Families w/member(s) who have a disability	28.5%
Young (25–39), single, not college educated	64%
Young (25–39), married, not college educated	62%
Older population	*75% (of U.S. population)*
Elderly: age 65 and over	*88% (of U.S. population)*
Population growth	1.3% (between April 2000 & July 2003)
Federal, state, local funding	$987 billion ($4,135 per resident)

* *Italics indicate the percentage of the United States' total population.*

(*Table 2.5 content sources*: Krout & Dwyer, 1991; Mather, 2004; U.S. Department of Agriculture, 2004; U.S. Census Bureau, 2006)

Applying what you have learned . . .

The Job Search

2.7. ***Refer to Table 2.1: Social Work Fields of Interest.*** List the fields that you think would be of interest to you. Keep your list handy.

2.8. ***Consider your list you developed in Exercise 2.7 Social Work Fields of Interest.*** Which education degree do you feel you would need in order to obtain a social work position practicing in each one of your listed fields of interest? Keep your list.

Rural and Urban Area Social Work Career Considerations

2.9. In which area, rural or urban, do you feel you would be most comfortable and successful practicing social work? Refer to *Table 2.4 and Table 2.5.*

2.10. Refer to the lists you made in *Exercise 2.7* through *Exercise 2.9*

    a. Which area, rural or urban, do you feel most needs your field of interest and would be most beneficial to the population?

    b. List the reasons you feel this way.

Section Three: Writing a Resumé and Cover Letter

Traditional Resumé

Your goal is to have your resumé remain at the top of the potential employer's stack of social work applicants so that you are sure to receive an invitation for an interview. Positive first impressions are extremely important in obtaining employment. Your resumé provides that first impression. You must develop a resumé that is impressive and professional, while remaining brief. Before going further, let's look at some key **Do's** and **Don'ts** of preparing your resumé (see Table 2.6).

Traditional Resumé Guidelines

Be Neat and Professional. Your resumé provides your *first impression* to a potential employer. It is therefore essential that it be neat and professional in appearance. It must also be completely free of errors. You can develop a neat, professional, and error-free document by doing the following:

1. ***Rough draft*** Preparing a rough draft of any writing is strongly advised. This process is used by most professionals and scholars.
2. ***Review and critique*** Having an adviser or someone in your field review and critique your resumé is a step that is beneficial to you. Another's eye can pick out errors and appearance flaws that may exist in your document. **Avoid** depending on your computer's spell-check because it does not know the context in which you are using words!
3. ***Additional resources*** Additional resources that can assist you in developing a professional resumé include writing and career development centers.

TABLE 2.6   Key DO'S and DON'TS of Developing a Professional Resumé

Do's	Don'ts
Be neat and use a professional format. **Must be completely free of errors!**	**Hurry!** This results in a sloppy/nonprofessional appearance.
Be brief when developing your resumé. Provide clear and specific information. Use powerful language!	**Lengthy!** May end up at the bottom of the stack, or worse. Generalizations and self-congratulation should be avoided.
Contact information, employment objective, education, employment history with dates, and skills are a must.	Salary on your resumé shortchanges you when it comes to negotiation time. **Don't write your resumé for your needs!**
One telephone number is sufficient. Make sure it is a number you check often and can have a calm and professional conversation on. Be sure to return the call in a timely fashion.	Providing your cell phone number is not a good idea. You can't have a dignified and professional conversation while sitting in traffic.
Be generous with margins. You should have a one-inch margin on all sides. Remember **symmetry** so that your resumé has a balanced appearance. Have adequate white space.	Cluttered, packed arrangement of information should be avoided. Paragraph structure and full sentences should be avoided.

(*Table 2.6 content sources*: Barthel & Goldrick-Jones, 2005; Beale, 2004; Hultberg, 2002; Hunter College Reading/Writing Center, 1999; Mansfield University Office of Career Development, 2005)

Be Brief, Precise, and Confident.   When developing your resumé, it is important that the document be brief. Because the potential employer is going to spend about 10 seconds scanning over your resumé the first time, it is important to choose your words wisely. Be confident in your abilities, and provide clear and specific information. The following suggestions will help you accomplish this clarity.

1. ***Active verbs*** Use active verbs when describing your skills, talents, abilities, and achievements. Examples of these verbs include:
   - lead, organize, participate, train, supervise, coordinate, direct, research
2. ***Adjectives and nouns*** Use adjectives and nouns that describe you in a positive and accurate manner. Examples include:
   - bilingual, capable, creative, diversified, motivated, experienced, flexible
3. ***Powerful language*** Be confident in your attributes and use powerful, honest wording. Avoid generalizations and self-congratulation!
4. ***Review and critique*** Do remember to have an adviser or someone in your field review and critique your resumé.

Resumé Contents.   Employers prefer a one-page resumé. Two-page (maximum) resumés are acceptable/preferred if you have a strong history of employment, leadership, and education, and have included your references.

Every resumé requires the following:

1. *Contact information* Your first/last name, current and/or permanent mailing address, telephone number, and e-mail address should be centered at the top of the page, with your name in bold print. **Avoid** using your cell phone number, "cutesy" e-mail address, and personal hobbies or interests that are not relevant to the position.

2. *Employment objective* The employment objective on your resumé is going to be slightly different for every job for which you apply. Make sure you tailor it to match the specific job for which you are sending it.

3. *Education* Your most recent education obtained should be listed first. Use the official name of each school you attended, along with the address that includes city and state. Be sure to use complete dates attended (start and completion), along with any honors earned. Listing relevant courses and an earned 3.0 grade point average and above are always impressive.

4. *Employment history* List your most recent employment first. Be sure to include company name, job title, date of employment, and a brief description of duties and accomplishments. **Never** list salaries on your resumé because this may be offensive and immediately sets the market value on your skills!

5. *Skills* Focus on what you know how to do in this section. Remember, use verbs because skills are *performable actions*.

6. *References* Three to five individuals who can support your skills and abilities may be listed in the reference section. Name, title, place of employment, and telephone should be listed for every individual reference. Be sure to ask permission to use them as a reference! **Avoid** personal references such as a boyfriend or a parent. References are optional.

7. *Additional sections* You can add additional sections to your resumé. Examples include honors, awards, and languages spoken.

8. *Review and critique* Having your resumé reviewed and critiqued by an adviser or someone in your field is an important step you should not skip.

Margins, Symmetry, and Space. Your resumé format will look impressive and professional if you follow these guidelines:

1. *Margins* Use a one-inch margin on all sides of your resumé.

2. *Symmetry* Make sure your resumé has a balanced appearance.

3. *Space* Leave adequate white space so that your resumé does not appear cluttered. Avoid a cluttered, packed arrangement. Do not use paragraph structure and full sentences.

4. *Font* The most appropriate typeface to use is *Times New Roman*, size 11 or 12 point.

5. *Review and critique* Again, take the beneficial step and have an adviser or someone in your field review and critique your resumé.

(*Traditional Resumé Guidelines sources*: Barthel & Goldrick-Jones, 2005; Beale, 2004; Hultberg, 2002; Hunter College Reading/Writing Center, 1999; Mansfield University Office of Career Development, 2005)

TABLE 2.7   Key DO'S and DON'TS of Developing a Professional E-Resumé

Do's	Don'ts
Be neat and use a professional format. **Must be completely free of errors!**	**Hurry!** This results in a sloppy/nonprofessional appearance.
Be brief when developing your e-resumé. Provide clear and specific information. Use powerful language!	**Lengthy!** May end up at the bottom of the stack, or worse. Generalizations and self-congratulation should be avoided.
Contact information, employment objective, education, employment history with dates, and skills are a must.	Salary on your e-resume shortchanges you when it comes to negotiation time. **Don't write your e-resumé for your needs!**
You should have a one-and-a-half inch margin on all sides.	Don't Clutter, information. Don't use paragraph structure and full sentences.
Use capital letters for section headlines. Align all text of the e-resumé to the left margin.	No characters should touch one another. *This also includes slashes used. Don't use columns.
Use asterisks or dashes to highlight specific features of your e-resumé.	Don't use decorative fonts, borders, bullets, etc. **For Scanning and Printing Purposes:
Font size should be 12–14 points (10 min. & 14 max.).	Don't use paper with speckles. Do not fold your resumé.
Keywords: It is important to use as many keywords as possible. Examples: subtitles, job titles, skills, accomplishments, education.	

(*Table 2.7 content sources*: Barthel & Jones, 2005; Beale, 2004; Hultberg, 2002; Hunter College Reading/ Writing Center, 1999; Mansfield University Office of Career Development, 2005)

E-resumé

The electronic resumé has advantages over the traditional resumé in that it is fast, convenient, and user-friendly. It is also cheaper than paper. When preparing your e-resumé, you should follow several important steps so that it is not lost in cyberspace.

First we will look at the key **Do's** and **Don'ts** of preparing and sending your e-resumé (see Table 2.7).

E-Resumé Guidelines

Be Neat and Professional.   The e-resumé provides your *first impression* to a potential employer. It is extremely important that it be neat and formatted in a professional manner. It must also be completely free of errors. You can develop a neat, professional, and error-free e-resumé by doing the following:

1. ***Rough draft*** Preparing a rough draft of any writing is strongly recommended. This process is used by most professionals and scholars.

2. *Review and critique* Having an adviser or someone in your field review and critique your e-resumé is beneficial to you. Another's eye can pick out errors and appearance flaws that may exist in your document. **Avoid** depending on your computer's spell-check because it does not know the context in which you are using words!
3. *Additional resources* Additional resources that can assist you in developing a professional e-resumé include writing and career development centers.

Be Brief, Precise, and Confident.   When developing your e-resumé, it is important that it be brief. Because the potential employer is going to spend about 10 seconds scanning over your e-resumé the first time, it is important to choose your words wisely. Be confident in your abilities, and provide clear and specific information. The following suggestions will help you accomplish this clarity:

1. *Active verbs* Use active verbs when describing your skills, talents, abilities, and achievements. Examples include:
   - lead, organize, participate, train, supervise, coordinate, direct, research
2. *Adjectives and nouns* Use adjectives and nouns that describe you in a positive and accurate manner. Examples include:
   - bilingual, capable, creative, diversified, motivated, experienced, flexible
3. *Powerful language* Be confident in your attributes and use powerful, honest wording. **Avoid** generalizations and self-congratulation!
4. *Review and critique* Do not forget to have your resumé reviewed and critiqued by an adviser or someone in your field.

E-resumé Contents.   Employers prefer a one-page e-resumé. Two-page (maximum) e-resumés are acceptable/preferred if you have a strong history of employment, leadership, and education, and have included your references. Prepare your e-resumé in *Word format* to avoid type distortion when potential employers print it out.
 The following are a must on every e-resumé:

1. *Contact information* Your first/last name and e-mail address should be the only information in this section. The potential employer may *not* be the only one with access to your e-resumé! This information should be at the left margin at the top of the page. **Avoid** using a "cutesy" e-mail address.
2. *Employment objective* The employment objective on your e-resumé is going to be slightly different for every job for which you apply. Make sure you tailor it to match the job you are seeking.
3. *Education* Your most recent education obtained should be listed first. Use the official name of the schools attended, along with the address that includes city and state. Be sure to use complete dates attended (start and completion), along with any honors earned. Listing relevant courses and an earned 3.0 grade point average and above is always impressive.
4. *Employment history* List your most recent employment first. Be sure to include company name, job title, date of employment, and a brief description of duties and accomplishments. **Never** list salaries on your resumé!

5. *Skills* In this section focus on what you know how to do. Remember, use verbs because skills are *performable actions*.

6. *Keywords* E-resumés are scanned using a keyword technique. It is important that you use as many keywords related to the position you are seeking. Examples of keywords include subtitles, job titles, skills, accomplishments, and education.

7. *References* Three to five individuals who can support your skills and abilities should be listed in the reference section. Name, title, and place of employment should be listed for every individual reference. Be sure to ask permission to use them as a reference! **Avoid** personal references such as boyfriend or parent. References are optional.

8. *Additional sections* You can add additional sections to your e-resumé. Examples include honors, awards, and languages spoken.

9. *Review and critique* Remember, having an adviser or someone in your field review and critique your e-resumé is a step that is beneficial to you. Do not skip this step prior to submitting your e-resumé to a potential employer.

Margins, Space, and Characters.   Your e-resumé format will look impressive and professional if you follow these guidelines:

1. *Margins* Use a one-and-a-half inch margin on all sides of your e-resumé.

2. *Left-justified* Make sure all your information on the e-resumé begins to the left. Do not indent.

3. *Space* Leave adequate white space so that your e-resumé does not appear cluttered. There should be a space between each character, including slashes. **Avoid** a cluttered, packed arrangement. Do not use paragraph structure and full sentences.

4. *Capital letters* Use ALL CAPITAL LETTERS for section headlines. Asterisks or dashes are used to highlight specific features of your e-resumé. Font size should be 12–14 points (10 min. & 14 max.).

5. *Review and critique* Again, having an adviser or someone in your field review and critique your e-resumé is a step that is beneficial to you.

Sending Your E-resumé.   There are a few steps you should take prior to sending your e-resumé to the potential employer. This will ensure that he or she not only receives it, but can read and print out your e-resumé in a professional format. They include:

1. *E-mail your e-resumé* to friends and/or colleagues so they may look over and critique it. This also ensures that your e-resumé sends properly and is received in a professional format.

2. *If possible, call the Human Resources Department* and get the name of the person responsible for the recruiting process. This will ensure that your e-resumé is not overlooked and/or lost among the many e-mails received.

3. *Send your e-resumé* as either a *Word attachment* or in the body of your e-mail. Before sending contact the Human Resources Department and find out what format it prefers.

(*E-Resumé Guidelines:* Barthel & Goldrick-Jones, 2005; Beale, 2004; Hultberg, 2002; Hunter College Reading/Writing Center, 1999; Mansfield University Office of Career Development, 2005)

Resumé Styles

You can use either of two styles when formatting your resumé; reverse chronological and functional.

Reverse Chronological Format. The reverse chronological format is the most popular resumé style used and is usually an employer's preference. Using this format, you list your most recent experiences first, and you proceed backwards through time. This is a good format to use if your most recent job and training closely fit with the position you are seeking. When developing your reverse chronological resumé, remember to do the following:

1. **If you start with the reverse chronological format**, all sections of your resumé should be in this style.
2. **Check your dates** to make sure the most current date is first and that remaining dates proceed backwards from there.
3. **Review and critique**. Have an adviser or someone in your field review and critique your resumé.

Functional or Skills-based Format. The functional or skills-based format reflects what you can do rather than where and when you did it. It is the best style to use ***only*** if:

1. You lack relevant work experience.
2. You are changing careers.
3. You have no time gaps in your employment and education history.
   - *FYI: This format is not always popular with employers!*

   ****Never Include in Your Resumé or E-Resumé***
1. Personal information such as height, weight, age, date of birth, marital status, gender, race, health, personal photo, and social security number
2. Reasons for leaving previous job (s) and salary history
3. Falsified information

   (*Resumé Styles sources:* Barthel & Goldrick-Jones, 2005; Beale, 2004; Hultberg, 2002; Hunter College Reading/Writing Center, 1999; Mansfield University Office of Career Development, 2005)

Cover Letter Guidelines

The second important document that is part of getting you an interview with a potential employee is your cover letter. The cover letter, like your resumé, needs to be done in a professional and error-free manner. To prepare a cover letter that will accent your resumé and highlight your professionalism, the following information should be present:

1. Your address, personal telephone number (not cell phone number), and e-mail address. It should be typed in this exact order, and located at the top, left-hand corner (do not indent). Double-space.

2. Full date (month, day, year) should be next (left-hand side). Double-space.
3. The contact name and title, and full business address (left-hand side). Double-space.
4. Write: Dear Mr./Mrs./Ms./Dr./Professor/etc. then the last name (left-hand side). Double-space. (Do not use: Sir, Madam, or To Whom it May Concern.)
5. The body of your cover letter should be typed in standard English format. Use full and complete sentences, with correct paragraph structure. Use professional, block-style format. Do not indent!

First Paragraph.   The first paragraph is your first chance to "grab the attention" of the potential employer. It should include:

1. Telling the reader who you are and the reason for writing
2. Informing the reader what position you are applying for
3. Stating why you believe the organization needs your services

Second Paragraph.   Your second paragraph should include:

1. The reason (s) you would like to work for the organization
2. A few qualifications and experiences you can bring to the organization

Third Paragraph.   Your third, and final, paragraph must contain:

1. A request for an interview and how you can be reached
2. A thanks to the reader for his or her time and consideration

Closure.   Close your letter with "Sincerely." Leave at least four spaces, then:

1. Type your name.
2. Sign your name in the space between the closing statement and your typed name.
3. Send the original to the potential employer—never send a photocopy!

(*Cover Letter Guidelines sources*: Hultberg, 2002; Mansfield University Office of Career Development, 2005; Purdue University, 2005)

Applying what you have learned . . .

Preparing a Resumé and Cover Letter

2.11. Prepare a traditional resumé using the reverse chronological format.
2.12. Prepare a cover letter that accompanies your traditional resumé.

2.13. a. Prepare an e-resumé using the reverse chronological format.
  b. E-mail your e-resumé to a classmate and/or instructor for feedback.

Section Four: The Interview

This section will guide you through the process of preparing for an interview. Professional etiquette surrounding appearance, arrival time, greeting, demeanor, and departing the interview are discussed. Captions reinforcing the proper protocol are displayed in the section. You will benefit from conducting a practice interview following the techniques and guidelines that are highlighted.

Preparation

You have a scheduled interview with a potential employer because your resumé and cover letter were presented in a professional manner. Researching the organization and practicing your responses to various interview questions are two ways to prepare yourself for the interview. This preparation will also help you maintain professionalism when meeting with the prospective employer.

Research the Organization.   You may be asking yourself, "Why do I need to research the organization? They will inform me of their goals, missions, and expectations during my interview." Yes, the *interviewer* will probably fill you in on the organization. However, you will have a better understanding of what the interviewer is talking about and can ask specific questions if you have done your homework.

There are several ways to research the organization. Your first step should be the organization itself. Brochures, newsletters, and annual reports can be requested from the organization. The Internet and library are also valuable tools to use for finding information about your prospective employer (Brantley & Miller, 2002; Mansfield University Office of Career Development, 2005).

Another important reason to research the organization before you have your interview is to enable you to respond to the interviewer's questions in an educated and professional manner. The interviewer may also be impressed to find that you took the initiative to become familiar with the organization. Keep in mind that the less time the interviewer spends explaining the organization means more time *selling yourself* (Mansfield University Office of Career Development, 2005).

Questions and Responses.   Most interviewers are interested in knowing three things about you.

1. ***Your education:*** what you know
2. ***Your transferable skills:*** your experiences that will be beneficial to them
3. ***Team fit:*** what type of employee will you be

You will appear more professional and be less anxious during the interview if you prepare your responses to these three items. In order to prepare yourself, you can ask yourself the following questions:

1. How do I want to express myself?
2. What are my key strengths?

3. What personal skills will best meet the job requirements?
4. What experiences have I had will be beneficial to the organization?
5. It is very important to remember that the interviewer may implement various job-related scenarios into his or her questions. An example is, "What would you do if a client asked you to behave unethically?" You need to prepare responses to meet this challenge!

(*Questions and Responses sources*: Brantley & Miller, 2002; Mansfield University Office of Career Development, 2005)

Nonverbal Communication

Your nonverbal communication is a critical element in the interview process. The interviewer will be listening to your responses while taking note of your body language. It is crucial that you become familiar with the Do's and Don'ts of nonverbal communication because of the impact they will have on your interview (Brantley & Miller, 2002; Mansfield University Office of Career Development, 2005; McDonald, 2004; Murray, 2005).

Body Language.   In order to be regarded as a competent professional, it is important that you display proper body language during your interview with a potential employer (Murray, 2005). You can maintain professionalism by following the guidelines presented in Table 2.8.

TABLE 2.8   Key DO'S and DON'TS of Professional Body Language

Do's	Don'ts
Appear confident.	Enter the room "sluggish."
Have a firm handshake = self-confidence & professionalism.	Have a weak handshake = may signify a weak personality.
Maintain eye contact.	Stare.
Smile when appropriate, express approval by nodding and keeping friendly eye contact.	Frown or make tense facial expressions.
Sit upright, yet be relaxed.	Cross your legs = presents awkward posture.
Keep your arms open & to the side, or loosely folded in your lap.	Cross your arms = says "defensive."
Remain in your own space.	Move into the interviewer's "comfort zone" by leaning forward in your chair.
Have a "natural response" nod when agreeing.	Nod persistently.
Use gestures to emphasize important points.	Overuse hand motions = distracting.
Stay calm and focus your energy on the conversation.	Fidget or tap your fingers or feet = indicates you are anxious to end the interview.

(*Table 2.8 content sources*: Brantley & Miller, 2002; Mansfield University Office of Career Development, 2005; McDonald, 2004; Murray, 2005)

Appearance

At this point, you may be asking yourself, "What do I wear to my interview?" It is important that all your clothing and accessories make a good impression on the interviewer (see Table 2.9). Always wear professional business attire because it is better to be *overdressed* than *underdressed!*

You can do a number of things to guarantee a professional appearance:

1. Make sure your breath is fresh and your teeth are clean. Avoid chewing gum or candy during the interview.
2. Make sure your hair is clean, recently cut, and neatly brushed. If your hair is long, you should pull it back so it remains away from your face.
3. Use deodorant or antiperspirant only.
4. Do not use perfume or cologne. The office staff and interviewer may have allergies.
5. Be clean-shaven. Facial hair may be acceptable if it is neatly trimmed.
6. Avoid open-toed shoes and tank tops.
7. Bring a pen, paper, and extra copies of your resumé.
8. Carry a clean portfolio or briefcase. Do not carry a backpack.

(*Appearance sources:* Brantley & Miller, 2002; Hultberg, 2002; Mansfield University Office of Career Development, 2005)

TABLE 2.9   Professional Appearance and Clothing Attire

MEN	WOMEN
Make sure fingernails are clean, trimmed, and buffed.	Use light nail polish colors. Avoid unusual colors and acrylic nails.
Use hair gel/mouse in moderation.	Use make-up in moderation.
Be sure to remove your piercings.	Go easy on the jewelry. Remove your piercings ("simple" earrings are fine).
Make sure you do not have things in your pockets that "jingle" (keys, change, etc.).	Invest in a basic, tailored suit with a knee-length skirt. Avoid anything above the knees. A pants suit is a good choice also. Both should be in plain colors (black, blue, gray).
Invest in a dark-colored suit (gray, black, blue). Coordinate your suit with a solid-colored dress shirt (white, beige, gray, or blue). Avoid polo shirts!	Wear skin-toned hosiery and polished shoes with a maximum heal of 2 inches.
Choose a tie that is "interesting" and in good taste. Polish your shoes.	Avoid tight-fitting clothing and clothing that is revealing.
Don't forget: Your clothing should be clean, pressed, and in good repair.	Don't forget: Your clothing should be clean, pressed, and in good repair.

(*Table 2.9 content sources:* Brantley & Miller, 2002; Hultberg, 2002; Mansfield University Office of Career Development, 2005)

The Appointment

Preparing and sending your professional resumé and cover letter, researching the organization, and shopping for the right professional attire have prepared you for your interview appointment. You now need to know how to "survive" the interview itself. The information in Table 2.10 is going to help you do this.

Follow-Up of the Interview Process

A "*Thank You*" note should be sent to the interviewer within 24 hours after your interview. Between ten days and two weeks after your interview, you should call the interviewer to

---

Applying what you have learned . . .

Interview Questions and Responses

2.14. Develop a list of your key strengths, personal skills, and experiences.

2.15. You have a scheduled interview. How do you think you will answer the interviewer's following questions? Refer to the list you developed in Question 1.

   a. The social work position requires you to travel to various rural areas and assist younger residents with household management. What classes and experiences have you had that you feel will enable you to properly assist the younger families?

   b. Our organization employs 15 social workers. Numerous families in the areas we cover require various types of intervention and prevention. How do you feel about collaborating with a coworker who may have special skills and experience to deal with a specific family situation?

   c. How would you handle the following client situation?

      1. You are visiting a single mom with two children who have been victims of domestic violence. The husband is out on bail and decides to visit his family while you are there. Your client lets him in the house. He is angry that you are there and the verbal abuse begins.

The Interview

It is time to put everything you have just learned into practice. The exercise should be spread out between at least two class time meetings (per instructor). You will be utilizing all the chapter's exercise materials you completed.

2.16. Pick a classmate with whom to do a "mock" interview. Both you and your partner will have an opportunity to take on the role of interviewer and interviewee.

2.17. Both of you *together* need to refer to your social work fields of interest lists you developed. Decide what type of social work position and area (urban or rural) each of you wants to interview for. Share this information with your partner.

2.18. You and your partner must then "individually" create questions and answers. Do not share your questions and answers with your partner.

   a. *Interviewer:* Create questions that match the field and area your partner is interested in.

   b. *Interviewee:* Develop a plan based on what you believe your partner's questions will be during the interview. The job opening is based on your field and area of interest.

   c. Switch roles.

TABLE 2.10   Proper Interview Protocol

Proper Protocol	Improper Protocol
Arrival Time Frame: Be on time or 5–10 minutes early *maximum*!	Do not be late or show up 30 minutes early. Have respect and remember, the interviewer is busy.
Proper Greeting: Smile and firm hand shake	A weak handshake.
Demeanor: Be in good spirits, confident, and positive	Leave your "cranky" mood and negative attitude at home.
Proper Exit: Let the interviewer end the interview. Use your manners and say "Thank you!"	It is not your role to end the interview. Forgetting your manners.
Follow-up: Send a "Thank you" note and say "Thank you!"	Forgetting to recognize the valuable time the interviewer spent with you.

(*Table 2.10 content sources*: Brantley & Miller, 2002; Hultberg, 2002; Mansfield University Office of Career Development, 2005)

find out the status of the position and your application. Be helpful if they ask for more information from you (Mansfield University Office of Career Development, 2005).

Summary

The first step in your exploration process brings about an understanding of social work expectations and practice. With this understanding, you can proceed to the second step, during which you become aware of your personal goals and values, and decide which field of social work fits your interests best. Exploring social work diversity and becoming familiar with the demographics of rural and urban populations help you gain a focus on a specific branch of practice that interests you. With this focus, you can also develop a successful educational plan that will lead to obtaining a position with an organization of your choice.

Self-promotion is the key to launching your career in social work. Initially, you do this through your resumé and cover letter. Both documents provide your *first impression* to a potential employer. It is extremely important that both your resumé and your cover letter be prepared in a professional format and be free of errors. As stressed throughout the section, you should complete a rough draft and have it reviewed and critiqued prior to submitting it to a potential employer. This will ensure that both your resumé and cover letter emphasize your professionalism, and that you stay at the top of the employer's interview call list.

Finally, preparation and familiarity with the organization you wish to join will equip you with impressive conversation pieces during the interview. *Don't forget*: your professional appearance, proper etiquette during the interview, and a follow-up *thank you note* are critical to your success in obtaining the position you are seeking.

KEY WORDS AND CONCEPTS

Section One
Exploring Expectations and
  Practice, p. 12
Internal Exploration, p. 13
Goodness of Fit, p. 14

Section Two
Job market, p. 14
  Fields of interest, p. 14
  Activity and competition,
    p. 14
  Employment, p. 15
Education, p. 16
Demographics, p. 17
  Rural, p. 17
  Urban, p. 18

Section Three
Traditional resumé, p. 19
  Professionalism, p. 19
  Brief, concise, p. 20
  Contents, p. 20
  Layout, p. 21
E-resumé, p. 22
  Professionalism, p. 22
  Brief, concise, p. 23
  Contents, p. 23
  Layout, p. 24
  Sending, p. 24
Resumé styles, p. 25
  Reverse chronological,
    p. 25

Functional or skills-based,
  p. 25
Cover letter, p. 25

Section Four
The interview, p. 27
  Preparation, p. 27
  Nonverbal communication,
    p. 28
  Appearance, p. 29
The appointment, p. 30
Follow-up, p. 30

REFERENCES

Barthel, B., & Goldrick-Jones, A. (n.d.). *Resumés*. Retrieved October 18, 2005 from The Writing Center at Rensselaer Web site: http://www.wecc.rpt.edu

Beale, A. V. (2004). Tips for writing winning resumes: Answers to students' most frequently asked questions. *Techniques, 79*(5), 22–25.

Brantley, C. P., & Miller, M. G. (2002). *Effective communication for colleges*. Cincinnati, OH: South-Western Educational Publishing.

D'Aprix, A. S., Dunlap, K. M., Abel, E., & Edwards, R. L. (2004). Goodness of fit: Career goals of MSW students and the aims of the social work profession in the United States. *Social Work Education, 23*(3), 265–280.

Hartley, D., LeBow, R., Longbotham, R., Parry, K., Phillips, D., & Watkins, B. (2006). *Rural America's health care safety net providers*. Retrieved from National Rural Health Association Web site: www.nrharural.org

Henslin, J. M. (2005). *Sociology: A down-to-earth approach*. Boston, MA: Allyn & Bacon.

Hultberg, R. (2002). Job search tips for social workers. *The New Social Worker, 9*(3).

Writing the resume (1999). Retrieved October 18, 2005 from Hunter College Reading/Writing Center Web site: http://rwc.hunter.cuny.edu

Krout, J. A., & Dwyer, J. W. (2004). Demographic characteristics of the rural elderly. *The future of aging in rural America: Proceedings of a National Symposium, 1991*. Retrieved March 22, 2006 from LookSmart Web site: http://www.findarticles.com

How-to help on interviewing (2005). Retrieved October 18, 2005 from the Mansfield University Office of Career Development Web site: www.mansfield.edu/~careserv

How-to help on resumes. (2005). Retrieved October 18, 2005 from the Mansfield University Office of Career Development Web site. www.mansfield.edu/~careserv

Martinez-Brawley, E. E. (1980). Identifying and describing the context of *rural* in social work. *Aretau, 6*(2), 21–32.

Mather, M. (2004). *America's rural children*. Washington, DC: Population Reference Bureau. Retrieved March 22, 2006 from Rural Families Data Center Web site: www.rfdcenter.org

McDonald, P. (2004). Nonverbal cues are great communicators. *USA Today, 132*(2708), 9.

Murray, J. (2005). *Quietly speaking volumes*. Retrieved February 16, 2005 from The Times Educational Supplement Web site: www.tes.co.uk

Practice. (2006). Retrieved March 3, 2006 from NASW Web site: http://www.naswdc.org

Specialty Practice Sections. (2006). Retrieved March 3, 2006 from NASW Web site: http://joblink. socialworkers.org/search/

Oldaker, A., & Olson, A. (2005). *Cover letters: Preparing to write a cover letter.* Retrieved October 26, 2005 from The Writing Lab & OWL Purdue University Web site: http://owl.english.purdue.edu/

Pugh, R. (2000). *Rural social work.* Dorset: Russell House Publishing.

Towle, C. (1954). *The learning in education for the professions. Education for social work.* Chicago: University of Chicago Press.

Census 2000: Urban and rural classification. (2006). Retrieved March 10, 2006 from U.S. Census Bureau Web site: www.ask.census.gov

Rural America at a glance. (2004). Retrieved March 22, 2006 from U.S. Department of Agriculture Web site: www.ers.usda.gov

Bureau of Labor Statistics Occupational Outlook Handbook. (2006). Retrieved March 8, 2006 from U.S. Department of Labor Web site: www.bls.gov

Finding and Communicating Current Knowledge

Deciding on a social work topic and/or issue you are interested in is the first step in the research process. Once you decide what you want to research, becoming familiar with the literature available and learning how to access and use up-to-date and current library resources related to your field of interest comes next. The chapter covers both the *Library of Congress* and *Dewey Decimal Classification System* so that you can find your way around the library and successfully access the information you are seeking.

The numerous components of peer-reviewed journal articles will be broken down and explained so that you will be able to understand the structure. Tools to develop your own professional and publishable research are provided. Finally, you will be assisted in planning and preparing your research for publication. All sections in the chapter are presented in an easy-to-understand format. This format, along with the exercises implemented throughout the chapter, will enhance your social work knowledge and research abilities, as well as increase your professional communication writing skills.

Section One: Research Topic and Resources

Choosing a Research Topic

Before venturing to the library, you need to decide what you want to research. For most people, this is the hardest part of the research process. In order to get past this "stumbling block," ask yourself:

1. What am I interested in researching?
2. What subject matter and/or issues do I want to learn more about?
3. Why do I want to expand my knowledge of this subject matter and/or issue?
4. Are you still unsure on what to research? Then browse current periodicals. You will eventually find a topic that sparks your interest.

(*Research Topic sources:* Rutgers, 2003)

Resources

No matter what topic or issue you decide to research, you will find an endless abundance of materials available and waiting for you in the library. The materials include books, microfilm, videos, and various periodicals (Rutgers, 2003).

Some examples of periodicals include:

1. *Scholarly*   Illustrations include charts and graphs; written by scholars and/or researchers in the field; original research or experimentation. Publishers include universities, research centers, and professional organizations. *Sources are always listed.*
   - *Health & Social Work*
   - *Social Science Quarterly*
   - *International Journal of Social Welfare*
   - *Family Relations*
2. *Professional or Trade*   Written for/by people in the specific field, some knowledge of the field assumed; some sources included; often published by a professional association.
   - *NASW Newsletter*
   - *American Libraries*
   - *Biography Teacher*
3. *Substantive News*   Writing geared toward the educated or well-read audience; may list sources.
   - *The Economist*
   - *National Geographic*
   - *Wilson Quarterly*
   - *Scientific American*
4. *Popular*   Articles written by staff or freelance writers; usually contain illustrations; seldom list all the sources used; geared toward general public.
   - *Newsweek*
   - *People*
   - *Sports Illustrated*

(*Periodicals source:* Rutgers, 2003)

Applying what you have learned …

What Do I Want to Research?

3.1. Make a list of subject matter and/or issues relating to your social work field of interest in which you would like to gain additional knowledge.

3.2. If you cannot decide on what to research, browse current periodicals. You can also speak with your instructor, classmates, and/or friends for research ideas.

3.3. Keep your list handy for your trip to the library.

Section Two: The Traditional Library

Have you ever wandered around a library trying to figure out where to find a book written by your favorite author or tried to locate research materials? *Section Two* is going to assist you in eliminating the time you spend wandering endlessly around the library with no success in locating the materials you are searching for. We will do this by exposing you to the types of book organization and shelving used in various types of libraries. **Reducing** the time you spend conducting your resource "hunt" **increases** the amount of time you have to develop your professional and publishable research.

The Library of Congress

The *Library of Congress* is the nation's oldest federal cultural institution. It is the largest library in the world, containing approximately 530 miles of bookshelves that hold 130 million items. The items include books, various other printed materials, recordings, photographs, maps, and manuscripts. Use of the *Library of Congress* was once for Congress *only*, but the staff's present-day mission is to extend the valuable resources to the American people (Library of Congress, 2005).

The Library of Congress Classification.   The *Library of Congress Classification (LCC)* is a book-organizing and arranging system first developed and used in the late nineteenth and early twentieth centuries at the *Library of Congress* in Washington, D.C. Academic and larger public libraries now utilize the LCC for shelving purposes rather than the *Dewey Decimal Classification System* (Library of Congress, 2005).

How-to of the LCC.   The *Library of Congress Classification* arranges materials on library bookshelves in alphabetical order, by subject. Because the books are all arranged by subject, additional resources relating to your topic will be located on the same shelf or in a nearby area of the library (Library of Congress, 2005; Rutgers, 2003).

Every book in the library is assigned a unique code, or call number, that tells you where to find it. The first sections of the call number represent the subject of the book. The letter-and-decimal section represents the author's last name. The last section is the year the book was published. Call numbers are written from top-to-bottom on the spine of a book and from left-to-right in the library catalog file system (Library of Congress, 2005; Rutgers, 2003).

The Library of Congress Classification
Families in distress: public, private, and civic responses, by Malcolm Bush (1988)
Book is shelved at the North Hall Library, Mansfield University (2006).

On the spine of a book
HV (Subject = Social Service)
699 (Read as a whole number)
.B88 (B=Bush, 88 = read as a decimal)
1988 (year book was published)

In the library catalog file system
HV 699 .B88 1988
(*LCC sources*: Library of Congress, 2005;
North Hall Library, Mansfield University, 2006; Rutgers, 2003)

The Dewey Decimal Classification System

In 1876, Melvil Dewey developed the *Dewey Decimal Classification System (DDC)* so that libraries could organize their literature collections. The DDC system is utilized in 135 countries, to include over 200,000 libraries. Smaller public libraries, as well as libraries in kindergarten through twelfth-grade schools, still utilize the traditional DDC for shelving purposes (Lorenzen & Guthrie, 2004).

How-to of the DDC. Libraries that use the *Dewey Decimal Classification System* arrange *nonfiction* books according to subject and number. By arranging nonfiction books by subject, you are able to find numerous other books on your research topic on the same shelf. *Fiction* books are shelved in alphabetical order by author's last name (Lorenzen & Guthrie, 2004).

The DDC has thousands of topics that are arranged into **ten main classes**. Each of the ten main classes listed in Table 3.1 continue to be divided (**100** = 110–190, 191–199, **200** = 210–290, 291–299, etc.). Each book is assigned a unique number. The book is then shelved according to the subject it falls under, in numerical order (Lorenzen & Guthrie, 2004).

The Dewey Decimal Classification System
Families in distress: public, private, and civic responses, by Malcolm Bush (1988)
If the book is shelved at a library using the DDC, it would be assigned a number
such as
(Nonfiction)
325.016
Bus

On the spine of a book, near the bottom
325.016 (300 = Social Science; 25.016 further breakdown of the subject)
Bus (first three initials of the author's name, sometimes only first letter is used)

TABLE 3.1   Ten Main Classes of the Dewey Decimal Classification System

000	Computer science, information, & general works
100	Philosophy & Religion
200	Religion
300	Social Science
400	Language
500	Science
600	Technology
700	Arts & Recreation
800	Literature
900	History & Geography

(*Table 3.1 content source*: Lorenzen & Guthrie, 2004)

In the library catalog file system
325.016 Bus
(*DDC sources*: Lorenzen & Guthrie, 2004)

Source Legitimacy Guidelines

It is important to keep in mind that the materials you refer to and use for your research must be legitimate sources. Ask yourself the following questions (Rutgers, 2003):

A. Author

   1. What are the author's credentials?
   - Educational background
   - Past writings
   - Experience

   2. Is the writing in the author's area of expertise?

   3. Have you heard of the author, or seen the author's name cited in other works?

   4. Refer to *Who's Who in America, Biography Index*, or biographical information in the publication itself.

B. Year of Publication and Edition Number

   1. When was the work published?
   - Located on the face of the title page, below the publisher's name.
   - Copyright date is on the reverse of the title page.

   2. Is the source current or out of date?
   - Science research demands current information.
   - Humanities often require material that was written years ago.

   3. Is this the first edition?
   - *Further editions.* Source has been revised and updated with new knowledge to meet readers' needs.
   - *Many printings/editions.* Work has become a standard and a reliable source in the field.

C. Publisher and Journal Title

   1. Who is the publisher?
   - *University press.* Likely to be a scholarly journal.
   - *Reputable.* Does not necessarily mean **quality**; could mean the publisher has high regard for the author/source.

   2. Is the journal scholarly or just popular?
   - Indicates level of complexity in conveying ideas.
   - Refer to *Types of Periodicals, Katz's Magazines for Libraries*, or ask a librarian if still unsure.

D. Intended Audience and Writing Style

   1. What type of audience is the author addressing, specialized or general?

   2. Is the source too elementary, technical, advanced, or just right for your research?

   3. Is the publication organized in a logical manner?

   4. Do you clearly understand the main points?

   5. Is the text easy to read?

   6. Is the author's argument repetitive?

Applying what you have learned...

Library Exploration   .

3.4. This exercise can be done individually or as a class.

3.5. Take a trip to the college/university or public library.

a. Inquire whether the library uses the Library of Congress Classification or the Dewey Decimal Classification System.

b. Once you know the library's shelving system, proceed to finding nonfiction books that pertain to the research interest list you developed in *Exercise 3.1.*

Legitimacy of the Sources

3.6. Develop a list of the research sources you found in the library.

3.7. Check off the sources that meet the A–F Source Legitimacy Guidelines.

E. Objective Reasoning and Coverage

1. Is the information fact, opinion, or propaganda? Remember:
   - Fact can be verified!
   - Be careful: opinion evolves from interpretation of facts. A skilled writer can make you believe opinion is fact!
2. Does the information appear to be valid and well-researched?
3. Is the author's point of view objective?
4. Does the author use language that is free of emotion-rousing words and bias?
5. Does the writing serve to update, substantiate, or add new information to the topic?
6. Is your topic covered extensively or just marginally?
7. Is the author using primary or secondary research, or both?
   - **Primary**—author uses his or her own raw material.
   - **Secondary**—author uses previously published research.

F. Evaluative Reviews

Consult a *Book Review Index* or *Book Review Digest* for answers to the following:

1. Did the author receive positive reviews for his research and writing?
2. Did the research/writing contribute valuable information to the field?
3. Are there better resources referred by the reviewer(s)?
4. Do various reviewers agree the work is valuable, or is there controversy?

(*Legitimacy Guidelines Source*: Rutgers, 2003)

Section Three: Web-Based Resources

Section Three provides you with the how-to of accessing social work Web-based resources. Guidelines assisting you in determining site reliability and usefulness will be highlighted. The goal of this section is to provide you with the necessary tools to conduct your own research. Current social work studies that exist on the local, national, and global levels pertaining to your research topic are within your reach!

Search Strategies

Analyze your topic.   Before turning on your computer and connecting to the Internet, you should develop a search strategy. By following the steps below, you will save yourself valuable time and also avoid the frustration of receiving Internet site information that has nothing to do with your topic.

Develop a list that includes:

1. Unique words, distinctive words and/or phrases, abbreviations or acronyms related to your topic
2. Societies, organizations, and/or groups that may have information about your topic
3. Other words pertaining to your topic that might be found in Web documents
4. Synonyms, variant spellings, and/or equivalent terms
5. Broader terms pertaining to your topic

(*Topic Analysis sources*: Barker, 2005; Calishain, 2004)

Conducting your search.   You decided on a topic to research, and your "search word analysis list" is done. You are sitting in front of your computer and start thinking, "How do I begin my search?" The first thing you need to do is to decide on a program, or Web ***search engine***, that will assist you in finding information on your topic (Barker, 2005; Barlow, 2004).

Search engines.   Various types of Web search engines are available (see Table 3.2); we will only focus on two. We will refer to the search engines as ***public*** and ***specific***.

Uniform Resource Locator (URL).   URL, or the address of a resource on the Internet, is a valuable piece of information that will take you directly to the specific site you want. The site may also provide you with additional links pertaining to your interests and/or topic of research.

TABLE 3.2   Search Engines

Public Web Search Engines	Specific Web Search Engines
Search engines available to anyone for accessing information and data	Found on library, government, organization, and company Web sites **May require a code to access and use*
Most popular include: Google Yahoo! AltaVista MSN	**Examples would include:** PILOT = Library Online Catalog EBSCOhost = Academic Search Premier InfoTrac = Expanded Academic ASAP LEXIS-NEXIS = Academic Universe PsyncINFO = primary for psychology research DOAJ = Directory of Open Access Journals CQ = Congressional Quarterly Researcher GALE (LRC) = Literature Resource Center

(*Table 3.2 content sources*: Barker, 2005; Barlow, 2004; Mansfield University, 2006; Rutgers, 2003)

TABLE 3.3 URLs for Social Workers

Organization	URL (web address)
Administration for Children and Families	http://www.acf.dhhs.gov/
Association of Social Work Boards	http://www.aswb.org/
Association for the Advancement of Social Work with Groups, Inc.	http://www.aaswg.org/
Association of Baccalaureate Social Work Program Directors	http://www.bpdonline.org/
Child Welfare League of America	http://www.cwla.org/
Council on Social Work Education	http://www.cswe.org/
Gateway to Statistics of 100 U.S. Federal Agencies (FedStats)	http://fedstats.gov/
Information for Practice (news/scholarships from around the world)	http://www.nyu.edu/socialwork/ip/
National Adoption Information Clearinghouse	http://naic.acf.hhs.gov/
National Association of Social Workers (NASW)	http://www.naswdc.org/
National Clearinghouse on Child Abuse and Neglect Information	http://nccanch.acf.hhs.gov/
National Institute of Health (NIH)	http://www.nih.gov/
University of Wisconsin School of Social Work	http://www.socwork.wic.edu/
U.S. Department of Health and Human Services	http://www.dhhs.gov/

By building a database of social work, specific URLs will save you time because you can then avoid having to "sift" through hundreds of Web sites that may lack information pertaining to your interests and/or topics of research. Developing your database will put current social work information at your fingertips! See Table 3.3 for a listing of URLs for social workers.

Reliability of Sites

The Internet contains a never-ending source of information on any topic you can imagine. A *filtering process* does not exist, which means that anyone can publish on the World Wide Web. It is important that you know how to distinguish reliable Web sites from sites that are motivated by profit, altruism, or malevolence (Benjamin, 2000; Rutgers, 2003).

Before using information you obtained from a Web site, check Table 3.4.

Section Four: Peer-reviewed Journal Articles

Social work journals provide valuable completed research, as well as research that is currently being conducted within the discipline. *Section Four* exposes you to various social work journals available and assists you in learning how to read and interpret the professional research data. This exposure will enhance your knowledge of social work research and your ability to develop your own research.

What Is a Peer-reviewed Journal Article?

A peer-reviewed article contains academic writings that have had some type of peer review process completed by *subject* experts in the field. This process is critical in ensuring that

TABLE 3.4 Reliability of Sites Checklist

Reliable Web Site	Unreliable Web Site
Author and credentials are listed.	Lacks author name and credentials.
Author's occupation, experience, and education are listed.	Lacks author's occupation, experience, and education.
Sponsor of Web site is reputable (company, government, university, organization, etc.).	No sponsor is listed on the site.
Site is updated frequently, and information is current.	Site is not updated; thus information may not be current.
Purpose of the site is clear.	Site is confusing and may have been created to sell products or persuade the user in some way.
Contains substantial coverage of the topic and includes relevant links.	Site lacks in-depth information about the topic and consists of *questionable links*.
Information sources are documented.	Site lacks source documentation.
Site information is nonbiased.	Site information is opinionated or biased, whichindicates an *ulterior motive and/or inaccurate information*.
Site is easy to navigate, and the additional links work.	Site is hard to navigate, and the links do not work.

(*Table 3.4 content sources*: Benjamin, 2000; Pask, Kramer, & Mandernack, 1993; Rutgers, 2003)

Applying what you have learned...

Topic Analysis

3.8. Decide on the social work topic you plan to research. You may have already done this in *Exercises 3.1–3.3*.

3.9. Analyze your topic by developing a list according to suggestions 1–5 in Section Three. Search Strategies (pg. 40).

Website Exploration and Reliability

3.10. Use the topic of research that you have picked.
  a. Choose a search engine (*public* or *specific*) to use to begin your search.
  b. Type in the topic that you are research-ing in the *search area, push enter*.
  c. Make a note of how many Web sites/ titles came up pertaining to your topic.

3.11. Choose 1 or 2 Web sites to visit.
  a. Using *Table 3.4*, check the site to see whether the information is reliable for use in your research.

3.12. Use the same topic you plan to research.
  a. Choose 1 or 2 specific URLs from *Table 3.3*.
  b. Scan the Web site for various links that may assist you in finding research on your topic.
  c. Using *Table 3.4*, check the site to see whether the information is reliable for use in your research.

3.13. Do a compare/contrast list on the various Web sites/addresses you visited.
  a. What Web sites/addresses were most reliable and helpful?
  b. What Web sites/addresses were least reliable and helpful?

the research information and data are accurate prior to being published. Because of this process, peer-reviewed journals are considered one of the most reliable academic sources (Leedy, 1981).

Types of peer-reviewed journals for the social worker.   You can refer to numerous social science journals when doing your research. Some of the most popular you may want to start with include the following:

1. ***Social Work*** is the official journal of the NASW and provides:
    - Insight into established practices
    - New techniques and research
    - Information relating to current social problems
    - Critical analysis in reference to the problems in the profession
2. ***Health and Social Work*** has provided information to Human Services professionals for 20 years. Topics/research you can expect to find in this journal include:
    - Latest advances in aging
    - Clinical work
    - Long-term care
    - Oncology
    - Substance abuse
    - Depression
    - Maternal health
3. ***Children & Schools: A Journal of Social Work Practice*** is a practitioner-to-practitioner resource that provides professional materials and information pertinent to social work services for children. Articles published in this journal focus on:
    - Student–authority relationships
    - Multiculturalism
    - Early intervention
    - Needs assessment
    - Violence
    - ADHD → Attention Deficit Hyperactivity Disorder
4. ***Social Work Research***, the outstanding journal in the social work field, provides:
    - Analytic reviews of research
    - Theoretical research
    - Evaluation studies
    - Diverse research providing knowledge about social work issues and problems
5. ***Social Work Abstracts*** has been NASW's abstracting service for more than 30 years. It is the starting point for literature searches in social work and social welfare. This journal provides:
    - Over 400 U.S. and international journal reviews
    - Approximately 450 abstracts in each issue
    - Availability on CD-ROM and the Internet (SilverPlatter)

(*Social Work Journals source*: NASW, 2006)

Components of a Peer-reviewed Journal Article

Intimidation and fear best describe the feelings students have when they are about to pick up a journal to read current research in the various fields of science. However, peer-reviewed journal articles communicate valuable results of social science investigations, and it is crucial that you overcome this anxiety so that you can read and comprehend the material within the articles. We will break down and explain each article component in the hope of eliminating your anxiety.

IMRAD.   As funding for research increased in the nineteenth century, scientists were writing more and more articles, and journal editors needed a more efficient way to establish consistency within the journals. Thus, *IMRAD* was developed between the late 1800s and the early 1900s for articles written in U.S. scientific journals. *IMRAD*, acronym for **I**ntroduction, **M**ethods, **R**esults, and **D**iscussion, is still used today to organize scientific research writings (Beebe, 1993; University of Wisconsin-Madison, 2004).

IMRAD represents the standard headings used in the various scientific field writings. However, required details and subheadings may vary according to the specific journals (University of Wisconsin-Madison, 2004). Let's discuss these variations.

Title Page.   The title page contains the following information:

1. Title of the research, representing a clear and precise description of the contents
2. Researcher(s), also known as author(s)
3. Institute and/or university with which author is affiliated
4. Name, date, volume, and number of the journal

Abstract.   When you read the abstract, you are actually reading the entire report in a "condensed form." The researcher has provided you with:

1. The what and why of the research
2. Methods used to do the research
3. Major conclusions and significance of the results

Introduction.   As you read the introductory section of the journal article, you will notice that the introduction:

1. Describes the problem researched
2. Summarizes the relevance of the research
3. Provides context, key terms, and concepts
4. Summarizes past research that is relevant to the conflict or unanswered questions the author has presently researched
5. Notes past findings the author is testing or expanding upon
6. Briefly describes the author's hypothesis(es) and/or research questions
7. Explains and justifies the experimental design or method used

Literature Review.   Prior to conducting the study, the researcher(s) has done his or her homework, and has reviewed past and present knowledge on the particular topic of interest. Thus, the literature review provides you with:

1. Historical and theoretical perspectives on the topic
2. Gaps that may exist in the literature
3. A summary of the study's purpose

Methodology.   The methodology section of the journal article tells you how the problem was studied. Various subheadings are used to divide the steps used. We will talk about the most common subheadings.

Participants.   The participants section gives you information pertaining to those who took part in the study, and usually includes:

1. Number of participants
2. Gender of participants
3. Age of participants
4. Other characteristics of the participants that are pertinent to the study

Materials.   The materials section of the article explains the apparatus that was used to conduct the study and may include:

1. Equipment used, such as a video camera or tape recorder
2. Type of survey used to collect the data
3. An explanation if the data collected was qualitative or quantitative

Procedures.   The procedures section of the article clarifies the materials used in the study. This section also explains the *how* and *why* of the data collected.

1. **Use of materials**—video cameras, tape recorders, cameras, etc.
   How: A video camera was used to collect qualitative data
   Why: in order to enhance the understanding of the behaviors being studied.
2. **Observations**—detached, participant, or enhanced
   How: Detached observations of several playground areas were conducted
   Why: so that several behaviors could be monitored and comparisons made.
3. **Surveys/questionnaires**—self-administered, mailed, or over-the phone; open-ended questions and/or closed-ended questions
   How: Self-administered surveys containing closed-ended questions were used
   Why: to collect quantitative data. The researcher stayed in the room in case the participants had any questions.
                            OR

>   *How:* In order to collect quantitative and qualitative data, surveys containing both closed and open-ended questions were mailed to 100 single-parents located in a rural area.
>
>   *Why:* The mailing process was implemented in order to ensure that all the single parents in the area would have the opportunity to be included in the study.
>
> 4. **Interviews**—face-to-face or telephone
>
>   *How:* Face-to-face interviews were conducted
>
>   *Why:* so that facial expressions could be observed as the questions were being asked.
>
> ***OR***
>
>   *How:* A tape recorder was used during the interviews
>
>   *Why:* so that all participants' information could be dictated accurately.

Analysis.   The analysis section explains what type of statistical program was used and the type of statistical analyses (tests) that were utilized to come up with the results of the study.

> *Example:*
>
> The Statistical Package for the Social Sciences (SPSS) chi square test was used to determine whether a statistical difference exists between home visits to the urban single parent and home visits to the rural and small town single parent (fictitious study).

Results.   The results section, also known as findings, explains what has been found by conducting the research. The section also includes the main tables and graphs that show the significant statistical results of the research.

 Let's use the foregoing example to show cross-tabulation and chi square test results when comparing the social worker home visits of single parents by community type. (See Tables 3.5 and 3.6)

Cross-tabulation.   In looking at the table, you can see that single parents in urban areas report a smaller number of positive social worker home visits *(121 positive visits)* when compared to reports from single parents located in rural and small-town areas.

TABLE 3.5   Positive Social Worker Home Visits by Community Type
Based on 705 interviews with single parents located in rural, small town, and urban areas

Home Visits	Rural Areas	Small Towns	Urban Areas
Positive Home Visits	174 (73%)	164 (65%)	121 (57%)
Negative Home Visits	65 (27%)	88 (35%)	93 (43%)
Total Number of Visits	239	252	214

Chi square results: 13.2 ($p < .001$)

(The study and numbers/percentages in the above table are fictitious.)

TABLE 3.6 Title—Positive Social Worker Home Visits by Community Type Headnote— *Based on 705 interviews with single parents located in rural, small town, and urban areas place about here*

Table heading Home Visits	Table heading Rural Areas	Table heading Small Towns	Table heading Urban Areas
Positive Home Visits	174 (73%)	164 (65%)	121 (57%)
Negative Home Visits	65 (27%)	88 (35%)	93 (43%)
Total Number of Visits	N = 239	N = 252	N = 214

Chi square results: 13.2 (*p* < .001)

(**Source:** Author(s) name and year would be located here)

Let's break down the parts of a table, using Tables 3.5 & 3.6 as the example.
Title—Positive Social Worker Home Visits by Community Type
Headnote—*Based on 705 interviews with single parents located in rural, small town, and urban areas*

1. *Title*—names the variables and states the topic
2. *Headnote*—provides information on how the study was done and on the number of participants and/or responses
3. *Table headings*—labels the variables
4. *N*—is an abbreviation for the total number of participants or responses in the study
5. *Source(s)*—provides information on where the data in the table originated (usually listed at the bottom of the table)
6. *Columns*—presents information arranged vertically
7. *Rows*—presents information arranged horizontally

Chi square.   The chi square is a nonparametric test used to compare expected frequencies to observed frequencies. The chi square was chosen for this example because it is the most popular statistical analysis used for testing differences that may exist in a cross-tabulation. The chi square also is easy to calculate by hand or computer, and requires only nominal level data (Levin & Fox, 2003; Royse, 1995).

When the chi square was computed, it was discovered that a value of 13.2 was obtained, using a .001 probability level ($p < .001$). This tells you that the existing differences are *not by chance*. Most social scientists, however, use the probability of at least $p < .05$ (Levin & Fox, 2003; Royse, 1995).

Keep in mind that this is just one example of a statistical analysis you will see in a journal article. Social researchers use various tests to analyze the data they collect. Therefore, you should keep a book on social research methods and statistics in your home library to refer to when needed.

Discussion and Conclusion.   The discussion and conclusion section of the journal article summarizes the most important findings of the study, and includes the following:

1. Brief summary of the findings
2. Observations on how the findings relate to expectations and to the literature cited in the *Introduction* section
3. Theoretical implications of the results
4. Practical applications of the results
5. Possible explanations for unexpected findings
6. Weaknesses and/or limitations of the study
7. Additional research that might resolve the contradictions, weaknesses, and/or limitations of the study
8. Extension of the findings to other situations in order to understand the broader issue

References.   The reference section of the journal article gives credit to all the sources the researcher referred to or cited when conducting the study. The reference section:

1. Provides the name(s), date, title and location (book, journal, Web site) of the source the researcher referred to and/or cited.
2. Lends credibility to the content of articles used, and can be checked by the reader.
3. Reduces editorial disputes, or resolves any that may arise (plagiarism).

Examples of sources found in a reference section

Babbie, E. (2001). *The practice of social research.* Belmont, CA: Wadsworth/Thomson Learning. (**book**)

National Association of Social Workers. (2006). *Practice.* Retrieved March 3, 2006 from NASW Web site: http://www.naswdc.org (**Web site**)

Neuman, K. (2006). Using distance education to connect diverse communities, colleges, and students. *The Journal of Baccalaureate Social Work, 11*(2), 16–27. (**journal**)

See Table 3.7 for the breakdown of these components.

TABLE 3.7   Components of Sources in the Reference Section

Author	Date	Title	Location
			Book
Babbie, E.	2001	The practice of social research	Belmont, CA: Wadsworth/Thomson Learning
National Association of Social Workers	2006	Practice	*Web site* http://www.naswdc.org
Neuman, K.	2006	Using distance education to connect diverse communities, colleges, and students	*Journal* The Journal of Baccalaureate Social Work, *11*(2), 16–27

Applying what you have learned…

Reading a Peer-Reviewed Journal Article

3.14. Visit the library of your choice and choose a social science peer-reviewed journal with an article that pertains to your social work field of interest. This exercise can be done individually or as a class.

a. Using legal size paper (turned sideways), make enough columns to include all sections of a peer-reviewed journal article discussed in *Section Four*. Label each column with one section only.

b. Read over each section at a time. Write what you believe are the most important details from each section of the article into the appropriate columns.

**Keep in mind that the sections in the journal articles may use titles/subtitles that differ from those mentioned in Section Four. Don't give up; using the suggested strategies and careful reading will help you find what you are looking for!

Appendix.   The appendix contains information that is important to the research but is not the main focus of the study. The appendix may also include tables and graphs, and a copy of the instrument (questionnaire) used to collect the data.

(Components of a Peer-reviewed Journal Article sources: Babbie, 2001; Henslin, 2005; Leedy, 1981; Levin & Fox, 2003; Monette, Sullivan, & DeJong, 2002; Neuman, 1994; Royse, 1995; The University of Wisconsin-Madison, 2004)

Strategies to Use When Reading a Peer-reviewed Journal Article

1. Read the title and abstract or summary first for an overall picture of the research topic.
2. Skim the article, making note of main headings and subheadings. This will provide you with the organization of the report.
3. Return to the beginning and carefully read the article. Make note of important details such as the problem researched and the method used to collect the data. Note exactly what the researcher has written.
4. Read the conclusions, then the problem again. Both should follow each other logically, along with complementing each other.
5. Remember: The main purpose of reading research is to know precisely what the researcher is saying.
6. Avoid assumptions and judgments. Do not interpret the results with your own wishes, desires, preferences, and ideas.

(Strategies sources: Leedy, 1981; Royse, 1995)

Section Five: Writing Tips and the APA Writing Style

Section Five provides you with writing tips, and the techniques and guidelines to follow when using the ***American Psychological Association (APA)*** writing style. The section contains how-to explanations, supplemented by examples assisting you in properly using the APA writing style. Because the social work field consistently uses the APA writing format, easy-to-read charts highlighting the important concepts are provided so that you can bookmark it and refer to it when writing.

Writing Tips

A sense of apprehension and confusion seems to envelope many students as they sit down to write a research paper. We hope to eliminate these feelings by offering you writing tips in a step-by-step format.

Step 1: *Topic*. "Brainstorming" is helpful when you are trying to decide on a topic to research. Find yourself a quiet place to sit and relax, and then:

1. Grab a pen or pencil, and a blank piece of paper.
2. Write down anything and everything that comes to mind about your social work interests. **Do not evaluate**, just write!
3. Once you run out of ideas, grab a new sheet of paper and refine your list.
4. Select your favorite topics and rate them according to appeal.
5. Number one on your list should be your favorite topic.

Step 2: *Purpose or goal*. Once you have chosen your topic, it is now time to decide why you want to research it. Remember, the purpose or goal of your paper is what drives your writing, so take the time to ask yourself the following questions:

1. What is the message that I want to convey to my readers?
2. Do I want to provide social work practice tips, details on a contemporary issue, or advocacy information?

Step 3: *Audience (readers)*. You must remember to write according to your readers. Ask yourself the following:

1. Who will be reading my research? A scholar, a colleague, or a supervisor?
2. If your goal is to publish your research in a peer-reviewed journal,
   - Consider who you would like to be the audience
   - Think about what peer-reviewed journal will reach your audience
   - Familiarize yourself with the journal's format and style

Step 4: *Outline*. An outline will provide you with organization and structure when you are working on your research. Your outline should include:

1. The material you plan to research
2. The content you want in your research
   - Be flexible—refining and expanding your outline will happen as you learn more about the topic.

Step 5: *Literature review*. By conducting a literature review, you are sure to expand your knowledge about your topic. As discussed in the peer-reviewed journal article components section, a literature review provides:

1. Background information on a topic
2. Finished studies and research currently being conducted on a topic and/or issue
3. Historical and theoretical perspectives on the topic

Step 6: *First draft.* You are now ready to begin writing that first draft. Refer to, and follow your sections, headings, and subheadings in the outline you developed in ***Step 4***. Once you complete your rough draft, have a colleague(s) review and critique it for you.

Step 7: *Refine draft.* It is now time to refine your rough draft. You can do this by:

1. Accepting the helpful hints and advice from your colleagues
2. Making sure that you have organized your writings in a professional format that the reader can follow by providing:
   - Headings and subheadings
   - Proper sentence structure—use complete sentences
   - Proper paragraph structure—a include maximum of six complete sentences per paragraph
   - Proper grammar
   - Proper punctuation
   - Language appropriate for your intended audience

Step 8: *Read out loud.* Once you have finished your revised draft, read it out loud to make sure that what you have written:

1. Makes sense
2. Sounds professional

(*Writing Tips sources*: APA, 2001; Beebe, 1993; Brantley & Miller, 2002; Pigg, 1996; Purdue University, 2001; Rutgers, 2003; University of Wisconsin-Madison, 2004)

American Psychological Association (APA) Style

The Publication Manual of the American Psychological Association, published by the American Psychological Association, contains over 400 pages (5th edition) of widely accepted instructions for social science writings. The APA style is used for writing research reports, manuscripts, and theses (APA, 2001). (This is an adapted version of sections of the APA Publication Manual. Please see this publication for full details.)

Format. By using the following APA format, your paper will be organized for the reader, along with providing a hierarchical (ranked) structure.

Title page. The title page of your report should include the following:

1. Header, or short version of your title, at the top, right margin—left of the page number
2. Title of your paper
3. Your name
4. Course name and number

Basics.   The APA format features certain basics that need to be followed.

1. *Margins*—One-inch margins should be used on all sides. Do not right-justify or break words at the end of a line.
2. *Spacing*—The entire paper should be double-spaced (including references), and the first line in each paragraph should be indented five to seven spaces—be consistent!
3. *Headings*—Heads help to organize your paper for the reader.
   - Running head—set your complete title in ALL CAPITAL LETTERS located at the top left margin.
   - Main headings—use appropriate upper- and lowercase lettering, and center them.
   - Second-level headings—start at the left margin, italicize, use appropriate upper- and lowercase lettering.
   - Third-level headings—(these headings start the paragraph) indent five to seven spaces, italicize, capitalize only first word, add period, then two spaces, and begin your first sentence.

Citations.   It is pertinent that you acknowledge every author's work used in your paper. The following are the most common examples of the APA format for citing references in the body of your paper:

1. ***One author:*** It is important to know who your intended audience is prior to writing your paper (Pigg, 1996).
   - You must always acknowledge the author and year throughout your paper when citing references (Pigg, 1996).
2. ***Two or more authors/sources:*** You can use technology to increase your workload efficiency (Schmolling, Youkeles, & Burger, 1993; Sheafor & Horejsi, 2006).
   - Note that a *semicolon* and *space* separate each source used.
   - When referencing a source with ***three or more authors***, use all the last names the first time you reference the work in your paper, then use et al. for subsequent citing(s): (Schmolling et al., 1993).

   (*Citations sources:* APA, 2001: Schmolling et al., 1993; Sheafor & Horejsi, 2006)

Quotations.   In order to avoid ***plagiarism***, using the proper format for a quote is mandatory. When quoting an author, use one of the following styles:

- According to Pigg (1996), "Some writers find 'brainstorming' helpful in topic selection" (p. 353).
  OR
- "Some writers find 'brainstorming' helpful in topic selection" (Pigg, 1996, p. 353). (notice that a quote requires that you provide a page number.)

References.   We have already discussed the importance of citing your references in the body of your text. It is now time to look at the APA format for recognizing your sources in the *References* page.

1. Sources are listed in alphabetical order.
2. Double-space is used between each line and each individual source.
3. Only the first word in the title is capitalized unless:
    - It is a two-part title, then the first word after the colon is capitalized. (Remember to follow the rules for capitalizing proper nouns!)
4. The first line of every source starts at the left margin.
5. The remaining lines of the source should be indented five to seven spaces. Be consistent!

Books Sheafor, B.W. & Horejsi, C.R. (2006). *Techniques and guidelines for social work practice*. Boston, MA: Pearson Education.
- **The title is italicized.**

Journals
Pigg, R.M. (1996). Ten steps towards professional writing. *Journal of School Health, 66*(10), 353–354.
- **The journal and volume number are italicized.**
- **The issue number is only included with the volume number if the journal is paginated by issue. If the pages are continuous throughout the issues for a given year, there is no issue number.**

Magazines
Richison, C. (2003, December). Clock testing in Dementia management. *Social Work Today, 3*, 6–7.
- **The magazine and volume number are italicized.**

ERIC documents
Roux, Y. (1997). *Teaching about global warming trends*. Yazoo, MI: National Conference of Concerned Educators. (ERIC Document Reproduction Service No. ED 987 321)
- **The title is italicized.**

Web resources
Guided search. (2006). Retrieved April 6, 2006 from North Hall Library, Mansfield University Web Site: http://lib.mansfield.edu
Lorenzen, M., & Guthrie, J. (2004). *How to find information in the information age*. Retrieved April 4, 2006 from the Library Instruction.com Web site: http://www.libraryinstruction.com
- **The first example does not have an author—title of the document is first.**
- **If there is no publication date, use "n.d" (stands for "no date") after the author, or title if there is no author listed.**

   The above examples are probably the most common sources that you will be using for your research. However, you may come across a source you would like to use, and the how-to of proper citing does not match any of the examples we covered. Don't panic! You can purchase the APA manual at any bookstore.

(*References source:* American Psychological Association (APA) Style, 5th ed., 2001. This is an adapted version of sections of the APA Publication Manual. Please see this publication for full details.)

Applying what you have learned …

Using the Writing Tips

3.15. You can use the topic you chose in *Exercise 3.8* or do *Step 1: Topic "Brainstorming"* to decide on a different topic to research.

3.16. Follow *Steps 2–6* of the *Writing Tips*. Keep all copies because you will be refining your rough draft in the next section's exercise.

Refining Your Rough Draft

For this exercise, make sure your surroundings are quiet, and choose a time that you feel you can fully focus on your writing.

3.17. Using the rough draft from *Exercise 3.16*, go back through it and make note of the comments your colleague(s) made. The suggestions can be accepted or rejected.

3.18. Check your rough draft to make sure you used proper:
  a. Grammar and punctuation
  b. Spelling
  c. Paragraph structure

3.19. As you are reading your rough draft, ask yourself the following questions:
  a. Did I meet the purpose or goal with my writing?
  b. Have I provided enough information for the reader?
  c. Is my writing clear for the reader?

3.20. Make sure you have used the proper *APA style* for citations/quotations in the body of your paper.

3.21. Read your refined draft out loud once you have made all the changes.
  a. Does it make sense?
  b. Did the reading flow nicely?

3.22. If you made all the necessary changes, and answered *Yes* to all the questions, your paper is ready to go!

Section Six: Tips on Getting Your Writing Published

Having current research available is important to the social work profession; thus *Section Six* focuses on assisting you in the process that will lead to a publishable product. Table 3.8 will guide you through the preparing, planning, submitting, and expectation process of getting your research out there for others to take advantage of.

Planning, Preparing, and Submitting

You have spent numerous hours researching and developing a paper. You are passionate about what you wrote and would like to share your information with others in the social science field. The best way to do so is through a peer-reviewed journal.

You may be thinking, "I'm just a student, I don't have what it takes to become published." You are wrong. It takes perseverance and planning. Remember, your hard work and perseverance have resulted in a research paper you are proud of, and you are anxious to share the valuable information with others (*Section Five*). You just need a plan! (Refer to Table 3.8).

TABLE 3.8   Steps to Preparing, Planning, and Submitting Research to a Peer-reviewed Journal

Done	Step 1: Preparation
_____	1. **Find** a faculty mentor.
_____	2. **Read** different types of journal articles to become familiar with various formats.
_____	3. **Decide** on a topic of interest/passion that you would like to research.
_____	4. **Follow** all the *Writing Tips* to prepare a "finished" research paper.
	Step 2: Planning
_____	5. **Search out** journals that you believe will reach your intended audience.
_____	6. **Narrow down** the list and **choose** the journal you feel is appropriate for publication of your research. **NASW's** *An Author's Guide to Social Work Journals* provides a national and foreign list of journals and the how-to of submission.
_____	7. **Know** the specific guidelines for the journal you have chosen and **follow** them!
_____	8. **Know** the style guide the journal uses and **follow** it! Do not assume APA is always used!
_____	9. **Know** the structure the journal requires and **follow** it! **(IMRAD and various subheadings)**
_____	10. **Test** your finished product by asking the following questions: a. Is your data true—findings support conclusions? b. Will your research have an impact on a situation, issue, etc? c. Is your information useful? d. Does your information add to the field? ****Journal editors will ask these questions when reading your paper****
	Step 3: Submission
_____	11. **Meet** with your faculty mentor for the final "ok" and any questions you have in reference to your paper and journal submission.
_____	12. **Examine** scientific journal ethics and protocol. a. Send your paper to only one journal at a time. b. Send the entire paper.

(*Table 3.8 content sources*: Linsley, 2002; NASW, 1997)

Expectations

Your paper contains valuable information prepared in a professional manner. However, be prepared for rejection. Actually, your paper may be rejected several times before it is accepted for publication. Do not take it personally. Journal editors receive hundreds of submissions a year and find it impossible to publish every one of the papers (Linsley, 2002; NASW, 1997).

If you are turned down, take careful note of the reviewers' comments and consider the suggestions they offered. Ultimately, do not give up! Take these suggestions seriously, revise, and resubmit.

Applying what you have learned...

Submitting Your Paper.

3.23. Make a copy of *Table 3.8.*

3.24. Place a check mark in the *Done* column as you finish each step.

3.25. Submit your paper to the journal.

Summary

Getting past the "stumbling block" of deciding what to research is the initial step in the writing process. Once you have found your topic of interest, you can begin looking for resources. An abundance of resources exist in the traditional library. Books, videos, microfilm, and various periodicals can be found in the library. These literature pieces are shelved using the Library of Congress Classification or the Dewey Decimal Classification System.

The Internet provides an endless amount of information right at your fingertips. Analyze your topic to find unique terms and variant spellings, choose a search engine or Web address, and begin your search. Be careful and analyze the sources you use because a filter process does not exist and anyone can publish on the World Wide Web.

Peer-reviewed journals are excellent academic resources you should use when doing your research. You can overcome the fear and anxiety of reading a journal article through the process of learning how to read the various components. Once you have all the resources, it is time to develop your paper.

Following the writing tips and APA writing style will help alleviate your anxiety over writing. The other benefit is that you will develop a professional research paper you are proud of, and you will want to share your information with others. Find a faculty mentor and prepare, plan, and submit your paper to a peer-reviewed journal. Prepare yourself for rejection simply because editors receive an abundance of papers every year. Don't take it personally; keep on submitting. Your persistence will pay off!

KEY WORDS AND CONCEPTS

Section One
Topic selection, p. 34
Research resources, p. 35

Section Two
Library of Congress
  classification, p. 36
Dewey Decimal classification,
  p. 37
Source legitimacy, p. 38

Section Three
Web search strategies, p. 40
  Topic analysis, p. 40

Conduct search, p. 40
Search engines, p. 40
URL, p. 40
Reliability, p. 41

Section Four
Peer-reviewed journal
  article, p. 41
IMRAD, p. 44
  Introduction, p. 44
  Methodology, p. 45
  Results, p. 46
    Chi square, p. 47

Discussion, p. 48
References, p. 48
Strategies for reading,
  p. 49

Section Five
Writing tips, p. 50
APA style, p. 51

Section Six
Publishing tips, p. 54
  Plan, prepare, submit
  p. 54
  Expectations, p. 55

E X A M P L E   O F   A N   A P A   S T Y L E
R E S E A R C H   P A P E R

Header: APA Style and Professional Communication 1
(Title Page—p. 1 of your paper)
title: The Effect of the American Psychological Association Style on Professional
Communication
your name: Denise L. Smiley
course: SWK 2249: Professional Communication Skills

Header: APA Style and Professional Communication 2
(Abstract page begins on p. 2 of your paper)
Abstract **(main heading)**
Start your typing here. Do not use indentation in your abstract page. Your
abstract page summarizes the following:
1. the what and why of the research
2. methods used to do the research
3. major conclusions and significance of the results

Header: APA Style and Professional Communication 3
(Introduction page begins on p. 3 of your paper)
The Effect of the American Psychological Association Style on Professional
Communication
(title/ main heading)
Indent five spaces and begin typing your introduction. The Introduction
should include a summary of:
1. Problem you research
2. Relevance of your research
3. Context, key terms, and concepts
4. Past research relevant to the conflict or unanswered questions
5. Past findings you are testing or expanding upon
6. Brief description of your hypothesis(es) and/or research questions
7. Explanation and justifications of the research method used

Header: APA Style and Professional Communication 4
Literature Review **(main heading)**
(New page)

History—second-level heading
Provide a one-paragraph introduction for your reader.

Founders.   **This is a third-level heading that is indented five spaces and**
italicized. The paragraph continues on the same line.

Organizations.   **The number of third-level headings is based on what you want**
to include.

Methods **(main heading)**
(Do not purposely start the Methods section on a new page.)

Participants—second-level heading

   Male.   **This is a third-level heading that is indented five spaces and italicized.**

   Female.   **This is a third-level heading that is indented five spaces and italicized.**

Apparatus (*or Materials*)—second-level heading

Procedures—second-level heading

Analysis—second-level heading

Results **(main heading)**

(Do not purposely start the Results section on a new page.)

The results section of your paper explains what you have found through conducting the research. This section also includes important tables and graphs pertaining to your study.

Discussion and Conclusion **(main heading)**

(Do not purposely start Discussion and Conclusion section on a new page)

The discussion and conclusion section of your paper includes:

1. Brief summary of the findings
2. How the findings relate to expectations and literature cited
3. Theoretical implications of the results
4. Practical applications of the results
5. Possible explanations for unexpected findings
6. Weaknesses and/or limitations of your study
7. Additional needed research to resolve contradictions, weaknesses, and/or limitations of the study
8. Extension of the findings to other situations in order to understand the broader issue

Header: APA Style and Professional Communication 5

References **(main heading)**

(start new page for References section of your paper)

Books

Sheafor, B.W., & Horejsi, C.R. (2006). *Techniques and guidelines for social work practice*. Boston, MA: Pearson Education. **(title is italicized)**

Journals

Pigg, R.M. (1996). Ten steps towards professional writing. *Journal of School Health, 66*(10), 353–354. **(journal and volume number are italicized)**. Note the issue number is only included with the volume number if the journal is paginated by issue. If the pages are continuous throughout the issues for a given year, there is no issue number.

Magazines

Richison, C. (2003, December). Clock testing in dementia management. *Social Work Today, 3*, 6–7. **(magazine and volume number are italicized)**

ERIC documents

Roux, Y. (1997). *Teaching about global warming trends*. Yazoo, MI: National Conference of Concerned Educators. (ERIC Document Reproduction Service No. ED 987 321). **(title is italicized)**

Web resources

Guided search. (2006). Retrieved April 6, 2006 from North Hall Library, Mansfield University Web site: http://lib.mansfield.edu.

Lorenzen, M., & Guthrie, J. (2004). How to find information in the information age. Retrieved April 4, 2006 from the Library Instruction.com Web site: http://www.libraryinstruction.com.

Header: APA Style and Professional Communication 5
Appendix **(main heading)**
(start a new page for your Appendix page)
After this page, you can attach various tables, graphs, and copy of the questionnaire you used while conducting your study.

(This content is to be used in conjunction with the "Publication Manual of the American Psychological Association (5th Edition).")

EXAMPLES OF PROPER GRAMMAR AND PUNCTUATION

Abbreviations

1. Use the customary abbreviations for titles immediately before and after proper names.
   Mr. Brandon Jones   Nancy Sidell, Ph.D.   Mrs. Joanne Smith
   Phillip Jones, M.D.

2. If using abbreviations such as:
   FBI YMCA AFL-CIO CIA NAACP IRS NASW
   **Write the full name and the abbreviation in parentheses the first time you use it in your paper. Just using the abbreviation is acceptable after that.

3. B.C., A.D., A.M., P.M., No., and $ should only be used with specific dates, times, numbers, and amounts.
   39 B.C.   A.D. 46   9:00 A.M.   7:00 P.M.   No. 18 $890

4. Do not use inappropriate abbreviations such as:
   Personal name: Rob.—use Robert
   Units of measurement: oz—use ounce
   Days of the week: Fri.—use Friday
   Months: Aug.—use August
   Holidays: Xmas—use Christmas
   Courses: Soc. Wk.—use Social Work
   Written works: chpt.—use chapter
   States: PA.—use Pennsylvania
   Countries: Aust.—use Austrailia
   Business names: Jones Cup Co.—use Jones Cup Company

Italics and Underlining

1. Italicize:

book titles	magazines	newspapers	pamphlets
films	software	plays	art works
television and radio programs		musical compositions	
choreographic works		comic strips	

2. Underline:

Names of spacecraft, aircraft, ships, trains

Foreign words—except those that have become part of the English language

laissez-faire   per diem

Numbers

1. Spell out numbers of one or two words and numbers that begin a sentence.

Two-hundred fifty books were found on the library floor.

The library was built about nine years ago.

2. If one number follows another, spell out one and use figures for the other.

Four 2-inch ply boards   75 four-legged chairs

3. Use figures for:

dates: May 18, 2006   addresses: P.O. Box 123   percentages: 10% (10 percent)

fractions: ¼   decimals: 0.979   scores: 8 to 6

statistics: average age 49   surveys: 2 out of 3   money amounts: $15.00

divisions of books: volume 11   divisions of plays: act III, scene iiii

identification numbers: serial number 209876   time: 2:00 P.M.

Punctuation

1. Commas separate parts of a sentence and elements in a series.

When your pager rings, please respond promptly.

The doctor wrote the prescription for pain killers, sleeping pills, and muscle relaxants.

2. Commas are used after introductory words, phrases, or clauses.

Actually, your situation is rare.

However, your situation is not destructive.

3. Commas separate adjectives.

She bit the hard, sour apple.

4. Commas separate quotations, dates, and addresses.

Mr. Jones said, "Please meet the others at the center."

The fundraiser is scheduled for Monday, May 5, 2006.

The fundraiser will be located at 123 Money Lane, Tax, PA 16942.

5. Semicolons separate main clauses and phrases in a sentence.

Professional writing is important; therefore, please follow the writing tips.

Write professionally; use your document for submission to a peer-reviewed journal.

Susan's article was accepted; Joan's article rejected.

6. Colons are used to introduce a list of items, a question, or a long quote, and between hours and minutes.

These are my least favorite things to do: filing, paperwork, and answering the telephone.

The question is: "Do you fulfill all your required duties prior to leaving for the day?"

Ms. Smith said: "The paper work is becoming overwhelming, the filing needs to be completed, and all the 25 phone messages must be dealt with before anyone can leave."

7. Quotation marks are used to enclose a direct quote, titles of articles, special words, and technical terms.

> Jonathan said, "I will not be able to do all the filing prior to 8:00 P.M. this evening."
>
> I read the article entitled, "The Working Administrator."
>
> One of the problems in most cultures is "ethnocentrism."
>
> Brandon's "CD-Rom" is scratched.

8. Single quotation marks are used to enclose a quotation within another.

> Bob said, "I have finished all the paperwork and remembered your advice: 'Shred all the documents containing identifying information.'"

9. Omission marks (ellipses) indicate an omission from a quotation and to mark a delay.

> ". . . was not part of the deal."
>
> Joseph asked, "Can we skip returning the telephone calls and just . . . ?"

10. Parentheses are used to set off references, give explanatory details, and provide additional information.

> The average number of telephone calls received (see Graph 2) each day is 190.
>
> Maintain professional communications skills by: (1) answering the phone promptly, (2) responding to messages, and (3) being polite.
>
> The American Psychological Association (APA) writing style is used frequently by social scientists.

11. Brackets are used when you insert your own words into a section of a quote, to mark an error made by the person quoted, or to enclose additional information within parentheses you already have.

> The social worker stated, "The paperwork has been completed [filing, messages] and it is time to go home."
>
> Dr. Smith wrote, "There are several issues in the home that need to be deal [*sic*] with."
>
> The average number of telephone calls received (see Graph 2 [possibly Graph 3]) each day is 190.

12. Hyphens are used to join compound words, separate certain prefixes, mark fractions and numbers, and show units.

> Up-to-date data   twenty-one   attorney-at-law
>
> one-half   two-, three-, or four credits

13. Dashes are used when you want to put a strong emphasis on material in your writing.

> Technology is changing the paperwork process—possibly for the better—so that more time can be spent with clients.

14. Apostrophes are used to indicate possession and other relationships using the letter "*s.*"

Singular possessive	**Plural possessive**
the child's sweater	children's clothing
administrator's file	administrators' duties
the social worker's clients	social workers' clients

15. Period, question mark, and exclamation point end a sentence.

She walked to work. (statement—period)

Joan asked, "Did you walk to work?" (question—question mark)

Oh my, get out of the way! (strong statement—explanation point)

Sentence Structure

1. Always use complete sentences when writing!

Possibly she can. *Reader is left wondering, "can what?"*

Possibly she can work the entire week.

2. As the writer, it is your duty to make sure your sentences are unambiguous for the reader!

Spelling

1. Your dictionary needs to become your *"best friend!"*

2. Discriminate between words that have the same sound but different spelling and meaning. Some of the most common include:

here, hair, heir	there, their	so, sew	know, no
which, witch	right, write, rite	one, won	ad, add
basis, bases	capital, capitol	cite, site, sight	do, dew, due
council, counsel	desert, dessert	eligible, illegible	ensure, insure
past, passed	whether, weather	who's, whose	your, you're
its, it's	conscience, conscious		affect, effect
compliment, complement	patients, patience	stationary, stationery	
all ready, already	accept, except	correspondence, correspondents	

Do not rely on Spell Check on your computer—it checks for misspellings but does not know the context in which you are using the word!!!!

(*Proper Grammar and Punctuation source:* Brantley & Miller, 2002)

REFERENCES

About the library. (2005). Retrieved April 4, 2006 from the Library of Congress Web site: http://www.loc.gov

Academic writing: Scientific reports. (2004). Retrieved May 2, 2006 from The University of Wisconsin-Madison Writing Center Web site: http://www.wisc.edu

An author's guide to social work journals. (1997). National Association of Social Workers. Washington, DC: NASW Press.

Babbie, E. (2001). *The practice of social research.* Belmont, CA: Wadsworth/Thomson Learning.

Barker, J. (2005). *Recommended search strategy: Analyze your topic & search with peripheral vision.* Retrieved April 13, 2006 from University of California Berkeley Web site: http://www.lib.berkeley.edu

Barlow, L. (2004). *The spider's apprentice.* Retrieved April 13, 2006 from Monash Information Services Web site: http://monash.com

Beebe, L. (Ed.) (1993). *Professional writing for the Human Services.* Washington, DC: NASW Press.

Benjamin, K. (2000). *Issues and concerns using information from the Web.* Retrieved April 4, 2006 from the National Network of Libraries Web site: http://eaccesshealth.org

Brantley, C. P., & Miller, M. G. (2002). *Effective communication for colleges.* Cincinnati, OH: South-Western Educational Publishing.

Calishain, T. (2004). *Web search garage.* Retrieved April 13, 2006 from Prentice-Hall Web Search Garage Web site: http://www.websearchgarage.com

Do we really know Dewey? (2004). Retrieved April 4, 2006 from the Library Instruction Web site: http://www.libraryinstruction.com

A guide to library research: How to write a better paper. (2003). Retrieved April 4, 2006 from Rutgers, The State University of New Jersey Paul Robeson Library Web site: http:// www.libraries.rutgers. edu/rul/libs/libres.html

Guided search. (2006). Retrieved April 6, 2006 from North Hall Library, Mansfield University Web site: http://lib.mansfield.edu

Henslin, J. M. (2005). *Sociology: A down-to-earth approach.* Boston, MA: Allyn and Bacon.

Leedy, P. D. (1981). *How to read research and understand it.* New York: Macmillan Publishing Co.

Levin, J., & Fox, J. A. (2003). *Elementary statistics in social research.* Boston, MA: Allyn and Bacon.

Linsley, J. (2002). Put it in writing: Tips on writing for professional publication. *The New Social Worker, 9*(4), 7–9.

Lorenzen, M., & Guthrie, J. (2004). *How to find information in the information age.* Retrieved April 4, 2006 from the Library Instruction.com Web site: http://www.libraryinstruction.com

Monette, D. R., Sullivan, T. J., & DeJong, C. R. (2002). *Applied social research: Tool for the human services.* Orlando, FL: Harcourt.

Neuman, K. (2006). Using distance education to connect diverse communities, colleges, and students. *The Journal of Baccalaureate Social Work, 11*(2), 16–27.

Neuman, W. L. (1994). *Social research methods: Qualitative and quantitative approaches.* Needham Heights, MA: Allyn and Bacon.

Pask, J., Kramer, R., & Mandernack, S. (1993). *The savvy student's guide to library research.* West Lafayette, IN: Purdue University, Undergraduate Library.

Pigg, R. M. (1996). Ten steps towards professional writing. *Journal of School Health, 66*(10), 353–354.

Planning. (2001). Retrieved May 2, 2006 from Purdue University Online Writing Center (OWL) Web site: http://owl.english.purdue.edu

Publication Manual of the American Psychological Association: Fifth Edition. (2001).Washington, DC: American Psychological Association Service Center.

Royse, D. (1995). *Research methods in social work.* Chicago, IL: Nelson-Hall Publishers.

4 What Are Verbal and Nonverbal Communication Skills?

Your main duty as a social worker is communicating in various contexts; thus it is important for you to learn proper and effective communication skills. A great percentage of communication is nonverbal, and social workers need to be acutely aware of the significance of nonverbal language and behavior. The PERCEIVE concept will assist you in securing the skills needed to successfully decode your client's various nonverbal communications.

Chapter 4 contains numerous concepts and terms that are relevant to establishing and maintaining effective communication with your client. Various themes surrounding effective communication are discussed: thus the *Applying What You Have Learned* exercises are implemented throughout the body of the chapter rather than consolidated at the end of the chapter. This process will allow you to take a breath, break down each communication theme, and work with the concepts in a productive manner.

Section One: The Significance of Verbal Communication

Voice Tone and Intensity

Paralanguage, or vocal cues, communicate the feelings, intentions, and emotions of the speaker. Paralanguage includes loudness of voice, pauses, silences, hesitations, rate, and inflections (tone). Paralanguage can also tell us a lot about a speaker such as age, gender, race, culture, and sex (LaPlante & Ambady, 2003; Porter, 1969; Sue & Sue, 2003).

We all know that the tone and intensity of an individual's voice tell us if he or she is feeling fear, sorrow, or happiness. We can also hear hostility, delight, and cooperation in another's voice. If you listen closely to the speaker, voice tone and intensity can also inform us of a person's abilities, bias, and personality (Ambady, Bernieri, & Richeson, 2000; LaPlante & Ambady, 2003; Porter, 1969).

As a social worker, it is important that you listen closely to your client's voice tone and intensity. This channel of verbal communication is extremely informative and powerful, and can reveal your client's internal state, attitude, and feelings. Be cautious! This verbal communication channel runs both ways. For example, your client decides to handle a situation in a way that you do not agree with due to strong inner convictions. Your personal attitude and feelings toward your client's decision will be revealed through your voice tone and intensity. If you are not careful, the communication process with your client will be damaged (DePaulo & Friedman, 1998; LaPlante & Ambady, 2003).

Verbal Content and Civility

Effective verbal communication always includes clear message content. In addition, both the sender and receiver must display politeness and respect toward each other in order for the communication process to be successful (Brantley & Miller, 2002).

Verbal content. The *Six C's*, careful planning, unambiguous word selection, and practice are strategies you can use to build and maintain effective verbal communication between you and your client (Brantley & Miller, 2002).

The Six C's of Effective Verbal Communication

1. *Courtesy.* Make sure you reflect your client's point of view and address the client's needs.
2. *Clarity.* Use appropriate vocabulary, and consider your client's background when choosing words (education, culture, race, class, etc.).
3. *Conciseness.* Eliminate unnecessary words, and remember that more is not always better.
4. *Concreteness.* Use specific words so that your client can build mental pictures.
5. *Correctness.* Verify the accuracy of information before discussing it with your client.
6. *Completeness.* Be sure to include all necessary information for your client's needs.

(*The Six C's source:* Brantley & Miller, 2002. The authors stress that the Six C's are effective strategies for both written and verbal communications.)

Civility. Civility is a "must have" social work attribute! Civility includes politeness and respect that serve to promote and maintain the dignity and worth of your client.

1. *Politeness.* When meeting with your client, be courteous!
   a. Develop the *you* attitude and remember the needs of your client.
   b. Use positive words and avoid insults.
   c. Select your words carefully and avoid prejudicial language at all times.
2. *Respect.* Remember, your client is a human being!
   a. Be kind and compassionate to your client.
   b. Display respect for your client at all times.
   c. Be empathetic with your client's situation.

(*Civility source*: Brantley & Miller, 2002)

Applying what you have learned...

Voice Tone and Intensity

For this scenario, the client lives alone and calling the home is not a confidentiality issue.

4.1. For some unknown reason a "new referral" client facing numerous problems has canceled the interview appointment. You feel that connecting with him/her is urgent, and you call the client's home. The person on the other end of the phone answers just as you normally would answer your phone at home. You introduce yourself, and now there is silence on the other end. After a few seconds of silence, the voice on the other end of the phone identifies him/herself as the client. The client's voice is very low, and you are struggling to understand what is being said. Silence again, and you decide to go forward with the interview process just as you would if it was taking place in your office. You ask your questions, and the client answers them in a slow, low voice. Throughout the phone conversation, some of your questions are answered after a brief period of silence. It is now time to discuss the problems that your client is facing. Your client's voice becomes louder, clearer, and rapid-paced as each problem is discussed. Every so often you hear a "crackling" in the client's voice.

a. List emotions you believe you heard in your client's voice. What voice tone and/or intensity caused you to believe your client was feeling this way?

b. As a group, compare and contrast your responses.

c. Keep a record of this exercise.

Verbal Content and Civility

4.2. **Read the following client scenario:** Your new client is 16 years old. He/she is not familiar with how the system works and is uncomfortable and angry about having to meet with you. He/she is failing eleventh grade and has been involved in various negative peer incidences at school over the past three months. Your client must receive ongoing counseling throughout the remaining school year or he/she cannot return to the school. Your client's parents have disclosed to you that their child's drinking and drug use are escalating, and they are concerned that it has turned into addictions. The police report you received shows your client was arrested for shoplifting. In reading your client's information received from the school's guidance counselor, you discover that all your client's time is being spent with his/her "first love." The parents are concerned that your client is sexually active.

a. Write what you believe will be the best way to begin, and continue, effective verbal communication with your new client (refer to the Six C's and Civility).

b. Verbally practice what you wrote with a classmate, noting any confusion and offenses, if any, your classmate experienced. Continue practicing with classmates, friends, and so on until you feel comfortable, and confident, that your verbal communication is not offensive, and your client would understand what you are saying.

Section Two: The Significance of Nonverbal Communication

What Is Nonverbal Communication?

Communication is a transmission of information in which the sender and receiver are always changing places while exchanging information. The exchange of information is not limited to written and verbal communication. You do not have to write or speak to communicate, and according to research, two-thirds of total communication may be nonverbal (Beall, 2004; Brantley & Miller, 2002). Often we are so focused on the words being spoken that we overlook the nonverbal aspect of communication (Beall, 2004; Brantley & Miller, 2002).

Every contact you have with your client is considered a communication cycle. You and your client are continuously changing roles from sender to receiver while exchanging verbal and nonverbal information. Being conscientious about selecting the appropriate words when communicating with your client is not enough. You must be aware of the significance of the nonverbal communication you and your client are exchanging during contact (Beall, 2004; Brantley & Miller, 2002).

Social Rhythms

Nonverbal communication is complex. Several environmental factors known as *social rhythms* influence these nonverbal communications. These influences can block productive communication and lead to problems between you and your client if you are not aware of the interaction between social rhythms and nonverbal communication (Beall, 2004; Brantley & Miller, 2002; Porter, 1969; Sue & Sue, 2003).

Influential factors.   The social rhythms you need to consider when communicating with your client include:

1. *Culture.* Culture includes more than just language, beliefs, clothing, and celebrating various holidays. Nonverbal communication and behaviors also vary in each culture; thus it is essential that you become both familiar and comfortable with your client's cultural background (Beall, 2004; Brantley & Miller, 2002; Henslin, 2005; Porter, 1969; Sue & Sue, 2003).

2. *Race.* Race is defined as "the physical characteristics that distinguish one group from another" (Henslin, 2005, p. 324). *Ethnicity*, on the other hand, applies to cultural characteristics that are not usually visible. Throughout the United States' history, racial and ethnic minority groups have faced both *prejudice* (negative attitudes/feelings) and *discrimination* (negative actions) (Henslin, 2005).

   Negative *stereotypes* of minority groups are formed when prejudice and discrimination exist. As a social worker, it is imperative that you refrain from discrimination because it is against the law and the NASW code of ethics. Although prejudiced attitudes and feelings can be hidden, both can become apparent when working with a client who is from a minority race and/or ethnicity. Prejudice causes negative "*stereotyping,*" which will inevitably influence your reactions and behaviors toward the client. Stereotyping will certainly block your ability to understand the client's nonverbal communication, thus preventing the fulfillment of the client's needs (Beall, 2004; Brantley & Miller, 2002; Henslin, 2005; Porter, 1969; Schmolling, Youkeles, & Burger, 1993; Sue & Sue, 2003).

3. *Gender.* The terms *gender* and *sex* are used interchangeably, but *sex* is the biological makeup of a person and *gender* is created culturally through society's behavioral and attitude expectations of the male and female (Henslin, 2005). Boys are rewarded for being active and independent, and are expected to get dirty and be defiant. Their bedrooms and clothes tend to be the primary colors of blue and green, and they receive

instrumental toys such as trucks and tools. Girls are rewarded for being passive and dependent, and are expected to be dainty and compliant. Their bedrooms and clothes tend to be the secondary colors of pink and white, and they receive *expressive* toys such as dolls and Easy-Bake ovens (Henslin, 2005).

This societal rearing process influences the manner in which males and females communicate verbally and nonverbally. The differences in nonverbal communication that exist between males and females can hinder your ability to successfully assist your client if you are not aware of the gender socialization differences (Henslin, 2005; Schmolling, Youkeles, & Burger, 1993).

4. *Social Class and Education Attainment.* Society is split into several classes, and these classes are ranked according to the amount of *valued resources* of status/prestige, power, and wealth present. This ranking and distribution of valued resources is known as *stratification* (Beeghley, 2000; Henslin, 2005; Kerbo, 1983; Tumin, 1985).

Because each level in society's stratification system has varied amounts of resources and educational attainment, distinctive *status symbols* and *cultural characteristics* within each class exist. Status symbols are a form of nonverbal, symbolic communication, including types of occupations, educational attainment, condition and location of homes, type of vehicles, merchant preferences, and club memberships. The symbols also provide individuals with an understanding of their place in society's class structure. Examples of cultural characteristics include public conduct, religious beliefs, values, attitudes, and ideologies (Beeghley, 2000; Kerbo, 1983; Porter, 1969; Tumin, 1985).

Status symbols and cultural characteristics affect both you and your client's nonverbal communication. It is important for you to understand society's class structure, together with the distinct symbols and characteristics within each. (See Table 4.1 and 4.2).

TABLE 4.1   Upper and Middle Class Characteristics

Physical health	Funds and insurance for personal physician Less likely to smoke, abuse alcohol, and use drugs. More likely to consume healthy-smart foods, exercise frequently, and practice safe sex
Mental health	Less stress due to resources and greater control over their lives Can afford vacations, and private psychiatrists or mental health professionals
Family life	Traditional view = stress ancestors, history, see family as a purpose and/or destiny in life Spouse affects entire family, thus marriage pool is limited, and parents play a major part in the child's mate selection Less divorce and single families
Education	Attend private and/or military schools, well-funded public schools, prestigious universities, and more likely to obtain degrees High parental expectations and motivation (aspirations)
Religion	Prefer reserved worship
Politics	Active, mainly Republican, conservative views on government spending, liberal views on social issues (abortion)
Crime	White-collar crime dealt with outside of the criminal justice system, arrests are rare

(Table 4.1. content sources: Beeghley, 2000; Henslin, 2005; Kerbo, 1983; Tumin, 1985)

TABLE 4.2 Working and Lower Class Characteristics

Physical health	Larger proportion of elderly and infants die yearly More likely to smoke, abuse drugs and alcohol, eat more fatty foods, exercise less, practice unsafe sex Unequal treatment and access to prime health care due to lack of funds and/or adequate medical insurance Waiting long hours in crowded public health clinics; may not be seen and has to return the next day Admitted to public hospitals that are usually underfunded and understaffed May lack medical/health progress follow-ups during hospitalization and after returning home
Mental health	Mental health is worse than that of the upper/middleclass due to less job security, lower wages, unemployment, threat of eviction, unpaid bills, divorce, vulnerability to crime, physical illness
Family life	Marital friction and divorce due to insecure jobs, inadequate/crowded homes, etc.
Education	High school education at best Attend public, low-funded, crowded schools Lack *new technology* resources and knowledge
Religion	Prefer more expressive worship services
Politics	Mainly Democratic, more liberal on economic issues (policies to increase government spending), conservative on social issues (abortion)
Crime	Street crimes, more likely to be in prison, on probation or parole More likely to be robbed, burglarized, or murdered

(Table 4.2 content sources: Beeghley, 2000; Henslin, 2005; Kerbo, 1983; Tumin, 1985)

- *Upper class.* The rich encompass a small percentage of the population, yet hold a disproportionally large percentage of the valued resources. They mainly attend preparatory schools and often have a college education from an Ivy League institution. Their wealth is either inherited or comes from an invention/creation that society values. Their homes include mansions and estates privately located in areas with little, if any, poverty and crime. Their cars of choice are the Rolls Royce and Mercedes Benz. The rich lead "intensely private lives" (Beeghley, 2000, p. 170), shop at very prestigious shops, and private clubs are their choice of membership. Their public conduct, values, attitudes, and ideologies are considered society's high-class norms.
- *Middle class.* The middle class encompasses nonmanual laborers, people found in white-collar occupations. Examples include doctors, lawyers, teachers, nurses, and various "desk job" occupations. They mostly have a college education and usually have high incomes. Society defines the middle class as hard-working, economically and occupationally successful, and possessing individual autonomy (independence). Their homes are located in what are considered "good neighborhoods," and these areas usually have low poverty and crime rates. The middle class is considered representative of *society's norms* of public conduct, values, attitudes, and ideologies.
- *Working class.* The working class includes manual laborers, who are usually found in blue-collar occupations such as manufacturing, garbage collection, custodial

work, and construction. Their job settings are frequently unpleasant and dangerous. Petty work rules, intense production pressures, and fear of layoffs usually are a large part of the blue-collar worker's existence. The terms *working poor* and *those living on a fixed income* are frequently used to describe the working class. Normally, they do not have a college education, and they reside in rural, poverty-stricken, and/or intermediate-crime areas. Since their education, housing, and lifestyles do not match those of the middle class, their public conduct, values, attitudes, and ideologies may be considered *deviant* rather than representative of society's norms.

■ *Lower class.* The lower class includes the poor, those living in *poverty*, and those who are homeless. It is difficult for the lower class to obtain food, shelter, and medical treatment. If employed, their work comes with low pay and few, if any, benefits. The lower class may or may not have a high school diploma. They mostly reside in rural areas, low-income housing developments, dilapidated buildings, and/or on the streets of cities with an abundance of poverty and criminal behavior. Society sees the lower class as untrustworthy, worthless, and deviant.

(*Social class and education sources*: Beeghley, 2000; Henslin, 2005; Kerbo, 1983; Tumin, 1985)

As a social worker, you will be less likely to have clients from the upper and middle social classes because they possess the financial and educational resources needed to deal with personal crises. The more resources one has, the more choices are available to one in handling a crisis (Beeghley, 2000; Henslin, 2005; Kerbo, 1983; Tumin, 1985).

For the most part, your clientele will consist of the working and lower-class population who lack financial, educational, and supportive resources, and the choices that come with these resources.

Applying what you have learned...

Culture Reflection

4.3. Think about the following scenarios and see if you can answer true or false correctly.

a. You have just started working with a young German boy who moved to your town three months ago. Your hour-long session with him has ended, and you walk him out to the reception area. His next appointment is scheduled and you "wave good-bye" to him. He will interpret this as a good-bye wave because "waving good-bye" is done the same in every culture.

b. You have been hired as a social worker in a small, multicultural public school. You begin your tour of the school in the second grade classroom where a Japanese girl is smiling at you. You smile back and think to yourself, "this young girl is happy," because the meaning of a smile is universal.

Race Reflection

4.4. Take a few moments to read and think about each of the following scenarios. How would you react to each situation? Reflect on your reaction, and be honest with yourself when answering the question, "Why did I react to the situation the way I did?"

a. The day has come for you to apply your education to practice. You leave your home and drive into the city to begin the first day of your new job as a social worker. Your morning appointments have gone well, and you feel comfortable with your abilities to help the clients and the urban community they live in. Your first afternoon appointment

Applying what you have learned... Continued

has arrived. He is a 25-year-old African American father who has not been able to find work since he was laid off last month. You close your office door and begin the interview. Your client is speaking loudly, and his voice sounds angry. His body movements are animated, and he appears to be confrontational.

b. Your husband has recently lost his job at the factory after working there 12 years. The bills are piling up, and Christmas is a month away. As a result, you must return to the social work field and leave your six-month-old son. The first client you are scheduled to interview on your first day on the job is a 22-year-old Latino male who is having problems with his boss and has been referred to your agency. He stresses to you that he has a wife and baby, Christmas is coming, and he just cannot lose his job.

Gender Reflection

4.5. Take a few moments to read the following list of problems.
   - The client is an unemployed single parent.
   - The client has three children and is living in a one-bedroom apartment.
   - The client does not have any money for food or this month's rent.
   - The weather is turning cold, and none of the family members has a coat.

4.6. How would you feel/react to the problems if your client were male? Why?
   How would you feel/react to the problems if your client were female? Why?

4.7. You are the social worker. Make two lists (male/female) comparing and contrasting what you believe would be your behavior and nonverbal communication according to the gender of your client.

4.8. You are the client. Make two lists (male/female) comparing and contrasting what you believe would be your behavior and nonverbal communication according to the gender of the social worker.

Social Class and Education Attainment Reflection

4.9. The following are problems your client is currently sharing with you:
   - She is having financial difficulties and cannot pay the rent this month.
   - Her car broke down, and now getting to school and work is difficult.
   - She has been feeling physically ill lately and fears she may be pregnant.
   - She is struggling with keeping up with her peers academically.
   - Her boyfriend has been drinking and using drugs, and told her he stole some jewelry and money to buy drugs.

You are a social worker from an inner-city neighborhood, and your client is from a middle-class suburban neighborhood. She was afraid to talk to her parents or to see their private family counselor, and so she has come to you for help.

1. Why do you think she feared sharing these problems with her family and private family counselor?
   a. In being honest with yourself, what do you believe would be your initial feelings and views of this client? Why?
   b. Consider your initial feelings and views of your client. List your nonverbal communications you think will be displayed during the interview based on your initial feelings and views of your client.
   c. You are the client in the scenario. What do you believe would be your initial feelings and views of the social worker? Why? List what you believe would be your nonverbal communications based on this.
   d. You are a social worker from a middle-class suburban neighborhood, and your client is from an inner-city neighborhood. She has no one to turn to except you.
   e. Apply 1b, 1c, and 1d to this scenario.
2. What do you think your feelings, views, and nonverbal behaviors would be if both you and your client came from the same social class?

Section Three: The Significance of Nonverbal Behavior

Both social workers and clients are very diverse, as can be seen in nonverbal behaviors. Being aware of your own nonverbal behaviors, and acclimating to your client's, is a necessary link in successfully understanding and assisting your client.

Body Language

Body language is always present when we communicate. Being less deliberate and mostly unconscious, body language is more meaningful than verbal statements. As a social worker, it is important that you be keenly aware of your body language and become skilled in displaying proper body language when working with your client. Remember, in order for your client to perceive you as genuine and sincere, your body language should match your verbal communication. This will also prevent client confusion (Beall, 2004; *Journal of Behavior Development*, 2001; *Journal of Nursing*, 2002; Kirch, 1979; Krim, 1953; Porter, 1969; Sue & Sue, 2003).

Kinesics.   It is imperative that you display proper kinesics, or body language, such as posture, gait, and body positioning when communicating with your client. Your facial expressions and eye contact should communicate interest, attention, concern, and respect. Caring and genuineness should also be displayed (Beall, 2004; *Journal of Behavior Development*, 2001; *Journal of Nursing*, 2002; Kirch, 1979; Krim, 1953; Porter, 1969; Sue & Sue, 2003).

Keep in mind that body movements vary with gender, class, and culture. It is beneficial to both you and your client that you investigate the common kinesics that exist within each group. This investigation will ensure that the initial interview with your new client is positive and nonthreatening (See Table 4.3 and 4.4). (Beall, 2004; *Journal of Behavior Development*, 2001; *Journal of Nursing*, 2002; Kirch, 1979; Krim, 1953; Porter, 1969; Sue & Sue, 2003).

TABLE 4.3   Proper Display of Kinesics

Type of Kinesic	Proper Display
Posture	Remain upright.
Facial Expression Most expressive part of the body	Smile, and make sure you display sincerity, concern, and respect.
Eye Contact Varies with the situation	Adopt seating or standing arrangements that *allow* for eye contact.
Gait Way of walking	Approach your client with a composed, slow gait.
Body Position Sitting Standing	If seated, place your hands on your lap. Allow your arms and hands to hang loosely along your sides when standing.

(*Table 4.3 content sources*: Beall, 2004; *Journal of Nursing,* 2002; *Journal of Behavior Development,* 2001; Kirch, 1979; Krim, 1953; Porter, 1969; Sheafor & Horejsi, 2006; Sue & Sue, 2003)

TABLE 4.4   Improper Display of Kinesics

Type of Kinesic	Improper Display
Posture	Slouching—displays fatigue or disinterest
Facial Expression Most expressive part of the body	Frowning and judgmental expressions
Eye Contact Varies with the situation	Forcing eye contact.
Gait Way of walking	Approaching client quickly
Body Position Sitting Standing	If seated, folding arms across chest, behind your head, or draped over an adjoining chair—displays inattention or non-receptiveness Tightly clasped hands, swinging legs or feet, pacing, and "watching the clock"—displays nervousness or impatience

(*Table 4.4 content sources*: Beall, 2004; *Journal of Nursing*, 2002; *Journal of Behavior Development*, 2001; Kirch, 1979; Krim, 1953; Porter, 1969; Sheafor & Horejsi, 2006; Sue & Sue, 2003)

Proxemics.   Proxemics, or spatial distance, varies with gender, class, and culture just as kinesics does. Spatial distance will also vary with your client's situation. Being familiar with your client's situation and social background is crucial in guaranteeing effective communication between you and your client (Beall, 2004; *Journal of Behavior Development*, 2001; *Journal of Nursing*, 2002; Sheafor & Horejsi, 2006).

Attending.   Substantial research has been done on spatial distance and the skill of attending. Attending is the process of nonverbally communicating to others that you are receptive,

TABLE 4.5   Key DO'S and DON'TS of Attending

DO'S	DON'TS
Face your client at a 90-degree angle, with 3–4 feet of distance between you and your client.	Do not face your client directly during the initial interview because this may threaten him/her.
Your office chairs should be at an angle of between 90 and 135 degrees so your client can direct his/her eyes and body toward or away from you. Your office chair should match your client's chair.	Do not have a table or other obstacles between you and your client. This may break the communication cycle. Do not have a desk separating you from your client. This suggests superiority over your client, and inhibits closeness and openness.
A slight lean or incline toward your client is recommended. **Watch your client's reaction.	**The leaning may be too intrusive during the initial interview, and you may have to lean away from your client.

(*Table 4.5 content sources:* Beall, 2004; *Journal of Nursing*, 2002; *Journal of Behavior Development*, 2001; Kirch, 1979; Krim, 1953; Porter, 1969; Sheafor & Horejsi, 2006; Sue & Sue, 2003)

Applying what you have learned…

Kinesics, Proxemics, and "Attending"

4.10 The following is a list of various *improper kinesics, proxemics,* and *"attending"* being displayed by a social worker while working with a new client.
- The social worker is walking fast and quickly approaches the new client for introductions.
- The social worker is sitting behind the desk, and the client's chair is snug to the front of the social worker's desk.
- Direct eye contact between the social worker and client is unavoidable.
- The social worker frowns when the client talks about his or her situation.
- The social worker is continuously looking at the clock on the wall.
- After some time spent with the client, the social worker leans back in the chair with arms crossed over his or her chest.
- Eventually, the social worker leans over the desk toward the client, and there is now only a few inches between their faces.
  a. How do you think the client will feel/react to the social worker's improper display of each kinesic, proxemic, and/or "attending"?
  b. List the proper body language, spatial distance, and/or "attending" for 1–7.

nonjudgmental, accepting of them as people, and concerned with what they have to say. The key to encouraging your client to express him or herself freely and completely is to have proper *attending* skills. Demonstrating attending skills and having respect for your client's personal space will eliminate discomfort for both of you (Beall, 2004; *Journal of Behavior Development*, 2001; *Journal of Nursing*, 2002; Sheafor & Horejsi, 2006).

Keep in mind that the DO'S and DON'TS listed in Table 4.5 pertain mainly to the initial interview with your client. As he or she becomes familiar with you and trust develops, attending and spatial distance with your client may change. Your client's nonverbal behavior will direct you (Beall, 2004; *Journal of Behavior Development*, 2001; *Journal of Nursing*, 2002; Sheafor & Horejsi, 2006).

Section Four: The Framework of "Decoding" Client Nonverbal Behavior Communication

Monitoring and displaying proper nonverbal behavior is important to successful communication with your client. Decoding your client's nonverbal behavior is just as important so that you can gain a significant understanding of your client. Decoding nonverbal behaviors in the social work field is done through the use of PERCEIVE.

The Use of PERCEIVE

A combination of behaviors will tell a story if you pay close attention to your client's nonverbal cues and decode these cues correctly through the use of PERCEIVE (Beall, 2004; Sheafor & Horejsi, 2006).

1. *Proximity* is the distance between individuals. The nearness of your client will indicate his or her feelings of interest and trust. Keep in mind that all clients will have a different *comfort zone* in terms of how close they want to be to you, and you need to read their body language and adjust accordingly. Remember, being too close may be threatening to some clients.

2. *Expressions* are observed on the face. The six universal expressions are happiness, sadness, anger, fear, surprise and disgust. If your client is trying to hide his or her feelings, the expression will be brief (1/15 of a second). When your client begins to experience an emotion he or she feels comfortable sharing with you, facial muscles are triggered and your client's feelings will be prominently displayed. Facial expressions may indicate whether your client is thinking one thing and saying something else.

3. *Relative orientation* is the degree to which individuals face each other. Interest and focus will be indicated by a parallel orientation. Various intentions and attitudes can be decoded through your client's body positioning. The key to decoding your client's level of interest and focus is to watch his or her foot placement and direction. Disinterest and inattention are indicated when your client angles his or her body and feet away from you.

4. *Contact* refers to physical contact. Closeness, familiarity, and degree of liking are indicated through the amount and frequency of touch. By touching your client's hand, arm, or shoulder, or by offering a hug, you convey reassurance, sympathy, or understanding. You must be cautious about touching your client, however, especially if he or she is of the opposite sex or from a cultural or ethnic background unfamiliar to you and different from yours. Depending on the client's background, a touch could be misinterpreted as a sexual advance. If your client has been physically or sexually abused, or has a certain mental disorder, a touch can be intimidating. You must carefully monitor and limit client touching.

5. *Eye Contact* is an extremely powerful means of communication. Your client's eyes will reveal to you emotion, sensitivity, and/or understanding of his or her situation. Your client's openness and willingness to communicate will be indicated by eye contact with you. Anxiety, intimidation, disinclination to communicate, and/or dishonesty will be indicated through the lack of eye contact. Remember, the amount of eye contact varies in cultures; never force eye contact.

6. *Individual gestures* are movements of the body when communicating. Gestures frequently indicate strong feelings. Arms and hands at the body's side or outstretched indicate openness, whereas crossed legs, arms folded across the chest, and body rigidity may mean defensiveness. Your client's impatience, nervousness, or preoccupation may be communicated through fidgety movements such as toe and finger tapping and leg bouncing. Clenched fists usually indicate anger or anxiety.

7. *Voice* reveals feelings. It is important that you listen closely to your client's tone of voice. Your client's voice may be barely audible if he or she is feeling withdrawn, fearful, and/or weak. If your client is disinterested, the voice will be monotonous. A loud and potent tone indicates aggressiveness, control, and/or strength. It is important to monitor your client's tone of voice at all times. If he or she begins to sound hostile, you must be prepared to handle the situation so that the environment remains safe for both of you.

8. *Adapters* are small behaviors that are exhibited when people are stressed or bored. Twirling a pen, playing with rings, or touching one's hair are the most common adapters. Your client may display various other adapters if communication has broken

Applying what you have learned...

Using PERCEIVE

4.11. The following is a list of behaviors being exhibited by a client.

- The client's body and feet are directed toward the door, away from the social worker.
- The client has been with the social worker for 15 minutes and still has not made eye contact.
- The client is continuously playing with the button on his or her jacket.
- The client's fists are clenched.
- The client's tone of voice is low, and the social worker is straining to hear what the client is saying.

- The client is sitting on the opposite side of the room far from the social worker and refuses to move closer.
- The client has been meeting with the social worker for 15 minutes and has not displayed any facial expressions that the social worker has been able to decipher.
- The client sits very close to the social worker. The client also keeps touching the social worker's arm.

a. Using PERCEIVE, decode the various client behaviors.

b. What do you feel you can do to change the client's behavior for 1–8?

down. Pay close attention to your client's behavior so that you can redirect your client and continue the effective communication cycle.

(*PERCEIVE sources:* Beall, 2004; Sheafor & Horejsi, 2006)

Summary

Paralanguage, or vocal cues, communicate the speaker's feelings, intentions, and emotions. Paralanguage is extremely informative and will assist you in determining your client's internal state, attitude, and feelings. It is important that you listen closely to your client's voice tone and intensity when communicating.

As a social worker, it is crucial that you become proficient in both speaking and listening. Practice, preparation, and the Six C's will assist you in perfecting your verbal speech. Your main duty is to promote and maintain the dignity and worth of your client, which can be achieved through courteous and humane treatment (civility) of your client. With civility, you will avoid frustrating and offending your client.

Speaking and writing are not always necessary in the communication process. It is estimated that two-thirds of total communication is nonverbal; therefore it becomes essential that you understand the social rhythms that influence nonverbal communication. Social rhythms include culture, race, gender, and class.

Body language is always present when we communicate. As a social worker, it is important that you be keenly aware of your body language and become skilled in displaying proper kinesics, proxemics, and "attending" when working with your client. Interpreting your client's nonverbal behavior is just as important as understanding your own. If you pay close attention to your client's body language, you can decode this nonverbal communication and complete your client's story through the use of PERCEIVE.

APPLYING WHAT YOU HAVE LEARNED

(Answers to the exercises implemented throughout the chapter)

Section One Exercises
Voice Tone and Intensity

4.1: The client in the scenario has just separated from an abusive partner after 15 years (scared, confused). The children have recently been pulled out of the home, and the abusive partner is in jail (confused, lonely, sad). The client has lost a job after 5 years, having missed several days of work (worried, angry). The client was released from the hospital three days ago and is still recuperating from the recent incident of abuse (tired, sore, maybe ill). **Now that you have background information on the client's problems, look back at the information you gathered for this exercise. How well do you believe you and your classmates did in figuring out how the client was feeling, having only voice tone and intensity to go by?**

Verbal Content and Civility

4.2: Remember, your client is 16 years old, is failing school, and has never been in the Human Services system. It is important that you do not use "scholarly" terminology or staff slang because this may confuse and frustrate your **new** and **young** client. Choose your words carefully so that insults and stereotyping do not enter into the communication cycle. Reflect your client's point of view, and address his or her needs. See your **young** client as a person who deserves respect and courteous treatment.

Section Two Exercises
"Social Rhythms" Reflections

4.3: Culture

    a. *False.* Your young male client will not understand your "good-bye" wave. In Germany, the hand is held horizontally, palm down, and the fingers are moved toward the departing person. In American culture, this is interpreted as "speeding one on their way" (Kirch, 1979).

    b. *False.* Japanese children are taught that a "smile" is a social duty. He or she must always appear happy so that inflicting sorrow on friends can be avoided (Kirch, 1979).

4.4: Race

    a. *White middle-class communication styles are usually detached, objective, impersonal, and nonchallenging. African American styles of communication are often interpersonal and confrontational.* The characteristics of communication include emotions, affects, and feelings. An advocacy stance is usually taken. It is not unusual for white mental health practitioners to describe these communication characteristics as hostile and angry, as a result of which they display anxiety, discomfort, or fear of the client through nonverbal communication. This includes leaning away from the client, tipping their chair back, and crossing their legs or arms (Sue & Sue, 2003).

b. **Be very cautious with this interview, and remain professional by assessing and assisting your client.** Remember, avoid the "immigrant" stereotyping of your client because your nonverbal communication and behavior will be quite apparent to your client (Sue & Sue, 2003).

4.5: Gender

Do not see gender and the client problems in this situation as "inseparable." Keep in mind that whether your client is male or female, the problems listed in the exercise can apply to both genders. The problems of the client are the same and require the same intervention plans. The strategies used to implement the plans, however, will vary according to gender because:

1. **Males** are socialized to be the "achievers" and "breadwinners." Your male client may feel guilt, embarrassment, and shame because of his inability to provide for his children (Henslin, 2005). He may also see the situation as a difference between right and wrong. Do not be quick to judge your male client if he lacks emotion during the interview. Public display of emotions is a "violation of their gender role" (Henslin, 2005, p. 73).

2. **Females** are socialized to be "compliant" and to base their success on relationships. Your female client is concerned about loyalty to her children and the harm that may come to them (Gilligan, 1982, 1990). Do expect displays of emotion from your female clients because it is socially acceptable for females to display happiness, delight, and sadness in public (Henslin, 2005).

4.6: Social Class and Education Attainment

It is extremely important that you become familiar with the social class system. Each class varies in status symbols and characteristics, which in turn affects nonverbal communication.

1. *Be cautious!* Remember, if you consider your middle-class client a spoiled rich kid, she will certainly see this opinion in your facial expressions and hear it in your voice.

2. *Remember,* the client is a human being and must be treated as such. Be careful with your facial expressions, body movements, and voice tone, which your client will surely see and hear even if she lacks a formal education.

   Avoid oversympathetic verbal and nonverbal communication.

3. *Be careful with this one!* You and your client are from the same social class and can understand each other's verbal and nonverbal communication.

   That is great, but as a result, both you and your client can experience the loss of role identity. Your experience is not your client's!

Section Three Exercises
Kinesics, Proxemics, and "Attending"
4.7(1): All the improper kinesics, proxemics, and/or "attending" displayed by the social worker have harmed or halted the effective communication process with the client.

1. The social worker is walking fast and quickly approaches the new client for introductions.

    a. The new client is probably going to be scared and/or intimidated by the social worker's quick approach.

2. The social worker is sitting behind the desk, and the client's chair is snug to the front of the social worker's desk.

    a. The client is going to see the social worker as superior.

    b. Sitting behind a desk inhibits closeness and openness.

    c. The client may feel uncomfortable sitting so close to, and directly facing, the social worker.

3. Direct eye contact between the social worker and client is unavoidable.

    a. Never force eye contact.

    b. The client may feel threatened by the social worker.

4. The social worker frowns when the client talks about his or her situation.

    a. Be careful! The client may think the social worker is being judgmental.

5. The social worker is continuously looking at the clock on the wall.

    a. The client may see the social worker as being nervous or impatient.

6. After some time spent with the client, the social worker leans back in the chair with arms crossed over his or her chest.

    a. The social worker is displaying inattention or nonreceptiveness toward the client.

7. Eventually, the social worker leans over the desk toward the client, and there is now only a few inches between their faces.

    a. The leaning may be too intrusive during the initial interview.

    b. Watch your client. You may have to lean away from your client.

4.7(2): "Attending." Refer to Table 4.3, Table 4.4, and Table 4.5.

Section Four Exercises
Using PERCEIVE

4.8(1): Decoding the various client behaviors

1. The client's body and feet are directed toward the door, away from the social worker.

> **Relative Orientation = Disinterest and inattention are being**
> **displayed by the client.**

2. The client has been with the social worker for 15 minutes and still has not made eye contact.

> **Lack of Eye Contact = 1. Client is feeling anxious or intimidated.**
> **OR**
> **2. Client is closed to communication.**
> **OR**
> **3. Client is being dishonest with the social worker.**

3. The client is continuously playing with the button on his or her jacket.

> **Existence of Adapters = Client may be bored and/or stressed.**

4. The client's fists are clenched.

Individual Gestures = Client is feeling angry or anxious.

5. The client's tone of voice is low, and the social worker is straining to hear what the client is saying.

Voice = Client is feeling withdrawn, fearful, and/or weak.

6. The client is sitting on the opposite side of the room, far from the social worker, and refuses to move closer.

Proximity = 1. Client is not interested in what the social worker is saying.
OR
2. Client does not trust the social worker.
OR
3. This may be common in the client's culture.

KEY WORDS AND CONCEPTS

Section One
Verbal communication, p. 64
 Paralanguage, p. 66
 Verbal content, p. 65
  The Six C's, p. 65
 Civility, p. 65
  Politeness, p. 65
  Respect, p. 65

Section Two
Nonverbal communication, p. 66
Social rhythms, p. 67
 Influential factors, p. 67
  Culture, p. 67
  Race, p. 67
   Race vs. ethnicity, p. 67

Prejudice vs.
 discrimination, p. 67
Gender, p. 67
 Sex vs. gender, p. 67
 Instrumental vs.
  expressive, p. 68
Social class and education
 attainment, p. 68
 Valued resources, p. 68
 Stratification, p. 68
 Status symbols, p. 68
 Cultural
  characteristics, p. 68
Class, p. 69
 Upper, p. 69
 Middle, p. 69

Society's
 norms, p. 69
Working, p. 69
 Deviant, p. 70
Lower, p. 70
 Poverty, p. 70

Section Three
Body language, p. 72
 Kinesics, p. 72
 Proxemics, p. 72
 Attending, p. 72

Section Four
"Decoding" nonverbal
 behavior, p. 74
 PERCEIVE, p. 74

REFERENCES

Ambady, N., Bernieri, F. J., & Richeson, J. A. (2000). Toward a history of social behavior: Judgmental accuracy from think slices of the behavioral stream. *Advances in Experimental Social Psychology, 32,* 201–207.

Beall, A. E. (2004). Body language speaks: Reading and responding more effectively to hidden communication. *Communication World, 21*(2), 18.

Beeghley, L. (2000). *The structure of social stratification in the United States* (3rd ed.). Needham Heights, MA: Allyn & Bacon.

Birdwhistell, R. L. (1970). *Kinesics and context.* Philadelphia: University of Pennsylvania Press.

Body Language. (2001). *Journal of Behavior Development, 25*(4), 344–353.

Body Language. (2002). *Journal of Nursing, 102*(1), 845.

Brantley, C. P., & Miller, M. G. (2002). *Effective communication for colleges*. Cincinnati, OH: South-Western Educational Publishing.

DePaulo, B. M. & Friedman, H. S. (1998). Nonverbal communication. In D.T. Gilbert, S.T. Fiske, & G. Lindzey (Eds.), *The handbook of social psychology* (4th ed., Vol. 2, pp. 3–39). New York: McGraw-Hill.

Gilligan, C. (1982). *In a different voice: Psychological theory and women's development*. Cambridge, MA: Harvard University Press.

Gilligan, C. (1990). *Making connections: The relational world of adolescent girls at Emma Willard School*. Cambridge, MA: Harvard University Press.

Henslin, J. M. (2005). *Sociology: A down-to-earth approach*. Boston, MA: Allyn & Bacon.

Kerbo, H. R. (1983). *Social stratification and inequality: Class conflict in the United States*. New York: McGraw-Hill Book Company.

Kirch, M. S. (1979). Non-verbal communication across cultures. *Modern Language Journal, 63*(8), 416–423.

Krim, A. (1953). *A study in non-verbal communications: Expressive movements during interviews*. Northampton, MA: Smith College School for Social Work.

LaPlante, D., & Ambady, N. (2003). On how things are said: Voice tone, voice intensity, verbal content, and perceptions of politeness. *Journal of Language and Social Psychology, 22*, 434–440.

Porter, G. W. (1969). Non-verbal communications. *Training and Development Journal, 23*, 7–8

Schmolling, P., Youkeles, M., & Burger, W. R. (1993). *Human Services in contemporary America*. Pacific Grove, CA: Brooks/Cole Publishing Company.

Sheafor, B. W. & Horejsi, C. R. (2006). *Techniques and guidelines for social work practice*. Boston, MA: Pearson Education.

Sue, D. W., & Sue, D. (2003). *Counseling the culturally diverse: Theory and practice*. New York: John Wiley & Sons.

Tumin, M. M. (1985). *Social stratification: The forms and functions of inequality*. Englewood Cliffs, NJ: Prentice-Hall.

Communicating in Supervision

The link between classroom learning and experiential education is examined in this chapter. Both work together to prepare you for a professional career in social work. The ability to understand your role and the role of your supervisor is the first step in getting the most out of your practicum or internship. The chapter will prepare you for supervision, along with providing the tools necessary to resolve supervision issues. By practicing the various supervision scenario exercises in the chapter, you will be able to increase your professional communication skills needed for your social work practicum.

Section One: The History of Social Work Supervision

Traditionally, social work supervision was emphasized as an educational and supportive role. By the 1980s, "supervisor" became an administrative function separate from practice. It was assumed that *supervision* meant "administrative duties" requiring a set of skills, behaviors, and attitudes distinct from those of the social worker. However, through research, it has been discovered that the supervisory role and process is more successful, and beneficial to both social workers and their clients, if partnered with practice skills and traits (Brashears, 1995; Harkness & Poertner, 1989).

What Is Social Work Supervision?

Even though a clear definition, specific duties, and a perfect length of time and amount of social work supervision have yet to be established, the necessity and importance of the supervisory role has been a fundamental part of practice since the 1880s. Throughout time, the social work supervisor has been considered a teacher, an enabler, and an administrator (Brashears, 1995).

Teacher. The 1880s charity organizations considered supervisors to be the overseers of the "friendly visitor volunteers." As a teacher, the supervisor was responsible for guiding, supporting, and monitoring the friendly visitor's communication, assistance, and efficiency with clients (Brashears, 1995).

Enabler.   The 1920s brought much change to the field of social work. The professionalism of the practice increased as the clientele expanded. Social workers began to specialize in child welfare, physical and mental illness, and the family in general (Brashears, 1995).

Due to field specialization, the social work supervisor became a "psychoanalytic therapist." In this process, the supervisor assisted social workers in recognizing and resolving their own inner conflicts. The supervisor *role-modeled* therapy behavior that the social workers could then use with their clients (Brashears, 1995).

Administrator.   By the 1970s and early 1980s, the social work supervisor began taking on an administrative role in the human services. Supervision and social work practice became separate entities with distinct roles (Brashears, 1995; Harkness & Poertner, 1989).

According to Christian and Hannah (1983), a supervisor should focus on "productivity and quality control" (p. 98, as quoted by Brashears, 1995). Soon the social work supervisor's duties changed and began to include:

1. Representing the agency
2. Managing agency services, programs, and resources
3. Maintaining agency standards
4. Networking with communities
5. Collaborating with various bureaucratic systems
6. Promoting and maintaining professional staff development

A bureaucratic work environment and hierarchical structure developed within the human services field. Competition and power struggles began as the basic framework of social work practice disappeared from the social work supervisor role. Researchers have discovered that the separation of roles has profound effects on both the social worker and supervisor, including disequilibrium, frustration, job stress, burnout, and turnover. These findings are causing concern, and returning to the social work supervision conceptual model based on client interests and relational point of view is being examined (Bramhall & Ezell, 1981; Brashears, 1995; Edelwich & Brodsky, 1980; Ganzer & Ornstein, 2004; Harkness & Poertner, 1989; Murphy & Pardeck, 1986; National Association of Social Workers, 1994).

Applying what you have learned...

Social Work Supervision

5.1. For this exercise, you will be exploring the changes in the social work supervisor role since the 1800s.

    a. Explore and develop a list of the various duties of social work supervisor prior to the 1980s.

    b. Explore and develop a list of the various duties of social work supervisor from the 1980s to present time. Compare the two lists. Note the existing similarities and differences.

Section Two: Role of Supervisor and Preparing for Supervision

When you enter the Human Services workforce, you will discover that supervision plays the central role in your social work practicum. It is important for you to understand the various supervisor duties, including:

1. Transmitting his or her professional knowledge and skills to you (teacher)
2. Monitoring, evaluating, and providing feedback on your work (enabler)
3. Performing administrative duties (administrator)

Knowledge and Skills

Supervision is a learning experience in which your supervisor will pass on his or her social work knowledge and skills to you. There is no set time period when you will learn everything you need to know for social work practice. It is a process that will continue throughout your career (Brashears, 1995; Harkness & Poertner, 1989; Rawls & Meehan, 1997).

Normally, several years of lengthy in-depth supervision is required for one to develop proficiency in counseling and listening skills. Your supervisor may set up a service delivery and training program to assist you in this development, which will include the following:

1. Individualized instruction and orientation
2. Self-reports of your field experiences
3. Role-playing of common and/or challenging situations
4. Agency training in a classroom setting—videotape viewing
5. Training sessions and workshops

(*Knowledge and Skills sources:* Rawls & Meehan, 1997; Sheafor & Horejsi, 2006)

Monitoring and Evaluating

Expect your work to be monitored and evaluated. Your supervisor will most likely work with you to develop a personal list of goals, along with service delivery plans that:

1. Verify that proper planning and intervention are continuous with clients
2. Monitor and ensure consistency and quality of client services
3. Monitor dependability and accountability of duties
4. Monitor training progress to ensure continuous knowledge and skill development
5. Monitor strengths and professional development

(*Monitoring and Evaluating sources*: Compton & Galaway, 1999; Miley, O'Melia, & DuBois, 1998; Sheafor & Horejsi, 2006)

A good supervisor will provide you with feedback. It is important to remain open-minded and objective. Do not take the feedback personally; learn from it!

Administrative Duties

The administrative role of your supervisor includes implementing policies and managing programs of the organization. He or she may oversee a specific program, a service unit, or an entire organization, and be responsible for:

1. Recruiting and selecting staff
2. Intervening and resolving staff conflict
3. Coordinating staff activities
4. Overseeing policy and program development, evaluation, and compliance
5. Conducting "consumer needs" assessments
6. Promoting professional standards
7. Budgeting–monitoring use of resources, acquisitions, buildings' maintenance, and the like.

(*Administrative Duties sources*: Compton & Galaway, 1999; Miley et al., 1998; Sheafor & Horejsi, 2006)

As you can see, your supervisor will be extremely busy and will require your patience and professionalism.

Strengths of a Successful Supervisor

The successful supervisor has several characteristics and skills that can prove beneficial to social workers in training.

1. Competence
2. Clinical knowledge
3. Practice knowledge
   - Skills
   - Experience
   - Ability to solve client problems
4. In-depth knowledge of available public social services
5. In-depth knowledge of social work theory
6. Ability to help social workers avoid or prevent burnout
7. Knowledge of social workers' strengths and weaknesses
8. Knowledge of problems and tasks social workers encounter daily
9. A successful supervisor is:
   - Supportive
   - Encouraging
   - Reassuring
   - Able to restore social workers' morale

(*Successful supervisor sources:* Kadushin & Harkness, 2002; Tsui, 2005)

What If the Supervisor Is a Non-Social Work Practitioner?

As you begin your practicum, you may find that your supervisor is a non-social work practitioner. While this is generally true of supervisors, your supervisor should still have the strengths and background knowledge in the social work field. In addition, your supervisor *must ensure* that the work environment and training he or she is providing are in compliance with the NASW *Code of Ethics* (NASW, 1996; Reamer, 2004). The *Code of Ethics* states that supervisor responsibilities include, but are not limited to:

1. Providing regularly scheduled and documented supervision (3.01[b])
2. Making timely and informative performance evaluations, fully explaining present competence or impairment, ethical and unethical behavior (2.09, 2.10, 2.11; 3.01[d], 3.03; 4.05)
3. Reviewing and critiquing case records and paperwork (3.04[a], [b], [c])
4. Providing information on obtaining proper informed consent from clients (1.03)
5. Knowing when clients should be reassigned or transferred or when treatment should be terminated (1.06 [a]; 1.16[a], [b], [e])
6. Monitoring proper boundaries between social worker and clients (1.06[c]; 1.09[a], [b], [c])
7. Setting clear, appropriate, and culturally sensitive boundaries (3.02[b])
8. Maintaining proper and professional boundaries with social workers (2.07[a]; 3.01[c])

(*Supervisor Responsibilities sources*: *Code of Ethics* NASW, 1996; Reamer, 2004)

Applying what you have learned…

Preparing for Supervision

5.2. As discussed in this section, preparing for supervision includes understanding the supervisor's role.
   a. *Knowledge and skills.* Make a list of the knowledge and skills you believe your future social work supervisor should have that can be passed onto you.
   b. *Monitoring and evaluating.* Suppose you have completed one month of your internship. Your supervisor has met with you and feels that your work with clients is unsatisfactory and that client service delivery plans are not being met. How do you believe you will react to your supervisor evaluation? Remember, don't take it personally; learn from it!
   c. *Administrative duties.* You really need to meet with your supervisor about a specific client; however, he or she is unavailable today. According to the office schedule, your supervisor has interviews and budget meetings all day. How will you handle the fact that you really need to speak with him or her but cannot do so until tomorrow? Remember, be patient and professional!

5.3. List the essential characteristics and skills you believe your supervisor should have so that your supervision is successful.

5.4. You have just started your supervision and have discovered your supervisor is not a social work practitioner. What are some responsibilities of your supervisor so that your work environment and training are in compliance with the NASW *Code of Ethics?*

Section Three: Role of Practitioner and Getting the Most Out of Supervision

Now that you have an understanding of the supervisory role, it is important that you know your role as practitioner. With this understanding, you will be able to get the most out of your internship and supervision experience, along with becoming a successful social work practitioner.

Role of the Social Work Practitioner

In order to begin fully understanding your role as a social work practitioner, let's re-visit the defining characteristics of social work discussed in *Part One: The Social Work Milieu and Context*. Social work is an applied science that focuses on:

1. *Empowerment* Assisting people in restoring their ability to function in society
2. *Resources* Assisting people in obtaining services
3. *Direct Services* Providing group, family, and individual mental and emotional support
4. *Advocacy* Actively participating in important legislative processes, producing societal changes that will increase the well-being of all people in a community

   (*Role of the Practitioner sources:* Barker, 2003; Compton & Galaway, 1999; Miley et al., 1998; NASW, 1973; Sheafor & Horejsi, 2006)

Empowerment.   As a social work practitioner, you will be assisting people in restoring their abilities to reenter and meet the expectations of society, thereby helping them to function in various settings and situations. You can accomplish this by:

1. Providing clients with effective ways to deal with various "life situations"
2. Instructing clients on how to anticipate and prevent crises in their lives
3. Offering advice, suggestions, and alternatives to deal with problems
4. Modeling appropriate behaviors
5. Assisting clients in changing dysfunctional behavior so that their social interaction is both positive and effective

   (*Empowerment sources*: Compton & Galaway, 1999; Miley et al., 1998; Sheafor & Horejsi, 2006)

Resources.   Becoming familiar with the numerous resources available in the community enables you to compile a database of valuable information. Compiling a community resource database that includes the agency names and the quality of staff, eligibility requirements, and costs of each agency's services is important in helping your clients. Of course, knowing the best way to gain access to the various agencies is pertinent to your clients' successfully acquiring various needed services (Barker, 2003; Compton & Galaway, 1999; Miley et al., 1998; Schmolling, Youkeles, & Burger, 1993; Sheafor & Horejsi, 2006).

Among the services your clients may need are financial assistance, insurance, employment, housing, public transportation, and education. Health and aging services may also be a client need. Through ongoing assessment, social workers learn about and respond to needed services (Barker, 2003; Compton & Galaway, 1999; Miley et al., 1998; Schmolling et al., 1993; Sheafor & Horejsi, 2006).

Direct Services.   As a social work practitioner, one of your goals is to assist your clients in understanding their feelings, modifying their behaviors, and teaching them how to cope with problems in various situations. This is done through providing direct services. Direct services is also known as a ***counseling*** or ***helping*** role (Barker, 2003; Compton & Galaway, 1999; Miley et al., 1998; Schmolling et al., 1993; Sheafor & Horejsi, 2006). Taking on the ***counseling*** or ***helping*** role requires that you:

1. Know and understand human behavior
2. Understand the impact of the social environment on people
3. Have the ability to assess client behavior, problems, and situations, and to determine a cause
4. Have the ability to use and teach clients proper interventions to deal with various stresses
5. Be able to provide long-term support, care, and knowledge to clients and their families in certain situations
6. Succeed in guiding your clients through the change process

(*Direct services sources:* Barker, 2003; Compton & Galaway, 1999; Miley et al., 1998; Schmolling et al., 1993; Sheafor & Horejsi, 2006)

Advocacy.   On the micro level, it is important that you know your own agency and the community services available to your clients. This knowledge will assist your clients in receiving services or resources needed. On the macro level, you may become an advocate for a segment of the population that is facing a common problem or concern (Barker, 2003; Compton & Galaway, 1999; Miley et al., 1998; Schmolling et al., 1993; Sheafor & Horejsi, 2006). This is known as ***class advocacy*** and can include:

1. Having contact and working with political and legislative staff
2. Building an alliance with various organizations that are trying to meet the same goals
3. Changing agency regulations, social policies, and/or laws
4. Removing barriers that may be preventing groups from receiving benefits and/or entitlements
5. Helping a group realize its civil rights

(*Advocate sources:* Barker, 2003; Compton & Galaway, 1999; Miley et al., 1998; Schmolling et al., 1993; Sheafor & Horejsi, 2006)

Keep in mind that your supervisor is going to support, educate, and lead you through the empowerment, resources, direct services, and advocacy functions. Working together will ensure that you have a successful supervisory experience.

Applying what you have learned …

Role of Practitioner

5.5. *Refer to the social work practitioners' various roles for this exercise.* You have a new client who has just been through a divorce, is struggling with finding and keeping a job, and is trying to locate an apartment. The client was released from the hospital a month ago and is finding it difficult to function in the community.

a. *Empowerment.* Make a list of skills, behaviors, advice, and alternatives that you could pass on/teach to your client in order to help the client reenter society and function positively in various settings and situations.

b. *Resources.* Make a list of services that you believe are needed in order to best assist your client in dealing with the divorce, unemployment, homelessness, and societal functioning.

c. *Direct Services.* Counseling or helping role: How is the social environment impacting your client? Assess your client's situation and determine what might be causing the problems. Make a list of the long-term support and care you believe your client requires.

d. *Advocacy.* You have gone through all the agencies in the local community and cannot find assistance for your client due to various service restrictions. As an advocate, what do you think should be your next step (s) in assisting your client (macro level)?

Section Four: Problem Solving in Supervision

Please keep in mind that it is impossible for every problem that can arise during supervision to be known or illustrated here. Thus, we will discuss the most common issues that can occur and the best techniques to solve these problems.

Bureaucracy Frustration and Change

As you know, a **bureaucracy**, or complex organization, operates using a **hierarchical structure**. This type of structure contains a well-defined chain of command and an obvious division of labor. Bureaucracies set specific rules and regulations, they are largely stable, and they provide fair and equal treatment of employees. Bureaucracies, however, are inflexible and impersonal, and slow to change. As a social worker, you will undoubtedly work in a bureaucratic organization, and you may find the administrative control, laws, agency rules, regulations, and policies frustrating at some point (Schmolling et al., 1993; Sheafor & Horejsi, 2006).

Along with the hierarchical structure comes the possibility of political control, self-serving superiors, and power struggles within agency departments and between various agencies. This ultimately can interfere with clients receiving services. The bureaucratic organization and hierarchical structure and functions seem to make up the bulk of social worker grievances (Schmolling et al., 1993; Sheafor & Horejsi, 2006).

Problem-solving Techniques. The first step in dealing with a bureaucratic organization is to be familiar with its the structure and function, which we covered earlier. Having knowledge of the organization will also prepare you for your supervisory sessions.

The second step is having the ability to work and function effectively in this type of structure so that your work with clients is successful. Suggestions for success in this area include the following.

1. Be familiar with the agency in which you plan to work, including knowing the agency's:
   - History
   - Mission
   - Goals
   - Structure
   - Culture
2. Understand the agency's special challenges, such as:
   - Funding sources and budgets
   - Chain-of-command and decision-making processes
   - External political and community forces
3. Keep in mind that bureaucracies are slow to change.
   - Research the agency rule, procedure, or policy to determine why it exists prior to pursuing change.
   - Make sure changes you want are both realistic and feasible.
   - Pursue only one or two issues at a time.
   - Be tactful and choose your strategies carefully.
   - Do not expect rapid change and avoid being aggressive!

(*Problem-solving techniques sources:* Schmolling et al., 1993; Sheafor & Horejsi, 2006)

Job Mismatch

Most of us have experienced job mismatch. Maybe you have taken a job that you disliked because you needed the money, or maybe you were forced into moving within an organization in order to remain employed. Other scenarios may exist, and ultimately, this mismatch leads to job dissatisfaction (Schmolling et al., 1993; Sheafor & Horejsi, 2006).

Problem-solving Techniques.   In order to avoid job mismatch and to achieve satisfaction in your career, consider the following:

1. Do not expect a "perfect fit." At the same time, your values, beliefs, and goals must be compatible with the organization.
2. Think of yourself as a "partner" rather than just an "employee!"
3. Believe in the agency's mission and recognize that your work is valuable in reaching these goals.
4. Do not "jump into" a new job or accept a promotion or transfer in your existing job without first considering the changes it will bring. You may end up missing the work you enjoyed, and be stuck with a job you dislike.

(*Problem-solving techniques sources:* Schmolling et al., 1993; Sheafor & Horejsi, 2006)

Noncooperation, Disagreement, and Miscommunication

In reality, we do not agree with everyone all the time, and this conflict can lead to discord if not handled professionally. It will inevitably lead to miscommunication among employees, cause tension in the organization, and ultimately stifle services to clients (Schmolling et al., 1993; Sheafor & Horejsi, 2006).

Personality Conflicts with Supervisor

As you enter the social work profession, you will find that agencies have a "pool" of professionals, each with his or her own unique personality. It is unrealistic for you to believe that you will "mesh" with every staff member, and a personality conflict may even arise between you and your supervisor. Personality conflicts can hinder both your career and the services clients receive.

Problem-solving Techniques. The *Code of Ethics* states: "Social workers should treat colleagues with respect and should represent accurately and fairly the qualifications, views, and obligations of colleagues" (NASW, Code of Ethics standard 2.01 [a], 1996). Negative criticism of colleagues when communicating with clients and other professionals needs to be avoided (NASW, Code of Ethics standard 2.01 [b] and [c], 1996).

Cooperation among employees, agencies, committees, and departments is necessary so that clients receive needed services. Consider the following problem-solving techniques:

Noncooperation, Disagreement, and Miscommunication
1. Maintain a "sense of humor" and a balanced perspective of both yourself and the organization for which you work.
2. Be courteous and use positive words when communicating with coworkers.
3. Be empathetic so that you can identify with, and understand the ideas, feelings, and thoughts of coworkers.
4. Be flexible and willing to make "reasonable" compromises.

(*Noncooperation, disagreement, and miscommunication problem-solving techniques sources:* Brantley & Miller, 2002; Schmolling et al., 1993; Sheafor & Horejsi, 2006)

Personality Conflicts with Supervisor
1. Know and accept your own personality traits.
2. Know and accept your own behaviors and emotional reactions to situations.
3. Understand and accept the diversity of personalities.
4. Be courteous and use positive words when communicating with your supervisor.
5. Be empathetic so that you can identify with, and understand the ideas, feelings, and thoughts of your supervisor.

6. Understand the leadership style of your supervisor. Several styles include:
   a. *Authority-compliance* Emphasizes tasks/job requirements, results-driven
      1. Controlling
      2. Demanding
      3. Strict
      4. Overpowering
   b. *Country club* Emphasizes interpersonal relationships, deemphasizes production
      1. Agreeable
      2. Helpful
      3. Comforting
      4. Uncontroversial
   c. *Impoverished* Not concerned with tasks or interpersonal relationships, just goes through the motions of leadership
      1. Uninvolved/withdrawn
      2. Indifferent
      3. Noncommittal
      4. Resigned
      5. Apathetic
   d. *Middle-of-the-road* Balance of tasks and interpersonal relationships/intermediate concern for both
      1. Practical
      2. Compromising
   e. *Team management* Strong emphasis on tasks and interpersonal relationships, promotes participation and teamwork, encourages employee involvement and commitment
      1. Open-minded
      2. Determined
      3. Positive/enjoys job

(*Personality conflicts with supervisor problem-solving techniques sources:* Brantley & Miller, 2002; Schmolling et al., 1993; Sheafor & Horejsi, 2006)

(*Leadership styles sources*: Blake & McCanse, 1991, p. 29; Blake & Mouton, 1985; Northouse, 2004, p. 68–72).

Lack of Time on Part of Supervisor or Social Worker

We have all been in the position of wishing for additional hours in a day so that we could accomplish more. Since we don't have this option, social work supervisors and practitioners must learn how to manage their time and workload effectively so that essential learning is not missed during supervision. Efficient management of both time and workload will also ensure that clients receive needed services (Morales & Sheafor, 1998; Sheafor & Horejsi, 2006).

Problem-solving Techniques.   Several techniques can help you manage both your time and workload so that services are provided to clients and your agency's job requirements are met (Sheafor & Horejsi, 2006). **Start** by logging your daily activities for a 5-day week, divided in 15–30 minute intervals. Look over your log to see how you used your time, then ask yourself:

    a. What times and days of the week were the busiest?
    b. What times and days of the week were most productive?
    c. What distractions and barriers prevented productivity?

Once you have finished examining your log and answering these questions, do the following:

1. Plan ahead by getting yourself a personal weekly planner. Your planner should include appointments, important telephone numbers, and daily to-do lists.
2. Develop a daily to-do list that includes major tasks that need to be done and the goals you want to reach. **Prioritize your to-do list!**
3. Reduce distractions by minimizing or eliminating the amount of time you allow people to interrupt you. Also, check your e-mail twice daily *only*—once in the morning and once before you leave for the day.

(*Lack of time problem-solving techniques sources:* Bates, 2006; Sheafor & Horejsi, 2006)

Inconsistent Expectations of Supervisor and Social Worker

Both supervisor and social worker need to have clear and consistent expectations of each other. With clear and consistent expectations, unclear job descriptions or directions can be avoided. Uniform expectations and reliable direction will ensure that services needed by clients are provided in a productive and timely manner (Johnson, 1998; Morales & Sheafor, 1998; Sheafor & Horejsi, 2006).

Problem-solving Techniques. In order to maintain consistency in both expectations and direction, these guidelines should be followed:

Expectations of Supervisor. To be an effective and successful social work practitioner, your supervisor will expect you to:

1. Know the agency's mission, program, and goals.
2. Know your job description and assume responsibility for your work.
3. Follow agency policies, procedures, and instructions at all times.
4. Maintain accurate and up-to-date client records.
5. Notify him or her if you are unclear about a client issue and/or agency procedure.

6. Inform him or her immediately about possible ethical, legal, or procedural violations that may injure the agency and/or clients.
7. Be enthusiastic about your work and the learning process.
8. Become more efficient and effective by accepting constructive criticism and suggestions.
9. Be cooperative and respectful of colleagues. Improve staff morale by exhibiting positive behaviors.

Expectations of Social Work Practitioner. In order to receive effective and successful supervision, expect the following from your supervisor:

1. Initial and continuance of on-the-job training and guidance.
2. Notification of agency policy and procedure changes.
3. Encouragement and support when you are confused and/or frustrated.
4. Regular performance evaluations.
5. Suggestions to improve your work.
6. Immediate and clear warnings if your performance is below agency standards.

Maintaining Professional Job Performance and Direction
1. Schedule weekly meetings with your supervisor.
2. Be prepared for meetings by having topics and questions ready for discussion.
3. Be an *adult learner* by behaving in a professional manner, understanding and carrying out assigned duties, and meeting all deadlines.
4. Prepare all records and reports in accordance with the agency's format.
5. Be present and on time to work. Give advance notice if you will be late or absent on a scheduled work day.
6. Take responsibility for your work.
7. Avoid claiming successes as "yours." Give credit to others who assisted you.
8. Never allow dishonesty to be part of your social work practice!

(*Expectations problem-solving techniques sources*: Johnson, 1998; Morales & Sheafor, 1998; Sheafor & Horejsi, 2006)

Supervisor or Social Worker Burnout

The social work field is both challenging and stressful, and the potential for supervisors and staff becoming victims of *burnout* is increasing. Dealing with "heavy doses of human and social problems over prolonged periods of time" (Johnson, 1998, p. 462) can cause *burnout*, or emotional exhaustion, alienation, and reduced personal accomplishments among supervisors and social work practitioners (Compton & Galaway, 1999; Johnson, 1998; Miley et al., 1998; Sheafor & Horejsi, 2009).

Problem-solving Techniques. The good news is that *burnout* can be prevented, reduced, or treated. The *impaired workers phenomenon*, or addictions, emotional, and mental health problems among social work practitioners, can also be avoided (Johnson, 1998).

You can take several measures to enhance your coping abilities, reduce your risk of *burnout*, and, ultimately, avoid *impaired workers phenomenon*:

1. Try to get adequate rest, nutrition, and exercise. Create a daily regimen for yourself.
2. Take mini-breaks throughout your day to provide you with diversion from the occupation's stress factors.
3. Maintain a positive self-image through support from peers, coworkers, and supervisors.
4. Place more emphasis on client self-responsibility and maintain a "detached concern for clients with reduced personal involvement in client's problems" (Johnson, 1998, p. 462).
5. Follow the time-management suggestions discussed in the *Lack of time on part of supervisor or social worker* section.
6. Take assertiveness training to improve your communication skills and enhance your ability to identify "stressors" in your work environment. This training will also help you in taking appropriate action to reduce or eliminate the stressors.

(*Supervisor or social worker burnout problem-solving techniques sources:* Compton & Galaway, 1999; Johnson, 1998; Miley et al., 1998; Sheafor & Horejsi, 2006).

Sexual Harassment

Sexual harassment is an abuse of power and is defined as "an unwelcome sexual attention at work [or at school], which may affect a person's job performance or create a hostile work environment" (Henslin, 2005, p. 314). According to the NASW's *Code of Ethics*, sexual harassment includes sexual advances, sexual solicitation, requests for sexual favors, and other verbal or physical conduct of a sexual nature (NASW, *Code of Ethics* standard 2.08, 1996). Social workers should never engage in sexual harassment activities with supervisors, colleagues, trainees, and clients. Sexual harassment can result in job loss and/or client injury (Henslin, 2005; Morales & Sheafor, 1998; Sheafor & Horejsi, 2006).

Problem-solving Techniques. It is important that you understand two strategies that deal with sexual harassment: *organizational* and *individual*.

Organizational Level
1. Understand the organization's sexual harassment policies.
2. Understand and follow the agency's procedure for reporting sexual harassment.
3. Attend periodic training (if available) that is offered to sensitize staff to the problem and prevention of sexual harassment.

Individual Level

1. As a victim, speak directly to the harasser first. Insist that the harasser stop the offensive behaviors. OR
2. Send a letter to the harasser that lists the incidents, when the incidents occurred, and how you were affected by the incidents. It is also recommended that you state how the conduct should change.
3. If the sexual harassment continues, it is important that you keep a log of events and a list of any witnesses, as well as consulting other workers, informing your supervisor, and using agency procedures to find a resolution to the problem.
4. If the problem cannot be resolved within the agency, you should consult a lawyer. You can also contact a state human rights commission or the U.S. Equal Employment Opportunity Commission to file a formal complaint. This should be done within 180 days of the incident.
5. It is important that you be prepared for negative reactions from both the harasser and others within the organization.

(*Sexual harassment problem-solving techniques sources:* Henslin, 2005; Morales & Sheafor, 1998; Sheafor & Horejsi, 2006)

The Concept of Balance

Balance.   Maintaining *balance*, or a sense of emotional stability and harmony, is important when working in the social work field. You must keep yourself emotionally healthy so that your occupation will be personally satisfying and your work with clients will be productive.

Achieving Balance.   You may be asking yourself, "How do I achieve personal balance?" Let's look at various steps you can take that will help you reach a sense of balance and ultimately help you in becoming a successful social work practitioner.

1. Know yourself and your abilities, along with accepting your weakness or areas in which you are less strong.
2. Recognize your vulnerabilities and explore various ways to deal with them.
3. Realize that you are *human* and will feel empathy. However, remain objective and limit close identity with client problems.
4. Limit the demands you place on yourself.
5. Realize that "human change is slow" (Compton & Galaway, 1999, p. 498) and that you cannot "transform" a client overnight.
6. "Go easy on yourself" when faced with disappointment and a sense of failure. We are often our harshest critic!
7. Remember, activities and relationships outside of the organization will give your life a sense of meaning, along with fulfilling your emotional and spiritual needs.

Applying what you have learned...

Problem Solving in Supervision

5.6. *Refer to the problem-solving techniques in this section.* You had an interview with a bureaucratic agency and were offered a social work practitioner position.

a. ***Bureaucracy frustration and change.*** Before accepting the position, what should you do in order to avoid frustration in your job?

b. ***Job mismatch.*** You researched the agency and decided to accept the job. You have been in the position for about six months and have been offered a promotion. What should you consider before accepting this promotion into the administration department?

c. ***Noncooperation, disagreement, and miscommunication.*** You feel your current clients need to have additional services. You decide to bring this matter to your supervisor's attention, and he or she angrily disagrees with you. How should you deal with the situation?

d. ***Personality conflicts with supervisor.*** You have been in your position for about a month and are still having problems with understanding your supervisor's personality and attitude toward you. How should you deal with this situation?

e. ***Lack of time.*** You have several clients who require your services, and additional responsibilities have been added to your list of "to do's." What can you do to manage your time and workload in a professional manner?

f. ***Inconsistent expectations.*** Lately, you have been unable to meet with your supervisor, and your role as social work practitioner is becoming confusing to you. What can you and your supervisor do to help you solve this problem?

g. ***Burnout.*** You have been feeling quite overwhelmed with your job responsibilities. You feel emotionally exhausted and believe your work with clients is not successful. What can you do to reduce your risk of burnout?

h. ***Sexual harassment.*** You feel uncomfortable because a colleague makes sexual remarks to you. You also realize that this specific colleague has worked in the organization longer than you have and could ultimately get you fired.

   i. Do you feel you are a victim of sexual harassment?

   ii. What are your alternatives for solving the problem?

5.7. *Refer to the Concept of "Balance" section.* You enjoy your career as social work practitioner and plan to stay in this field. What can you do to maintain a sense of balance so that your job continues to be both satisfying and successful?

Summary

Traditionally, social work supervision was considered an educational and supportive process. Through the years the supervisor role changed, and by the 1980s, supervision was considered an administrative process that dealt with various management functions. Even though the supervisor role has changed, supervision still remains the central element in your social work practicum and in your employment success.

Your supervisor can be considered a teacher, an enabler, and an administrator who guides you through the social work supervision and learning process. The successful supervisor's strengths include competence, knowledge, and support. It is also important that the supervisor have the ability to encourage, reassure, and restore social workers' morale. Keep in mind that whether or not your supervisor is a social work practitioner, he or she must still have the strengths and background knowledge of the field. Your supervisor must also adhere to NASW's *Code of Ethics.*

As a social work practitioner, your job includes providing empowerment, resources, direct services, and support (advocacy) to clients. You may find yourself working for an inflexible and impersonal bureaucratic organization with a hierarchical structure. However, being familiar with the agency's history, mission, goals, structure, and culture will help you maintain patience within this type of system. Being tactful and understanding that bureaucracies are slow to change are important to your success as a social worker.

Although there may not be a "perfect fit" between you and your agency, your values, beliefs, and goals should at least be compatible with those of the organization. Remember, cooperation among employees, agencies, committees, and departments is essential to the successful delivery of client services. Having the ability to resolve personality conflicts with your supervisor takes knowing and accepting yourself and understanding that personality diversity exists.

Management of time and workload, as well as consistent expectations of both you and your supervisor, are important in the social work field. Professional job performance and direction can be maintained through weekly supervisory meetings. It is important that you be an *adult learner* and meet all required deadlines. Maintaining a sense of humor, a balanced perspective, and an emphasis on client self-responsibility can reduce or prevent *burnout.*

Sexual harassment includes sexual advances and solicitation, requests for sexual favors, and other verbal or physical conduct of a sexual nature. Social workers should never engage in sexual harassment activities with supervisors, colleagues, trainees, and clients. Job loss and/or client injury can occur.

Finally, maintaining *balance,* or a sense of emotional stability and harmony, is important in the Human Services field. Being self-aware, realizing that human change is slow, and fulfilling your emotional and spiritual needs will help keep you emotionally healthy. Taking care of yourself is vital to your successful career in social work.

KEY WORDS AND CONCEPTS

Section One
Social work supervisor
  history, p. 82
  Teacher, p. 82
  Enabler, p. 82
  Administrator, p. 83

Section Two
Supervisor role, p. 84
  Knowledge and skills, p. 84
  Monitoring and evaluating,
    p. 84
  Administrative duties, p. 85

Inconsistent expectations,
    p. 93
Professional job performance,
    p. 94

Adult learner, p. 94
Burnout, p. 94
Impaired workers
    phenomenon, p. 95

Sexual harassment, p. 95
Organizational, p. 95
Individual, p. 96
Balance, p. 96

REFERENCES

Barker, R. L. (2003). *Social work dictionary, (5th ed.).* Washington, DC: NASW Press.

Bates, R. (2006). Take control of your day! *JCK Reed Business Information.* Retrieved October 24, 2006, from http://www.reed.elsevier.com.

Blake, R. R., & McCanse, A. A. (1991). *Leadership dilemmas—Grid solutions.* Houston, TX: Gulf.

Blake, R. R., & Mouton, J. S. (1985). *The managerial grid III.* Houston, TX: Gulf.

Bramhall, M., & Ezell, S. (1981). Working your way out of burnout. *Public Welfare, 39*(2), 32–39.

Brantley, C. P., & Miller, M. G. (2002). *Effective communication for colleges.* Cincinnati, OH: South-Western Educational Publishing.

Brashears, F. (1995). Supervision as social work practice: A reconceptualization. *Social Work, 40*(5), 692–699.

Christian, W. P., & Hannah, G. T. (1983). *Effective management in Human Services.* Englewood Cliffs, NJ: Prentice Hall.

Compton, B. R., & Galaway, B. (1999). *Social work processes.* Pacific Grove, CA: Brooks/Cole Publishing Company.

Edelwich, J., & Brodsky, A. (1980). *Burn-out stages of disillusionment in the helping professions.* New York: Human Sciences Press.

Ganzer, C., & Ornstein, E. D. (2004). Regression, self-disclosure, and the teach or treat dilemma: Implications of a relational approach for social work supervision. *Clinical Social Work Journal, 32*(4), 431–449.

Harkness, D., & Poertner, J. (1989). Research and social work supervision: A conceptual review. *Social Work, 34*(2), 115–120.

Henslin, J. M. (2005). *Sociology: A down-to-earth approach.* Boston, MA: Allyn & Bacon.

Johnson, H. W. (1998). *The social services: An introduction.* Itasca, IL: F.E. Peacock Publishers.

Kadushin, A., & Harkness, D. (2002). *Supervision in social work.* New York: Columbia University Press.

Miley, K. K., O'Melia, M., & DuBois, B. L. (1998). *Generalist social work practice: An empowering approach.* Needham Heights, MA: Allyn & Bacon.

Morales, A. T., & Sheafor, B. W. (1998). *Social work: A profession of many faces.* Needham Heights, MA: Allyn & Bacon.

Murphy, J. W., & Pardeck, J. T. (1986). The "burnout syndrome" and management style. *Clinical Supervisor, 4*(4), 35–44.

National Association of Social Workers. (1994). Public child welfare. In *Social Work speaks: NASW policy statements* (3rd. ed., pp. 221–222). Washington, DC: NASW Press.

National Association of Social Workers. (1996). NASW *Code of Ethics.* Washington, DC: Author.

Northouse, P. G. (2004). *Leadership theory and practice.* Thousand Oaks, CA: Sage Publications.

Rawls, A. W., & Meehan, A. J. (1997). The application of interactional analysis to an applied study of social work. *Applied Behavioral Science Review, 5*(1), 113–140.

Reamer, F. G. (2004). *Ethical standards in social work.* Washington, DC: NASW Press.

Schmolling, P., Youkeles, M., & Burger, W. R. (1993). *Human Services in contemporary America.* Pacific Grove, CA: Brooks/Cole Publishing Company.

Sheafor, B. W., & Horejsi, C. R. (2006). *Techniques and guidelines for social work practice.* Boston, MA: Allyn & Bacon.

Standards for Social Service Manpower. (1973). Washington, DC: National Association of Social Workers.

Tsui, M. (2005). *Social work supervision: Contexts and concepts.* Thousand Oaks, CA: Sage Publishing.

Wren, J. T. (1995). *The leader's companion: Insights of leadership through the ages.* New York: The Free Press.

6 Communicating About Confidentiality

As a social worker, your primary mission is to enhance human well-being and assist in meeting the basic human needs of all people in a community. In order for you to reach this goal, you need to earn the trust of the clients and the community you are serving. Thus, Chapter 6 defines *right to privacy, confidentiality*, and *privileged communications* that provide the link to building client trust. Justifications for privilege, exceptions to the rule, and threats to confidentiality are also discussed in the chapter. Understanding all these components of confidentiality increases your ability to communicate with your client professionally.

Section One: What Are Right to Privacy, Confidentiality, and Privileged Communications?

Defining Right to Privacy, Confidentiality, and Privileged Communications

Right to Privacy.   As a social worker, it is important for clients to trust you so that they do not avoid seeking treatment or withhold important information that is needed in obtaining services (Luepker, 2003). This trust is earned as you spend time with your clients in a private, professional, and responsible manner (NASW, 1996).

According to the NASW *Code of Ethics,* "Social workers should respect clients' right to privacy. Social workers should not solicit private information from clients unless it is essential to providing services or conducting social work evaluation or research. Once private information is shared, standards of confidentiality apply" (NASW, *Code of Ethics* standard 1.07 [a], 1996).

Confidentiality. According to the NASW *Code of Ethics*, ***confidentiality***, or being entrusted with private information, is a necessity in the social work profession (NASW, 1996). It is vital that the "helping relationship" you have with your client contains the utmost possible confidentiality. However, you must also realize that you cannot guarantee "absolute confidentiality" to your clients, and you need to make them aware of this (Dickson, 1998; Roberts & Greene, 2002). The NASW *Code of Ethics* contains a provision explaining that it is ethical to inform a client of the possible limits of confidentiality (NASW, *Code of Ethics* standard 1.07 [d], 1996; Roberts & Greene, 2002). We will discuss these limitations and "exceptions to the rule" later in the chapter.

Privileged Communications. A confidential conversation or correspondence that does not have to be disclosed in a court of law is known as ***privileged communication***. Privileged communication applies to doctor-patient, attorney-client, husband-wife, and priest-penitent relationships. Rarely does it extend to a social worker-client relationship (Dickson, 1998; Gibelman, 1995; Sheafor & Horejsi, 2006).

The extent of privileged communication is governed by state statutes, and this privilege belongs to the client *only*, not the social worker. A client whose confidential information has been subpoenaed can request the judge to recognize his or her privilege in order to prevent the disclosure of information to the court. The judge makes the determination as to whether or not there is a compelling need to reveal the client's information in a trial (Dickson, 1998; Miley, O'Melia, & DuBois, 1998; Sheafor & Horejsi, 2006).

There is a standard in the NASW *Code of Ethics* that you need to be aware of when client records have been subpoenaed or requested by the courts and there is no existing client consent:

> Social workers should protect the confidentiality of clients during legal proceedings to the extent permitted by law. When a court of law or other legally authorized body orders social workers to disclose confidential or privileged information without a client's consent and such disclosure could cause harm to the client, social workers should request that the court withdraw the order or limit the order as narrowly as possible or maintain the records under seal, unavailable for public inspection (NASW, *Code of Ethics* standard 1.07 [j], 1996)

Applying what you have learned ...

Right to Privacy, Confidentiality, and Privileged Communications

6.1. Define *right to privacy, confidentiality,* and *privileged communication.* What are the differences between the three concepts?

Section Two: Threats and Exceptions to Maintaining Client Confidentiality and Privileged Communication

Threats to Client Confidentiality and Privileged Communication

Threats to clients' confidential information can arise during the use, exchange, and storage process of files. The organization for which you work should have certain technical and administrative procedures in place that will safeguard client information. This is especially important when information is stored in a computer or is transferred electronically.

To reduce or prevent threats to client confidentiality, the following should be done:

1. All files and client information must be stored in locked files. Only legitimate, need-to-know professionals or agency employees should have access to files.
2. Files, computer screens, and appointment books should be kept away from, and out of the sight of other clients, people in the waiting room, and maintenance and janitorial staff.
3. Professional discussions with those who have a need to know about clients should be done "behind closed doors!"
4. Telephone conversations with clients or about clients should be held in private areas so that the risk of others hearing the conversation can be eliminated.
5. When working with a client's file, always place it face down so that the name and other information on the file cannot be read by others.
6. Always evaluate the possibility and risks of violating a client's privacy before sending any correspondence via mail, e-mail, and facsimile.
7. Records and notes to be discarded must be shredded. Never place a "whole" document in a waste container.
8. Remember, the client's records belong to the client. The client has the right to decide whether and to whom information is to be released.

(*Threats to Confidentiality sources*: Morales & Sheafor, 1998; NASW *Code of Ethics*, 1996; Reamer, 1998; Roberts & Greene, 2002; Sheafor & Horejsi, 2006)

Exceptions to Maintaining Client Confidentiality and Privileged Communication

Ultimately, it is the responsibility of the social worker to protect the confidentiality and privileged communication of clients so that no harm comes to them. However, there are *exceptions to this rule*. The exceptions are in instances of child abuse or neglect, elder abuse, clients with HIV, and those threatening harm to others. As a social worker, it is important that you have the knowledge and ability to professionally handle these specific exceptions that may arise when working with clients.

Child Abuse. State laws require social workers to report ***all cases*** of suspected child abuse or neglect to the proper authorities. As a social worker, you must be able to differentiate ***physical abuse*** from ordinary spanking or ***corporal punishment*** (striking a person's body as a form of punishment).

Indicators of a Child Who Is Being Physically Abused

Physical Indicators
- Bruises or welts on the face or body, including back, buttocks, and/or torso
- Bruises that appear to be in different stages of healing
- Multiple bruises clustered in one area on the body, forming symmetrical patterns or shapes of instruments such as loop marks, lineal or parallel marks, punch marks
- Bruises that appear regularly after a weekend or a visit
- Bruises in the shape of a hand and fingers found on the shoulder or neck
- Cigarette burns on palms, soles, back, or buttocks
- Hot water or dunking burns that have a sock-like, glove-like, or doughnut shape found on the buttocks or genitalia
- Burns shaped like an electric stove burner, hot plate, or curling iron
- Rope burns and tie marks on wrists or ankles
- Broken teeth, broken bones, or head injuries
- Human, adult-size bite marks
- Retina detachment or whiplash injuries (violent shaking)
- Internal injuries caused by "punching"
- Poisoning from alcohol, prescription medications, household chemicals, or street drugs

Behavioral Indicators
- Appears reluctant to talk about injuries, embarrassed about the injury
- Attempts to hide injuries with clothing
- Fears human touch, especially by adults—this includes his or her parents
- Appears excitable, apprehensive, and cautious around adults
- Exhibits extreme adaptive behavior in order to meet parent needs
    - Takes care of and comforts parent(s)
    - Tries to keep things calm to prevent abusive episodes
- Becomes anxious when another child cries or acts up—associates crying with pain of abuse
- Exhibits serious behavioral problems: self-mutilation, suicide attempts, violence, withdrawal, and/or running away

(*Indicators of Child Physical Abuse sources*: Gibelman, 1995; Miley et al., 1998; Morales & Sheafor, 1998; Reamer, 1998; Roberts & Greene, 2002; Sheafor & Horejsi, 2006)

Indicators of Child Neglect

- Underweight, bald patches on scalp; begs, steals, and hoards food
- Primitive eating and toilet behaviors
- Fatigue and sluggishness
- Poor hygiene, filthy and/or inappropriate clothing for weather
- Medical and dental problems untreated, even though parent has insurance/resources for medical services
- No supervision or protection from dangerous activities
- Poor school attendance or stays at school for extended periods of time
- Stays in public places or at others' homes for extended periods

(*Indicators of Child Neglect sources*: Gibelman, 1995; Miley et al., 1998; Morales & Sheafor, 1998; Reamer, 1998; Roberts & Greene, 2002; Sheafor & Horejsi, 2006)

Elder Abuse.   By 2025, the U.S. Census Bureau projects that approximately 60.8 million Americans will be 65 years of age and older (Koff & Park, 1999; Roberts & Greene, 2002). With this increase in the elderly population will come an increase in elder abuse. As with child abuse and neglect, social workers are mandated by law to report elder abuse and neglect.

Signs and symptoms of elder abuse.   Elder abuse is defined as "the mistreatment of aged or relatively dependent people by their adult children, relatives, legal custodians, or others who provide their care" (Roberts & Greene, 2002, p. 723). Social workers need to be familiar with, and able to detect signs and symptoms of, elder abuse and neglect.

Signs and Symptoms of Elder Abuse and Neglect

Physical Indicators
- Injuries that appear untreated; client is vague or defensive when asked to explain the injury—bruises, welts, scratches, burns, fractures, lacerations, and/or punctures
- Missing patches of hair or bleeding under scalp
- Unexplainable genital infections or venereal disease
- Unexplained weight changes
- Inappropriate clothing for the weather
- Unpleasant odors relating to personal hygiene

Psychological Indicators
- Eating patterns change
- Depression and crying, low self-esteem
- Extreme fearfulness, paranoid references, disinterest or distress
- Confusion and disorientation—does not recognize you, may not know day, time, or where they are
- Wanders outside at odd hours or into dangerous areas

Financial Indicators
- Lack of food, complains of hunger
- Unpaid bills—eviction notice, utility(ies) shutoff, and so on
- Overinvolvement of family relative in client's financial affairs (Roberts & Greene, 2002, p. 724)
- Adequate finances, but client or caregiver refuses to pay for needed services
- Withdrawals from bank accounts, or client complaints about "being taken to the bank" (Roberts & Greene, 2002, p. 724)

Other Indicators
- Strange activity or no activity around the client's residence
- Several days of mail, newspapers, and/or deliveries that have not been picked up
- Unpleasant odors in the home

> (*Indicators of Elder Abuse and Neglect sources*: Gibelman, 1995; Roberts & Greene, 2002; Schmolling, Youkeles, & Burger, 1993; Sheafor & Horejsi, 2006)

Clients Who Are HIV-Positive. *Acquired Immune Deficiency Syndrome* (**AIDS**) is a disease caused by the *Human Immunodeficiency Virus*, or **HIV.** HIV is spread through having sexual relations or sharing drug injection needles with a person infected with the virus. The virus can also be passed to an unborn child during pregnancy and delivery if the mother is infected. In rare instances a child has been infected with the virus through breastfeeding (Sheafor & Horejsi, 2006). Approximately 930,000 people in the United States were diagnosed with HIV between 1999 and 2003 (Centers for Disease Control, 2003).

Clients who are HIV-positive present social workers with a significant ethical challenge in reference to client confidentiality. As a social worker, it is your duty to ensure that the client's sexual partner(s) is/are informed about this medical situation. It is important that you discuss the situation with your client so that a joint plan to inform the client's sexual partner(s) can be developed. Discuss the issue with your supervisor too! A follow-up is necessary to make sure your client has followed through with the plan you both have developed. If your client has not informed his or her sexual partner(s), it now becomes your responsibility to do so, per the ***Duty to Warn*** legal requirement. Discuss this legal and ethical responsibility with your client prior to informing his or her sexual partner(s) (Compton & Galaway, 1999; Dickson, 1998; Miley et al., 1998; NASW *Code of Ethics,* 1996; Reamer, 2004; Sheafor & Horejsi, 2006; *Tarasoff v. Regents of the University of California*, 1976).

Duty to Warn. The ***duty to warn*** and the ***duty to report*** refer to situations in which client confidentiality must be breached (broken) to prevent harm to others (Compton & Galaway, 1999; Miley et al., 1998). The ***duty to warn*** is a legal requirement established through the *Tatiana Tarasoff* case in which a third party was not warned of dangerous threats from a client. The client confided to his therapist that he was going to kill Tarasoff; the therapist then shared the confidential information with his supervisor and police. This led to the client's brief detainment; however, there were no grounds to keep him and he later killed Tarasoff. The therapist was sued by Tarasoff's family for his *failure to warn her* of the danger from the client

(Compton & Galaway, 1999; Dickson, 1998; Miley et al., 1998; NASW *Code of Ethics,* 1996; Reamer, 2004; *Tarasoff v. Regents of the University of California,* 1976).

As a social worker, you have an ethical duty to warn third parties of possible danger from your clients. It is also your duty to inform the client that serious threats must be disclosed to the parties he or she has threatened. Both the client and your supervisor should be involved in deciding what procedure will be used to notify third parties of this danger (Compton & Galaway, 1999; Miley et al., 1998; NASW *Code of Ethics,* 1996; Reamer, 2004).

Other Exceptions.   Other exceptions to maintaining client confidentiality and privileged communication include:

1. Client need for emergency services
2. Guardianship hearing
3. Committal procedures
4. Client lawsuits filed against social workers
5. Colleague, consultant, and attorney consultations
6. Quality assurance procedures, internal audits, or peer reviews—case records should be nonidentifiable

(*Other Exceptions* source: Miley et al., 1998)

Applying what you have learned ...

Threats and Exceptions to Maintaining Client Confidentiality

6.2. As discussed in this section, threats to the client's confidentiality and privileged communication exist. What are some procedures you can institute to ensure that your client's information remains as confidential as possible?

6.3. Refer to the *Exceptions to maintaining client confidentiality and privileged communication* section for the following exercises.

a. You have been placed in a public school setting for your social work internship, and the first child you work with is quite cautious about discussing his or her home life. You notice the child has on dirty clothes, does not appear healthy, and has a black eye. Should you immediately assume "child abuse and neglect?" Why or why not?

b. After looking over the list of physical and behavioral child abuse and neglect indicators, along with consulting other professionals, it is concluded that the child is being abused and/or neglected. You also discover that the child is your best

friend's sister's child. Should you just speak to them or report the incident to the proper authorities? Why or why not?

c. You believe that your elderly aunt is being abused by her daughter. Your aunt cries when you visit, you notice weight loss, and she no longer has a telephone or cable television to watch her favorite show. Should you speak to your aunt's daughter in order to resolve the problem, or should you report your suspicions to the proper authorities? Why or why not?

d. You have been working months with a certain client who suffered from depression and loneliness after his or her divorce. Your client has found a compatible companion, and you believe the relationship is positive for your client. At one appointment, your client discloses to you that he or she has been diagnosed with HIV. Your client is crying hysterically and has already decided not to tell his or her partner. Your client is begging you not to tell the companion either. What should you do to handle the situation? Why?

Section Three: Waiver of Confidentiality or Privileged Communication

What Is a Waiver?

Situations in which client information is accessed by persons other than the social worker and client occur in social work practice. Thus, it is important that you know how to properly and legally share your client's confidential information with others who do not fall into the *exceptions categories* covered earlier. This process is done through the use of a **waiver**, or a legal form in which your client has **voluntarily waived** his or her right to confidentiality and privileged communication.

Consent for Release of Information

The Client's written permission to share confidential information with others is known as the **Consent for the Release of Information** form. Most agencies have developed a standard release of information form, and in most cases, the signed form will expire six months from the date signed. From a legal and ethical standpoint, the client's permission must indicate **informed consent**, or a thorough understanding of what he or she has signed (Dickson, 1998; Sheafor & Horejsi, 2006).

Before having your clients sign the **Consent for Release of Information** form, consult specific state statutes, regulations, and policies for disclosing client information (Dickson, 1998). Make sure your client has a concise understanding of **what, who** and **why** the confidential information is being shared. You can do this by carrying out the following steps:

1. Inform the client of:
   a. **What** information is being requested
   b. **Who** is requesting the information
   c. **Why** the information is needed
2. Allow the client to read the material that is being requested. If necessary, read and/or explain in words he or she can understand.
3. Allow the client to read his or her records. Make sure any errors are corrected prior to the release of any client information.
4. Inform the client of possible negative consequences if information is released.
5. Inform the client of the possible consequences if information is *not* released.
6. Inform the client that the signed consent form can be **voided** (canceled) at a later date.
7. Make sure a copy of the signed consent form is present in the client's case file. Make sure both the client and the professional requesting the information receives a copy of the signed consent form.
8. **Do not release** any letters or information in the client's file that were received by a third party (doctor reports, other agency reports, etc.) because these reports are not part of your agency's records.

9. If drug treatment information is present in a client's file, *federal confidentiality laws supersede the agency's consent form*. The client information cannot be *released without* specific consent on a federal form or through a court order.

(*Client information* sources: Dickson, 1998; Miley et al., 1998; Morales & Sheafor, 1998; NASW *Code of Ethics*, 1997; Sheafor & Horejsi, 2006)

HIPAA: Notice of Privacy Practices

As a social worker, it is imperative that you understand the *Health Insurance Portability and Accountability Act of 1996* (HIPAA), which gives various agencies and professionals the right to access your clients' records. HIPAA also explains the rights and procedures for client/patient access to his or her own records. Items on the HIPAA notice include:

1. *Client Understanding of Health Record/Information*   This understanding serves to provide:
   - A record of each visit
   - A basis for planning and providing care and treatment
   - A means of communication between health professionals contributing to client/patient care
   - A legal document describing the care received
   - A way to educate health professionals and provide a source of data for research
   - Information for public health officials overseeing the delivery of health care in the United States
   - A tool to assess and improve care to client/patient
2. *Agency Responsibilities*   Requirements of the agency include:
   - Terms of this notice
   - Privacy maintenance
   - Notice of agency's legal duties and privacy practices
   - Notifications of the inability to agree to requested restriction(s)
   - Accommodations of reasonable requests to communicate health information by alternative means and/or locations
3. *Procedures for the Use and Disclosure of Client/Patient Information*
   - *Treatment.* Health information shared among client/patient health care team (case manager, doctor, psychologist, therapist, clinical director)
   - *Payment.* Health information shared with third-party payer
     *Medical information is limited to what is necessary to establish a claim for reimbursement.
   - *Health Care Operations.* Client information used in assessing and improving the care and outcomes of treatment
   - *Notification.* Information and notification provided to the person responsible for client/patient care (family member, personal representative). Information related to care, location, and general condition of client is provided.

- ***Communication with Family.*** Health information disclosed to family member, relative, close personal friend, or any other person client designates to receive the information.

  *Requires written permission from client.

- ***Research.*** Information disclosed to researchers.

  *Institutional review board reviews the research proposal and establishes the protocol that ensures the privacy of client health information.

- ***Administration.*** Certain client/patient information disclosed to administrator responsible for overseeing the facility/agency operations

- ***Commitment Proceedings.*** Client/patient health care information disclosed to mental health reviewer, attorney, and/or court conducting the involuntary commitment proceeding, per ***Mental Health Procedures Act.***

- ***Food and Drug Administration (FDA).*** Client/patient information disclosed pertaining to adverse events with respect to food, supplements, product, and product defects; marketing surveillance information posted for product recalls, repairs, or replacements

- ***Public Health.*** Client/patient health information disclosed to public health or legal authorities to prevent or control disease, injury, or disability

  *Required by law.

- ***Correctional Institution.*** Client/patient information disclosed to health care professionals if client is an inmate requiring health treatment

- ***Business Associates.*** Client/patient information disclosed when services are contracted

  *Business associates must adhere to the agency's procedures for safeguarding client/patient information.

- ***Coroners, Medical Examiners, and Funeral Directors.*** Client/patient information disclosed so that duties required by law can be completed

- ***Law Enforcement.*** Client/patient information disclosed for:
  1. Subpoena, court order, warrant, summons or similar process
  2. Identification and location of a suspect, fugitive, material witness, missing person, or victim of a crime
  3. Investigation of a death that may be due to criminal conduct
  4. Investigation of criminal conduct at the agency
  5. Emergency circumstances: report of a crime, location of crime or victims; identity, description, or location of person who committed the crime

- ***Military and Veterans.*** Client/patient information disclosed to military command officers or appropriate foreign military authority

  *If client/patient is member of armed forces.

4. ***Client Health Information Rights***   Health information in the record belongs to the client/patient, and he or she has the following rights:
   - Written request that health information not be disclosed or used

     *Request will be considered, but agency obligation to accept it or abide by it does not exist.

Applying what you have learned...

Waiver of Confidentiality of Privileged Communication

6.4.   What are a *waiver, Consent for the Release of Information*, and *HIPAA?*

6.5.   Prior to having your client sign the Consent for the Release of Information and HIPAA forms, what should you do? Make a list of the suggested procedures.

■ Written request to change manner and location of where the clients are receiving health information and communication if dissatisfied

*Agency will attempt to accommodate reasonable requests.

■ Written request to inspect and/or obtain health information in their file

*Agency to provide this information in the time frames established by law; may charge fees for requested copies of material.

5. *Additional Information and Reporting a Problem* Clients use information regarding the agency's process to request additional information on the HIPAA form or to report a problem:
   ■ Agency's Privacy Officer and address
   ■ Federal Department of Health and Human Services contact information

(*Sources:* Centers for Disease Control, 2003)

Summary

Your primary mission as a social worker is to enhance human well-being and assist in meeting the basic human needs of all people in a community. To reach this goal, you need to establish a feeling of trust with your clients and the community you are serving. As discussed in the chapter, you can do this by knowing what the *right to privacy, confidentiality,* and *privileged communication* mean.

Threats to confidentiality and privileged communication do exist. You can reduce or avoid these threats to your client's information by following the safeguards the organization you work for has implemented. Safeguards include, but are not limited to, locked file cabinets, limited access to files by need-to-know professionals, and holding client-related conversations in privacy. Remember, the information in the client's file belongs to the client!

Exceptions to maintaining client confidentiality and privileged communication include child abuse, elder abuse, and HIV-positive clients. Reporting child and elder abuse is mandatory. According to the *duty to warn* law, it is essential that you and your client notify his or her sexual partner(s) about the HIV disease. Other exceptions include guardianship hearing, client need for emergency services, and committal procedures.

A waiver, or a legal form your client voluntarily signs to release his or her information, is known as the *Consent for Release of Information* form. It is important that your client fully understand the what, who, and why of the information that is being released. The organization that you work for will also have the *Health Insurance Portability and*

Accountability Act of 1996 (HIPAA) federal form that your clients must sign. Taking the time to go over the forms and the client's information in his or her file, and explaining the release of information process are important prior to the client signing these forms. As a social worker, you must become familiar with the NASW *Code of Ethics* and the federal and state laws surrounding client confidentiality and privileged communication.

KEY WORDS AND CONCEPTS

Section One
Right to privacy, p. 100
Confidentiality, p. 101
Privileged communications, p. 101

Section Two
Threats to client confidentiality,
    p. 102
Exceptions to maintaining client
    confidentiality, p. 102
    Child abuse, p. 103
        Physical abuse, p. 103

Corporal punishment, p. 103
    Physical indicators, p. 103
    Behavioral indicators, p. 103
Child neglect, p. 104
Elder abuse, p. 104
    Physical indicators, p. 104
    Psychological indicators,
        p. 104
    Financial indicators, p. 105
    Other indicators, p. 105
HIV-Positive clients, p. 105
    AIDS, p. 105

Duty to warn, p. 105
    Tarasoff case, p. 105
Other exceptions, p. 106

Section Three
Waiver, p. 107
    Voluntarily waived, p. 107
Consent for the release of
    information, p. 107
    Informed consent, p. 107
    What, who, and why, p. 107
HIPAA, p. 108

REFERENCES

Barker, R. L. (2003). *Social work dictionary* (5th ed.). Washington, DC: NASW Press.

Centers for Disease Control. (2003). Health Insurance Portability & Accountability Act of 1996. Retrieved October 31, 2006 from CDC Web site: http://www.cdc.gov/

Compton, B. R., & Galaway, B. (1999). *Social work processes.* Pacific Grove, CA: Brooks/Cole Publishing Company.

Dickson, D. T. (1998). *Confidentiality and privacy in social work: A guide to the law for practitioners and students.* New York: The Free Press.

Gibelman, M. (1995). *What social workers do.* Washington, DC: NASW Press.

Koff, T. H., & Park, R. W. (1999). *Aging public policy: Bonding the generations* (2nd ed.). Amityville, NY: Baywood.

Luepker, E. T. (2003). *Record keeping in psychotherapy and counseling: Protecting confidentiality and the professional relationship.* New York: Brunner-Rutledge.

Miley, K. K., O'Melia, M., & DuBois, B. L. (1998). *General social work practice: An empowering approach.* Needham Heights, MA: Allyn Bacon.

Morales, A. T., & Sheafor, B. W. (1998). *Social work: A profession of many faces.* Needham Heights, MA: Allyn & Bacon.

National Association of Social Workers (1996). NASW *Code of Ethics.* Washington, DC: Author.

Reamer, F. G. (2004). *Ethical standards in social work.* Washington, DC: NASW Press

Roberts, A. R. & Greene, G. J. (2002). *Social workers' desk reference.* New York: Oxford University Press

Schmolling, P., Jr., Youkeles, M., & Burger, W.R. (1993). *Human services in contemporary America.* Pacific Grove, CA: Brooks/Cole Publishing Company.

Sheafor, B. W., & Horejsi, C. R. (2006). *Techniques and guidelines for social work practice.* Boston, MA: Allyn Bacon.

Tarasoff v. Board of Regents of University of California, 33 Cal. 3d 275 (1973), 529 P. 2nd 553 (1974), 17 Cal. 3d 425 (1976), 131 Cal. Rptr. 14 (1976).

7 Communicating About Clients

As a social worker, it is important for you to understand that proper service documentation is critical in the social work field to make sure that the client's situation is correctly assessed and understood, and that appropriate planning and intervention are implemented. This chapter discusses the content and types of case note recordings, as well as the importance of keeping accurate client service documentation. Scenarios and hands-on documentation exercises will enhance the professional communication skills you will need when preparing social work documentation.

Section One: Purpose and Importance of Accurate Case Note Documentation

The Purpose of Case Notes

Social workers provide both direct and indirect services to clients in the community. *Direct practice* involves face-to-face interaction with an individual or family, whereas *indirect practice* involves the social worker partaking in activities that will benefit clients (Sheafor & Horejsi, 2006). In this chapter, the main focus is on proper documentation surrounding *direct practice*.

When social workers provide direct services, their interactions with clients are recorded using casework documentation. It is important to remember that documentation should be done each time you have contact with a client. This process provides organization, reflection, and a guarantee of proper, continuous client care in your absence (Darowski, 2005).

The Importance of Accuracy

Accurate casework documentation is critical in the social work field so that the client's situation can be correctly assessed and understood (see Table 7.1 and 7.2). In order to assist

TABLE 7.1   Characteristics of ACCURATE Case Note Documentation

Accurate Case Note Documentation Characteristics	The Result
Clear and comprehensive documentation	Correct client assessment and understanding, solid foundation to design and deliver high-quality services
Careful and thoughtful information collection	Adequate foundation for clinical reasoning and intervention plans
Continuity and coordination	Ensures up-to-date client information and continuation of appropriate services
Strong recordkeeping practices	Maintains integrity of programs offered to clients

(*Table 7.1 content sources*: Compton & Galaway, 1999; Miley, O'Melia, & DuBois, 1998; Reamer, 2005, p. 326; Schmolling, Youkeles, & Burger, 1993; Sheafor & Horejsi, 2006; Wilson, 1976)

the client in obtaining appropriate services, professional planning and intervention need to be implemented. Thus, proper casework documentation serves three functions:

1. Assessment and planning
2. Service delivery
3. Continuity and coordination of services

Assessment and Planning.   Clear and thorough documentation of all facts and circumstances of the client's situation is essential to the assessment and planning process. Accurate assessment and planning documentation provides:

1. An adequate foundation for the social worker's clinical reasoning and intervention plans
2. A reliable source of measuring client performance and outcomes

Service Delivery.   The social worker's thorough documentation provides a solid foundation for the design of high-quality services. The social worker can provide competent delivery of clinical, community-based, and agency-based services by keeping comprehensive client records.

TABLE 7.2   Characteristics of INACCURATE Case Note Documentation

Inaccurate Case Note Documentation Characteristics	The Result
Incomplete client records	Inadequate planning and intervention services
Carelessness and thoughtless documentation	Critical judgment errors and poor outcomes for the client
Inconsistent and disordered	Lack relevant client information and appropriate services
Weak recordkeeping practices	Integrity lost for programs beneficial to clients

(*Table 7.2 content sources*: Compton & Galaway, 1999; Miley, O'Melia, & DuBois, 1998; Reamer, 2005, p. 326; Schmolling, Youkeles, & Burger, 1993; Sheafor & Horejsi, 2006; Wilson, 1976)

Applying what you have learned…

Accuracy of Case Work Documentation

7.1. The following is a case note documentation record full of various types of mistakes.

    a. Read through the record and list the various mistakes you found.

    b. Type this case note documentation record, fixing the mistakes.

    John apeared in mi office today. He seamed a bit antsy about getng caut drinking last Saturday. He knows this violats his parole guidelines (what an idiot)! He is beginning to get aggistated that I am "putting things on the line" for him. He begins to walk towards me. I am feeling scarred, and wondering if I should "buzz" the front disk. I will quicly call Drug & Alcohl. I hope Jim is not the one on-call. You can't count on him du to his own addiction. Because John is agitated, it probably isn't wort discussing his plan today.

Continuity and Coordination of Services.   Appropriate documentation assists the professional social worker in collaborating and organizing proper services for their client. Accurate and up-to-date client information guarantees that suitable services for the client will continue.

(*Importance of Accuracy:* Compton & Galaway, 1999; Miley, O'Melia, & DuBois, 1998; Reamer, 2005, p. 326; Schmolling, Youkeles, & Burger, 1993; Sheafor & Horejsi, 2006; Wilson, 1976).

Remember: "Your client's chart is a legal document and needs to be treated with care. This means: be neat, make sure your content is accurate, and that it presents your client in his or her best light." (Darowski, 2005, p. 22)

Section Two: Types and Content of Case Note Recordings

Various types of case note recordings are used in the social work field. The format used is determined by state and federal laws and regulations, the individual agency, and the types of social work being performed. In some cases, the type of case note recording may be based on who has access to the records (Sheafor & Horejsi, 2006; Wilson, 1976).

Narrative (Process) Recording

Narrative Recording is a type of comprehensive process recording that is still used in some direct-service agencies. When using the Narrative Recording, everything that took place in the interview with the client and social worker must be written down. Because of the process and in-depth details required when using the Narrative Recording, it is beneficial to you to employ this format when developing your first case note documentation. The benefits for you include enhancing self-awareness, improving assessment skills, and assisting you in learning to work effectively with clients (Miley et al., 1998; Sheafor & Horejsi, 2006; Wilson, 1976).

Steps in Properly Completing a Narrative Recording.   You must take two important steps, as follows, when preparing a narrative recording properly after it is taped.

1. ***Create*** many handwritten notes documenting everything that was said (verbatim, word for word) in the interview. It is important that you and your client's actions and nonverbal behaviors are also logged. (See Table 7.3.)
   - You can organize your handwritten notes by dividing legal-size paper into labeled columns, then placing the notes in a loose-leaf notebook. It is extremely important that you record the interview details immediately when using this style of client documentation to ensure everything from the interview is documented.
2. ***Review*** your handwritten notes. Completing paperwork is not exciting for most social workers, but it is one of the most important parts of the job. Procrastination will quickly lead to a tower of paperwork on the corner of your desk!

   (*Steps in narrative recording*: Miley et al., 1998; Sheafor & Horejsi, 2006; Wilson, 1976)

Narrative Recording Summary Report Contents.   A properly prepared Narrative Recording summary report includes: (See Table 7.4)

1. Identifying data for both the client and social worker
2. Date of the interview

TABLE 7.3   Sample of Handwritten Notes from Mrs. Smith's Interview

Client: *Betty Smith*		Case Number: *1234*	Cross Reference: *Foster home name, if applies*
Date	**Type of Contact**	**Verbal**	**Nonverbal**
12/10	Client in office	Betty said, "The house is so small that nobody has privacy." I said, "Could you give me an example?"	At this time, Betty appears to be upset. She is crying
		Betty said, "The apartment has only 2 bedrooms and Jenny and Billy share a room. Jenny is 12 and does not want to share a room anymore. The kids are fighting so much, I can't stand it." I said, "There are housing programs that will help you find a 3 bedroom apartment or house. Do you want to call an agency?"	Betty is rubbing her hands together and still crying. The crying has increased to the point where Betty's breathing has changed and her words are hard to interpret. At this point, I am moving closer to Betty so I can understand what she is saying. The crying is making me feel a little uncomfortable. I am confused on how to best approach this situation.
		Betty said, "Yes, can you help me get in contact with them?" I said, "Yes, we can call from here to inquire about their services and to begin the process of finding a bigger residence for you and your family."	Betty has now stopped crying. She leans back in her chair sluggishly. I believe she is relieved by the housing suggestion, and exhausted from the crying.

(*Table 7.3 format source*: Sheafor & Horejsi, 2006)

TABLE 7.4 Sample of a Narrative Recording Summary Report for Mrs. Smith

Client: *Betty Smith*		Case Number: *1234*		Cross Reference: *Foster home name, if applies*

Type of Contact	Date	Time Spent	To Do	Notes
Client/office	12/10	1 hour	Call HUD	Betty says home is crowded and nobody has privacy.
			Find different/ bigger housing	Betty says she will start doing the HUD paperwork today and look in the newspaper for rentals.
				I told Betty I will help her with the HUD paperwork and application.
				I also told her I will assist her in finding a larger residence to rent.

(*Table 7.4 format source*: Sheafor & Horejsi, 2006)

3. Full details of the interview, using the "I said then he/she said" style
4. Description of actions and nonverbal behaviors of both the client and social worker
5. Social workers' "reflection" of the interview (internal thoughts, feelings, questions)
6. Diagnostic summary or analysis of the interview, including summary of observations, analytical thoughts, and impressions
7. Treatment plan for intervention, goals, and so on.

(*Narrative recording summary*: Miley et al., 1998; Sheafor & Horejsi, 2006; Wilson, 1976)

Problem-Oriented Recording (POR)

Most practicing social workers use the summary recording style to record client case notes. The most popular summary recording type is *Problem-Oriented Recording (POR)* (Sheafor & Horejsi, 2006; Wilson, 1976).

Problem-oriented recording is a recordkeeping method that consists of four components:

1. Client database
2. List of specific problems, each assigned an identifying number
3. Action development for each problem
4. Plan implementation

Client Database.   The client database is the identifying information collected during the intake. Information gathered from the client interview should include:

1. Client's full name, including any aliases (false name, nickname)
2. Identifying number such as social security number, patient or case number
3. Interview date
4. Recording date
5. Your name as the "Social Worker"
6. Purpose of the interview

(*POR sources*: Reamer, 2005; Sheafor & Horejsi, 2006; Wilson, 1976)

TABLE 7.5   Problem List for the Smith family

Problem Number	Problem	Date
1.	Crowded housing	12/10
2.	Short of food money	12/10
3.	Jenny (age 12) needs braces	12/15
4.	Billy (age 7) failing reading	12/20

(*Table 7.5 format source*: Sheafor & Horejsi, 2006)

List of Specific Problems.   When documenting specific problems, the concerns of both the client and social worker can be included. Usually each problem is listed individually and explained in a behavioral language. (Refer to Table 7.5).

Some agencies use a ***master problem list*** in which each problem is assigned a number. "Crowded housing" may be assigned the number 2, and "Short of food money" may be assigned the number 5. Having a master problem list allows agencies to achieve greater consistency in their recordkeeping process. It also assists agencies in program evaluations, and client problems and services research (refer to Table 7.6). (Sheafor & Horejsi, 2006).

Action Development.   Action development is the type of reaction to each client problem on the list (Refer to Table 7.6). There are three basic actions (Sheafor & Horejsi, 2006):

1. Initiate intervention.
2. Secure additional information to assist in understanding the problem(s) better.
3. Monitor the situation(s) and wait for further developments.

Plan Implementation.   Once the client problems and plans of action have been identified, it is time to implement the plans. When using the **Problem-Oriented Recording (POR)**, and intervention is required to solve the problem, it is helpful to use the **SOAP** format to describe the proposed action and rationale for the action (Sheafor & Horejsi, 2006).

TABLE 7.6   Problem and Action List for the Smith Family

Problem Number	Problem	Date	Action
1.	Crowded housing	12/10	Rental assistance for larger residence
2.	Short of food money	12/10	Enroll in food stamp program
3.	Jenny (age 12) needs braces	12/15	Find a dentist and secure insurance
4.	Billy (age 7) failing reading	12/20	Assist in scheduling Parent/Teacher Conference, assist parent in locating a reading tutor

(*Table 7.6 format source*: Sheafor & Horejsi, 2006)

Applying what you have learned ...

Types and Content of Case Note Recordings

7.2. Narrative (Process) Recording and Problem-Oriented Recording (POR) Now that you have fixed the mistakes in the previous record, (Ex. 7.1) ask yourself, "What is missing?"

   a. Make a list of data that you believe is missing from the scenario in Ex. 7.1.

   b. Create a *Narrative Recording* using the data in Ex. 7.1 scenario, adding the data you felt was missing.

   c. Create a *Problem-Oriented Recording (POR)* using the data in Ex. 7.1 scenario, adding the data you felt was missing.

SOAP Format. The SOAP acronym represents **s**ubjective information, **o**bjective information, **a**ssessment, and **p**lan: (see Table 7.7).

   1. *Subjective information.* The subjective information is derived from the client. It describes how the client perceives his or her situation. Subjective information cannot be validated.

   2. *Objective information.* The objective information is derived from professional staff. It can include the social worker, clinical examinations, and/or data collection. Objective information can be verified and validated.

   3. *Assessment.* Using both the subjective and objective information, the social worker is able to assess the client's problem.

   4. *Plan.* The plan clearly spells out how the social worker and client intend to address and/or resolve the problem.

   (*SOAP format:* Sheafor & Horejsi, 2006)

TABLE 7.7   Sample of SOAP Entry Format for the Smith Family

Subjective	Mrs. Smith states Billy does not read very well and I (Mom) didn't either when attending school. Mrs. Smith worries that Billy will have to repeat the reading class next year and his peers will pick on him. She is intimidated by the school staff at Billy's school.
Objective	School records indicate that Billy's reading comprehension test scores are poor.
Assessment	Family does not have many literature pieces in the home for the children to read. Mrs. Smith probably does not have any money for children's books. Mrs. Smith's intimidation prevents her from scheduling Parent/Teacher conferences and requesting a reading tutor for Billy.
Plan	Need to support Mrs. Smith in scheduling a Parent/Teacher Conference. The support will extend to assist her in obtaining a reading tutor for Billy by 1/10. Need to assure her that the school staff is not there to intimidate her, and she has the right to request additional help for her child. Begin a plan to assist Mrs. Smith in building self-confidence.

(*Table 7.7 format source:* Sheafor & Horejsi, 2006)

Section Three: Risk-Management Guidelines for Case Note Documentation

Risk-Management Guidelines

Practicing social workers have developed detailed risk-management guidelines to increase delivery of services to clients. The guidelines have also been created to protect social workers in the event of ethics complaints and lawsuits contending professional negligence (Reamer, 2005).

The risk-management guidelines relating to case recording documentation fall into four individual categories:

1. Documentation content
2. Language and terminology
3. Credibility
4. Accessing records and documentation

(*Risk-management guidelines source*: Reamer, 2005)

Documentation Content.   Case note documentation must be thorough. Adequate information ensures that service to the client is appropriate and that all parties involved are protected. Guidelines in preparing professional case note documentation include the following:

1. ***Serve and protect.*** Sufficient detail should be documented so that appropriate client services take place. Sufficient detail will also protect you in the event of an ethics complaint or lawsuit.
2. ***Strike a balance.*** This is difficult and usually takes time and practice. Striking a balance results in properly assessing clients' needs and being accountable to clients, various providers, the courts, and utilization review bodies.
3. ***Avoid overdocumentation in a crisis.*** Excessive detail in a crisis can serve as a "red flag" during an ethics hearing or litigation. "Was the situation handled in an unusual way?"
4. ***Use caution with personal notes.*** Personal notes can quickly become the property of the courts if subpoenaed by a lawyer. The information contained in personal notes could be a risk to you and your client.
5. ***Be cautious in documentation of services for families and couples.*** Keeping separate records for sensitive information is suggested so that you can protect each client in the event of a dispute. Routine assessments and summaries of services could be combined in joint files.
6. ***Do not air agency "dirty laundry."*** Never put details and personal opinions of agency and/or staff programs and competencies in clients' files. This information should be in administrative files only!

(*Documentation content source*: Reamer, 2005)

Remember: "A primary function of documentation is to serve and protect. The content, however, must tread a careful line, striking a balance between too much and too little information." (Reamer, 2005, p. 328)

Language and Terminology. Case note documentation should be done in a professional manner. Remember, appropriate language and terminology should be used because you always have an audience (supervisor, agency, or court)!

The guidelines for appropriate language and terminology include the following:

1. *Gain clarity.* Be clear, precise, and specific in your wording. This practice results in better delivery of service to clients, along with strengthening your ability to explain and defend prior decisions and actions. Avoid using jargon, slang, and abbreviations that could cause confusion and misunderstandings. Ambiguity can be a disaster for both you and the client!
2. *Draw conclusions.* Always provide supporting details when drawing conclusions. "The client was hostile" should be followed by "as evidenced by. . . ."
3. *Avoid defamatory language.* Protect yourself against yourself! Avoid *libel* (written) or *slander* (spoken), the two forms of defamation of character.
4. *Write for an audience.* Remember, the records that you keep will be viewed by supervisors, managed care authorities, utilization review personnel, and third-party payers. Be thorough and professional in your writing.

(*Language and terminology guidelines source*: Reamer, 2005)

Credibility. Case documentation and records provide essential evidence of your credibility. Thorough documentation defends your actions, but this is not enough. You need to follow guidelines for maintaining credibility (Reamer, 2005).

1. *Document in a timely fashion.* Documentation is time consuming, but it is necessary in social work. Complete your documentation of decisions and actions in a timely manner. **Avoid** procrastination because this failing can be used to challenge your credibility with adversaries, such as opposing legal counsel, and can negatively affect client services.
2. *Avoid prognostic documentation.* **Do not** record planned interventions and events until they happen. Premature recorded notes can lead to inaccurate reflection and will undermine your credibility.
3. *Strive for professional elocution.* Write or print legibly, using proper grammar and spelling. **Avoid** illegible entries, as well as grammar and spelling errors. This inattention to detail can destroy your credibility as a professional.
4. *Acknowledge errors.* Always acknowledge your errors. Make sure you clear up any confusion with a new entry acknowledging and correcting the error. Draw a line through the error, initial, date, and label it "error." This should be done as soon as the error is discovered. Never change, hide, lose, or destroy records. Never use white-out to change errors. This will destroy your credibility quickly!

(*Credibility source*: Reamer, 2005)

Accessing Records and Documentation. In reality, truly confidential case records do not exist. It is beneficial for you to be familiar with laws and rules that surround the disclosure of confidential documents, and security risks in the age of technology.

Applying what you have learned…

Risk Management Guidelines

7.3. In using the Narrative Recording and the Problem-Oriented Recording (POR) you developed in *Exercise 7.2*:

a. Check to make sure that your entries follow the various risk-management guidelines.

b. Change the entries that do not meet the risk-management guidelines.

In order to protect yourself and your clients, you should (Reamer, 2005):

1. *Acquire legal know-how.* There is a difference between subpoenas to *appear* with documents and a court order to *disclose* the document's contents. According to the 1996 NASW *Code of Ethics*, social workers are obligated to take steps to protect the confidentiality of relevant documents during legal proceedings (Reamer, 2005, p. 333):

   ■ Social workers should protect the confidentiality of clients during legal proceedings to the extent permitted by law. When a court of law or other legally authorized body orders social workers to disclose confidential or privileged information without a client's consent and such disclosure could cause harm to the client, social workers should request that the court withdraw the order or limit the order as narrowly as possible or maintain the records under seal, unavailable for public inspection. (Standard 1.07[j])

2. *Know relevant statutes and regulations.* There are many federal and state laws and regulations pertaining to the handling of confidential information and records. Resources include:

   ■ Federal Health Insurance Portability and Accountability Act (HIPAA), which addresses personal health-related information, to include psychotherapy notes (P.L. 104-91).

   ■ Family Educational Rights and Privacy Act (FERPA), which deals with the confidentiality of school records (34 C.F.R. Part 99).

   ■ Confidentiality of Alcohol and Drug Abuse Patient Records which deals with the confidentiality of mental health records (42 C.F.R. Part 2).

3. *Secure records.* Exercise caution at all times. Clinical records should be stored in secure locations to prevent unauthorized access. Social workers should be careful when using computer data entry systems and should take precautions so that information cannot be accessed by unauthorized personnel.

** When records are destroyed or disposed of, it is extremely important that a client's confidentiality still be protected. See NASW *Code of Ethics*, standards 1.07[l],[m], for further information and guidance in reference to disposing of client records.

(*Protection source*: Reamer, 2005)

Summary

Social workers employ case note documentation when providing direct services to clients. The documentation provides organization and reflection, and guarantees the proper continuous care of the client in your absence. Proper service documentation is critical in the social work field to make sure that the client's situation is correctly assessed and understood, and appropriate planning and intervention are implemented.

Social workers use various types of case note documentation. The two most popular types in are Narrative Recording and Problem-Oriented Recording (POR). **Narrative Recording** is a comprehensive process recording still used in various agencies. It is the best tool for teaching students the "know-how" of preparing professional case note documentation. **Problem-Oriented Recording (POR)** is the most popular type of case note documentation among social workers because it is condensed, and requires less time spent on paperwork.

Risk-management guidelines have been created to protect social workers in the event of ethics complaints and lawsuits contending professional negligence. The risk-management guidelines relating to case recording documentation fall into four individual categories: documentation content, language and terminology, credibility, and accessing records and documentation. It is extremely important that your case note documentation be accurate and that the contents be completed in a balanced manner.

KEY WORDS AND CONCEPTS

REFERENCES

Compton, B. R., & Galaway, B. (1999). *Social work processes*. Pacific Grove, CA: Brooks/Cole Publishing Company.

Darowski, W. A. (2005). *In the field: A real life survival guide for the social work internship*. Boston, MA: Allyn & Bacon.

Miley, K. K., O'Melia, M., & DuBois, B. (1998). *Generalist social work practice: An empowering approach*. Needham Heights, MA: Allyn & Bacon.

Reamer, F. G. (2005). Documentation in social work: Evolving ethical and risk-management standards. *Social Work, 50*(4), 325–334.

Schmolling, P., Jr., Youkeles, M., & Burger, W.R. (1993). *Human services in contemporary America*. Pacific Grove, CA: Brooks/Cole Publishing Company.

Sheafor, B. W., & Horejsi, C.R. (2006). *Techniques and guidelines for social work practice*. Boston, MA: Pearson Education.

Wilson, S. J. (1976). *Recording: Guidelines for social workers*. New York: The Free Press.

CHAPTER

8

What Is Cultural Diversity?

As a social worker, you must be able to relate to, and understand, various cultures so you can help your client in the most effective and positive manner. Increasing your cultural competence will give you a personal awareness of your own culture, while equipping you with the tools to understand various client cultures. The importance of remaining open-minded and empathetic to various client cultures is stressed in this chapter. Hands-on exercises will help reinforce the concepts learned so that you will enter the diversified social work field equipped with professional communication skills.

Section One: Essential Characteristics of Culture

Defining Culture and Subculture

Culture is defined as "the language, beliefs, values, norms, behaviors, and even material objects that are passed from one generation to the next" (Henslin, 2005, p. 36). Cultural characteristics and influences are not limited to just race and ethnicity. Cultural characteristics actually include, but again, are not limited to, gender, social class, level of education, occupation, and religion. All these characteristics are *social agents* that influence one's beliefs, values, and cultural norms, and are fundamental in determining how individuals behave. These characteristics also play an important part in the way one communicates and views the world (Henslin, 2005; Sheafor & Horejsi, 2006).

Subculture. *Subcultures*, or cultures existing within the larger, dominant culture, are distinctive in that their values, norms, religion, and language differ from those of the larger culture surrounding them (Henslin, 2005). Your client's *subculture* must be considered and understood thoroughly so that you can envision "society" the way your client does. By seeing society through your client's eyes, you can gain a clear understanding of his or her behavior. Empathy surrounding your client's issues will develop, and problems can be addressed and solved in a positive, culturally sensitive manner (Galambos, 2003; Mama, 2001; Miley, O'Melia, & DuBois, 1998; Seaton, 2003).

Applying what you have learned . . .

Contrasting Culture and Subculture
8.1 List the differences between a culture and a subculture.

8.2 What are the two main challenges when researching various subcultures?

Challenges in Developing MultiCultural Competence

First Challenge.   The first challenge you must face when researching various clients' distinctive subcultures is acceptance of "difference." Differences in beliefs, values, norms, and language will exist between your culture/subculture and theirs. Thus, the way your client views society will differ from your view.

Second Challenge.   The second challenge you will be presented with is relating to, and understanding, these accepted differences with an open mind. You can overcome this challenge by gaining a sense of cultural relativism, which enables you to understand a behavior in the context in which it takes place. This will ultimately lead you to multicultural competence and an understanding of social diversity.

Section Two: Developing Multicultural Competence

NASW *Code of Ethics* Cultural Competence and Social Diversity

According to the NASW *Code of Ethics* (2001):

1. Social workers should understand culture and its function in human behavior and society, recognizing the strengths that exist in all cultures (1.05 [a]).
2. Social workers should have a knowledge base of their clients' cultures and be able to demonstrate competence in the provision of services that are sensitive to clients' cultures and to differences among people and cultural groups (1.05 [b]).
3. Social workers should obtain education about and seek to understand the nature of social diversity and oppression with respect to race, ethnicity, national origin, color, sex, sexual orientation, age, marital status, political belief, religion, or mental or physical disability (1.05 [c]).

The first step in meeting the cultural competence and social diversity requirements of the NASW *Code of Ethics* is achieving an understanding and acceptance of *your* cultural beliefs, values, and behaviors.

The Road to Multicultural Competence

As a social worker, you need to understand and feel comfortable with your cultural characteristics and actions before you can gain a *thorough* and *productive* understanding of your client's cultural/subcultural characteristics and behaviors.

Enlightened consciousness, or having a sound, open-minded understanding and acceptance of facts surrounding your own beliefs, values, and behaviors is vital to becoming multiculturally competent. As a social worker, you must be free of ignorance, prejudice, or superstition toward your own culture and that of others so that you can successfully understand and assist your clients (Fong, 2001; Galambos, 2003; Henslin, 2005; Mama, 2001; Miley, O'Melia, & DuBois, 1998; Seaton, 2003).

Steps to "Self." You can take several steps to reach your "conscious use of self" (Garvin, 1997, p. 90, as quoted by Seaton, 2003, p. 54). These steps require an "open mind and heart" (Okayama, Furuto, & Edmondson, 2001, p. 89):

1. Acknowledge and accept your personal strengths and weaknesses.
2. Become aware of your behaviors, habits, and customs.
3. Be willing to increase your awareness of your own culture and cultural identity.
4. Develop an appreciation of your own cultural heritage and identity.

   (Fong, 2001; Okayama, Furuto, & Edmondson, 2001; Sue & Sue, 2003)

When you reach an enlightened consciousness and sense of "self," you will be ready to learn about, and accept another's, culture and cultural identity. You will also discover that cultural sensitivity, flexibility, a sense of humor, and openness exist when working with your diverse clients (Seaton, 2003).

What is Cultural Relativism?

Cultural relativism, or the ability to understand another's culture within its context without prejudice (Henslin, 2005; Sheafor & Horejsi, 2006), is essential to the social work field. Understanding your client's cultural characteristics is the first step in building a trusting and communicative relationship with your client. Relating to your client's values, norms, and behaviors in a positive manner will lead to a productive social worker–client relationship (Fong, 2001; Galambos, 2003; Mama, 2001; Miley, O'Melia, & DuBois, 1998; Seaton, 2003; Sheafor & Horejsi, 2006).

Communication Reminder!

Don't forget that it is essential to listen carefully to your client's verbal tones and various languages used. Pay close attention to his or her nonverbal facial expressions and behavior. (Refer back to Chapter 4, Section One, to refresh your memory about verbal and nonverbal communication, and Chapter 4, Section Two, to review social rhythms and influential factors.)

Applying what you have learned . . .

Exploring the "Self"

8.3 What is "enlightened consciousness"?

8.4 What are the steps you should take in order to reach the "self"?

8.5 What does the term *cultural relativism* mean? Why is it important to be able to relate to your client's culture/subculture?

Section Three: Cross-Cultural Model of Practice

Client Individualism

As a social worker, you will have clients from various cultural and racial backgrounds. You should be aware of human diversity so that you can *individualize* each client and avoid stereotyping values, beliefs, and behaviors in relation to your client's physical features, ethnic identity, and socioeconomic status. In order to individualize each client, you must become culturally sensitive (Henslin, 2005; Hyde, 2004; Morales & Sheafor, 1998; Sheafor & Horejsi, 2006).

Becoming Culturally Sensitive

A *culturally sensitive* social worker will acknowledge and understand that prejudicial feelings and stereotyping affect the interactions between people. The willingness to learn about another's culture and respect for existing differences are necessary in reaching cultural sensitivity (Fong, 2001; Okayama et al., 2001).

Cumulative skill proficiency, or the ongoing process of developing skills, is also necessary in the Human Services field. Social workers need to consistently expand their understanding and acceptance of difference if they are to successfully engage in a culturally diverse client population (Galambos, 2003).

Grounded Knowledge Base

The most efficient way to become culturally sensitive, and accumulate multicultural competence and skills, is to continuously gain knowledge about your various clients' cultures and subcultures. You can gain this knowledge by doing your "homework." Once you have gathered your client's physical information such as gender, age, and race, research your client's social environment and existing influences in his or her distinct culture or subculture. Collect client information on the following:

1. *Socioeconomic status*—income, occupation, and education
2. *Religious beliefs*—in most cases, strongly intertwined with culture
3. *Family structure*—single, married, divorced, children, strong or weak
4. *Family behavioral patterns*—functional or dysfunctional, level of influence

5. *Residence location*—neighborhood, town, county
6. *Support network*—family, friends, organizations
7. Any other details important in gaining a precise understanding of your client's culture/subculture

(Houston, 2002; Morales & Sheafor, 1998)

By collecting in-depth client information, you gain an appreciation for difference, along with sensitivity toward your client's culture. With this knowledge, you will be able to connect your client's behaviors to the possible effects of his or her social environment. You may also discover that your client's behavior is actually meeting the social expectations (norms) within his or her subculture (Fong, 2001; Galambos, 2003; Henslin, 2005; Okayama et al., 2001; Seaton, 2003). As your cultural and subcultural database grows, so does your proficiency in working with diverse clients.

What Is Ethnocentrism?

As a social worker, one important concept warrants your full attention. *Ethnocentrism*, or the tendency to use one's own culture as a standard in which to judge other cultures, must be avoided so that you do not form an insolent and disapproving attitude toward your client's values and norms. Ethnocentric views will lead to a judgmental and negative evaluation of your client's behavior. Obtaining a concise understanding of your client becomes difficult, and the social worker–client communication process is hindered (Henslin, 2005; Sheafor & Horejsi, 2006). Ultimately, ethnocentric views do not belong in the field of social work.

Summary

Understanding the difference between culture and subculture is pertinent to becoming multiculturally competent. It is necessary for you to understand that differences exist between cultures and subcultures. You must establish an enlightened consciousness and

---

Applying what you have learned . . .

Exploring Client Diversity

8.6 In order to become culturally sensitive and to individualize each one of your clients, what must you do first?

8.7 As a social worker, you must have a grounded knowledge base. What are some characteristics you need to know about your client so that you can gain a thorough understanding of his or her behavior?

8.8 What is ethnocentrism?

8.9 As a social work student, what can you do now to prepare yourself to work with diverse clients? Make two separate lists: *Action Ideas* and *Internal Ideas*.

acceptance of your "self" before you can understand, accept, and relate to your client's culture/subculture.

Your first step in becoming culturally sensitive is to establish a grounded knowledge base by collecting information about your client's cultural/subcultural characteristics. By remaining open-minded and accepting to the differences found, you can avoid ethnocentric thought in relation to your client. By avoiding judgmental and negative evaluations of your client, communication and understanding will flourish.

KEY WORDS AND CONCEPTS

Section One
Culture, p. 123
  Social agents, p. 123
Subculture, p. 123

Section Two
Cultural relativism, p. 125
Enlightened consciousness, p. 125

NASW *Code of Ethics* cultural
  competence and social
  diversity, p. 124
"Self", p. 125

Section Three
Client individualism, p. 126
  Individualize, p. 126

Culturally sensitive, p. 126
Cumulative skill
  proficiency, p. 126
Ethnocentrism, p. 127
Grounded knowledge
  base, p. 127

REFERENCES

Fong, R. (2001). *Culturally competent social work practice: Past and present.* Boston, MA: Allyn & Bacon.

Galambos, C.M. (2003). Moving cultural diversity toward cultural competence in health care. *Health & Social Work, 28*(1), 3–4.

Garvin, C. (1997). *Interpersonal practice in social work: Promoting competence and social justice* (2nd ed.). Boston, MA: Allyn & Bacon.

Henslin, J.M. (2005). *Sociology: A down-to-earth approach.* Boston, MA: Allyn & Bacon.

Houston, S. (2002). *Reflections on habitus, field and capital: Towards a culturally sensitive social work.* London: Sage Publications.

Hyde, C.A. (2004). Multicultural development in human services agencies: Challenges and solutions. *Social Work, 49*(1), 7–10.

Mama, R.S. (2001). Preparing social work students to work in culturally diverse settings. *Social Work Education,20*(3), 373–383.

Miley, K.K., O'Melia, M., & DuBois, B. (1998). *Generalist social work practice: An empowering approach.* Needham Heights, MA: Allyn & Bacon.

Morales, A.T., & Sheafor, B. W. (1998). *Social work: A profession of many faces.* Needham Heights, MA: Allyn & Bacon.

National Association of Social Workers. (2001). *NASW Code of Ethics: Cultural competence and social diversity.* Washington, D.C.: NASW.

Okayama, C.M., Furuto, S.B.C.L., & Edmondson, J. (2001). Components of cultural competence: Attitudes, knowledge, and skills. In R. Fong, *Culturally competent social work practice: Past and present* (pp. 89–99). Boston, MA: Allyn & Bacon.

Seaton, C. (2003). Empowered use of self in social work: Understanding personal narrative through guided autobiography. *Social Work & Christianity, 31*(1), 51–77.

Sheafor, B.W., & Horejsi, C.R. (2006). *Techniques and guidelines for social work practice.* Boston, MA: Pearson Education.

Sue, D.W., & Sue, D. (2003). *Counseling the culturally diverse: Theory and practice.* New York: John Wiley & Sons.

9 Client Spirituality and Empowerment

This chapter provides a contrast of spirituality, religion, and secularism to assist you in understanding the tenets of social work. Maintaining diversity and sensitivity to spirituality is emphasized. Another topic in this chapter, client empowerment, is a central theme in professional social work because it emphasizes the client's strengths, resiliency, coping style, and ability to succeed. Thus, the chapter discusses the importance of accentuating your client's empowerment process. Strategies that encourage client empowerment are highlighted to assist you in learning the how-to of facilitating the empowerment process that lies within each client. We have combined the concepts of spirituality and empowerment because both work together in the team-oriented helping relationship you will have with your client.

Section One: Spirituality, Religion, and Secularism

Defining and Contrasting Spirituality, Religion, and Secularism

Spirituality, or striving to find a sense of meaning, purpose, value, and fulfillment in life, is different from religion in that spirituality is a quality of "inner self" or soul, whereas religion is community and group-based. Through spirituality, we become conscious of who we are and we learn our meaning and purpose in life. Our individual views of right and wrong are defined through spirituality. The essence of spirituality is culturally based in that existing opportunities or deprivation in our social environment, and our overall life experiences, shape the view of our inner "self" (Compton & Galaway, 1999; Sheafor & Horejsi, 2006; Van Hook, Hugen, & Aguilar, 2001).

Understanding and fostering your client's search for spirituality is an important part of being a social worker. You must also recognize the value of your client's sense of "inner self," along with being conscious of the consequences if your client sees life as having no meaning (Compton & Galaway, 1999). According to Patricia Sermabeikian (1994), "spirituality is a human need; it is too important to be misunderstood; avoided; or viewed as regressive, neurotic, or pathological in nature. Social workers must . . . acknowledge

**TABLE 9.1   Individual and Environmental Influences
That Develop the "Inner Self"**

Individual	Environmental Influences
Genes	Social Structure—Government, Laws, Class System
Senses	Economic Resources/Opportunities
Intelligence	Occupation
Temperament	Education
Emotional Strength	Familial Values, Beliefs, Traditions
Needs and Desires	Cultural Behavior, Language, Beliefs
Health/Energy through Food	Group Affiliations/
Consumption	Interactions
Physiological Functioning	Religious Affiliations/Beliefs
Psychological Functioning	Meaningful "sense of belonging"
	Life Successes and/or Failures
	Overall Life Experiences

(*Table 9.1 content sources:* Compton & Galaway, 1999; Henslin, 2005; Sheafor & Horejsi, 2006)

that spirituality in a person's life can be a constructive way of facing life's difficulties" (p. 181). Let's look at various pieces of the "individual" and factors that influence one's development so that you can gain a better understanding of how your client's sense of "inner self" and spirituality are fostered or discouraged. Refer to Table 9.1.

The individual (nature) and the environment (nurture) are constantly intertwined and working together as one grows and develops physically, mentally, emotionally, and spiritually. Experiences of joy or distress can bring change to one's beliefs and values, along with new insights into life in general (Sheafor & Horejsi, 2006; Van Hook et al., 2001). Spirituality is considered a life-long, dynamic journey (Sheafor & Horejsi, 2006). As a social worker, you assist and support your client in his or her spirituality excursion.

Religion is defined as "a set of beliefs, stories, traditions, and practices that nurture and support particular approaches to spiritual growth" (Sheafor & Horejsi, 2006, p. 33). Religion is also public and institutional in that a group's beliefs and practices center around sacred things, and a moral community or institution (church) is developed through these group interactions (Henslin, 2005; Sheafor & Horejsi, 2006; Van Hook et al., 2001).

As a social worker, it is important for you to understand and respect your client's religion, especially if it differs from yours. You must try to avoid ethnocentric and judgmental thoughts that may become apparent to your client through either your verbal or nonverbal communication and behavior.

Secularism is defined as "a process by which worldly affairs replace spiritual interests" (Henslin, 2005, p. 536). The secularization process results in the decline of an individual's focus on otherworldly issues (e.g., the afterlife) as he or she shifts focus to worldly affairs such as homelessness. According to research, secularization does not signal the death of religion; rather, it changes, liberates, and expands religious views. For many, this means that the practices of various religious organizations need to be

Applying what you have learned . . .

Defining Spirituality, Religion and Secularism
9.1 Compare and contrast the characteristics of spirituality, religion, and secularism.

9.2 How do you personally define/describe spirituality, religion, and secularism?

brought into line with social attitudes. One example of change is allowing the ordination of women, a change that supports society's general view of gender equality (Macionis, 2005).

Even though the belief in the afterlife is declining, religious affiliation has increased (Macionis, 2005). Research continues surrounding secularism and religion, and keeping up-to-date on the various data is suggested.

Section Two: Tenets of Social Work with Spirituality

Spirituality is a popular practice in our society, especially in the various helping professions. Currently, you can find the concept of spirituality in medicine, nursing, psychology, marriage and family therapy, and social work. There has been a steady growth in teaching students the importance and use of spirituality when working with clients in the social work field. The *Society for Spirituality and Social Work* is an international organization consisting of social work practitioners, educators, and students who consider **spiritually sensitive practice** a key component in the successful empowerment of clients (Canda & Furman, 1999; Sheridan, 2001).

The How-To's of Spiritually Sensitive Practice

Understanding and Assessing.   First, and foremost, you must be clear and honest when assessing your personal spiritual or religious values and beliefs systems. You need to realize that your values and belief systems will filter into your social work profession so that you can control your personal influences on your client that may be detrimental to his or her values and beliefs. Being aware and accepting the fact that religious or spiritual diversity exists leads to respect for differences. Respect for religious or spiritual diversity will lead you to sensitive and competent personal growth, along with promoting the personal growth of your client (Canda & Furman, 1999; Sheridan, 2001).

Using Skills and Techniques.   Using a holistic approach that includes integrating spirituality with biological, psychological, and sociological dimensions of human experience results in a better understanding and acceptance of human behavior. Creating a spiritually sensitive social work practice requires knowledge and skill in all these areas. You must also understand and accept the fact that your clientele will be diverse in most aspects. Being aware of various successful techniques utilized is critical to the success of your relationship with your clients (Becvar, 1997; Canda & Furman, 1999; Sheridan, 2001). Because spirituality and empowerment work together in helping your client, the various techniques that have been used successfully in the field of social work will be discussed in *Section Four* of the chapter.

Keep in mind that, even though you and your client's personal values and beliefs will be present internally, spirituality will probably not be discussed between you and your client at his or her initial meeting. Focusing on the reasons your client has sought help should be the first topic of discussion. As you and your client interact and build a relationship of trust and respect, spirituality will inevitably begin to filter into your future communication and collaboration (Becvar, 1997).

Applying Ethical Guidelines.   Each of us has a personal code of ethics that teaches us the difference between right and wrong. These personal ethics are influenced by various social agents, including family, peers, teachers, and clergy. Our moral standards are developed, and sometimes changed, as we experience life. As a student and future social worker, you need to decide which teachings and experiences you truly subscribe to in your personal code of ethics. Remember that your conduct when working with clients will be influenced by your personal code of ethics (Canda & Furman, 1999).

Another set of ethics that influences your conduct when working with clients is the NASW *Code of Ethics*. It is extremely important that both your personal ethics and the ethics of the NASW are consistent so that you will service your clients in a positive and successful way (Canda & Furman, 1999; NASW *Code of Ethics,* 1997; Reamer, 2004).

Six values central to social work in the *Code of Ethics* are as follows.

1. *Service*   The primary goal of social workers is to "help people in need and to address social problems" (Reamer, 2004, p. 14; NASW *Code of Ethics,* 1997, p. 1).
2. *Social Justice*   "Social workers challenge social injustice on behalf of oppressed individuals and groups of people" (Reamer, 2004, p. 15; NASW *Code of Ethics,* 1997, p. 5).
3. *Dignity and Worth of the Person*   Social workers must respect people and "treat each person in a caring and respectful fashion, mindful of individual differences and cultural and ethnic diversity" (Reamer, 2004, p. 15; NASW *Code of Ethics,* 1997, p. 6).
4. *Importance of Human Relationships*   "Relationships between and among people are an important vehicle for change, and that social workers need to engage people as partners in the helping process" (Reamer, 2004, p. 15; NASW *Code of Ethics,* 1997, p. 6).
5. *Integrity*   Social workers should "act honestly and responsibly and promote ethical practices on the part of the organizations with which they are affiliated" (Reamer, 2004, p. 15; NASW *Code of Ethics,* 1997, p. 6).
6. *Competence*   "Social workers should achieve reasonable levels of skill before offering their services to others" (Reamer, 2004, p. 15; NASW *Code of Ethics,* 1997, p. 6).

Controversial Issues of Spirituality in Social Work

Every profession confronts controversial issues surrounding various practices used. Spirituality is not exempt from this process. As we look at the existing controversial issues involved in spirituality as used in social work, we need to keep an open and positive mind. Controversy is not always negative, for it can broaden one's understanding of a concept, thus creating a clearer awareness of the specific practice. To better comprehend the controversial issues, let's first look at some questions researchers have posed surrounding the use of spirituality in social work practice:

1. Is utilizing spirituality appropriate in social work practice?
2. Can the use of spirituality be logically justified?
3. Is spirituality part of the challenges the client faces?
4. Should the use of spirituality be further explored?

   (Roeder, 2002)

To answer the questions of whether using spirituality in social work is appropriate and justified, and to determine whether spirituality is part of a client's challenges, let's revisit the definition and various characteristics of spirituality. At the same time, we will compare spirituality to the primary mission (preamble) in NASW's *Code of Ethics*. See Table 9.2.

Spirituality is described as the striving to find a sense of meaning, purpose, value, and fulfillment in life; spirituality is a quality of "inner self" or soul. We need to understand that:

1. We become conscious of who we are and our meaning and purpose in life through spirituality.
2. Our individual views of right and wrong are defined through spirituality.
3. The essence of spirituality is culturally based in that existing opportunities or deprivation in our social environment, and our overall life experiences, shape the view of our "inner self".

   (*Spirituality sources:* Compton & Galaway, 1999; Sheafor & Horejsi, 2006; Van Hook et al., 2001)

TABLE 9.2   Comparing Spirituality and the NASW *Code of Ethics* Mission

Spirituality	NASW *Code of Ethics* Mission
Sense of meaning and purpose in life	Enhance human well-being
Existing opportunities or deprivation in our social environment	Help meet basic human needs of all people, with particular attention to the needs and empowerment of people who are vulnerable, oppressed and living in poverty

(*Table 9.2 content sources:* Compton & Galaway, 1999; NASW *Code of Ethics*, 1997; Roeder, 2002; Sheafor & Horejsi, 2006)

Applying what you have learned . . .

Exploring Your Spirituality and Religious Beliefs

9.3 List your personal spiritual and/or religious values and beliefs.

9.4 List your personal spiritual and/or religious values and beliefs that you feel would fit into your personal code of ethics and would be beneficial in the field of social work.

9.5 List the NASW *Code of Ethics* that you believe matches your personal code of ethics.

Now let's revisit the mission (preamble) to the NASW *Code of Ethics*:

> The primary mission of the social work profession is to enhance human well-being and help meet basic human needs of all people, with particular attention to the needs and empowerment of people who are vulnerable, oppressed and living in poverty. (NASW *Code of Ethics*, 1997, p. 1; Roeder, 2002, p. 10)

Ultimately, when comparing the concept of spirituality to the NASW *Code of Ethics* mission, we can see similarities. One of your goals as a social worker should be to explore the available research on using spirituality in the social work field. Becoming familiar with the advantages, as well as any present disadvantages, of using spirituality is necessary prior to your working with clients.

Section Three: Defining and Understanding Empowerment

Over the past 25 years, social work has slowly moved from a paternalistic medical model of practice to a client self-determination and involvement model. By including the client in the helping process, the client gains independence and empowerment (Hancock, 1997).

What Is Empowerment?

Empowerment, or the process by which one gains a sense of confidence or self-esteem, is important to your client's success in dealing with his or her various issues successfully. As a social worker, emphasizing client strengths and abilities is more advantageous than focusing on the weaknesses and inabilities of the client. In essence, the client takes control over his or her life through the empowerment process (Colby & Dziegielewski, 2001; Hancock, 1997; Hasenfeld, 1987; Sheafor & Horejsi, 2006).

Principles of Empowerment

As a social worker, you need to familiarize yourself with the following key principles of empowerment.

Applying what you have learned . . .

Defining and Understanding Empowerment

9.6 Define empowerment and describe, in your own words, what the principles of empowerment mean.

9.7 Develop a list of words describing what empowerment means to you.

9.8 Develop a list of words describing what empowerment may mean to a client.

9.9 Compare and contrast the list of words you developed in *Exercises 9.2* and *9.3*. Are your two lists similar or different? Explain why your lists are similar or different.

---

1. *Client power*   Believing your client has the ability to acquire a sense of personal, interpersonal and political power, and can take control of his or her life.
2. *Firm conviction*   Believing that every client has the capacity to understand his or her situation and the strength to bring about desirable changes.
3. *Client as the "expert"*   Viewing your client as the expert in defining his or her situation, and believing your client has the ability to decide on solutions.
4. *Self-confidence and self-respect*   Believing in your client's ability to take risks that are necessary in learning new skills that will build self-confidence and self-respect while eliminating the thwarting and self-limiting beliefs and behaviors.

(*Principles of Empowerment sources:* Colby & Dziegielewski, 2001; Hancock, 1997; Hasenfeld, 1987; Pinderhughes, 1983; Sheafor & Horejsi, 2006)

As social workers, we believe that clients are capable of change and have the strength necessary to improve their functioning. They might not know it!

Section Four: Strategies for Fostering Client Empowerment

You can use numerous strategies to foster your client's empowerment process. As we discuss these strategies, take note of how these useful tools fulfill the principles of client empowerment.

Understanding Power and Powerlessness

The key component in effective intervention and empowerment is knowing and understanding how feelings of power or powerlessness influence human behavior. For example, when people live in poverty and lack various resources, the environment for them is stressful and they feel powerless. Growth, development, and potential for change become out of reach for these individuals. As a social worker, it is important for you to assist your client in breaking this "cycle of powerlessness." In helping your client acquire a sense of personal, interpersonal, and political power, he or she learns to take control of his or her life, along with gaining the ability to bring about desired change (Colby & Dziegielewski, 2001; Hancock, 1997; Hasenfeld, 1987; Henslin, 2005; Pinderhughes, 1983; Sheafor & Horejsi, 2006).

Believing in Client Abilities

Believing that your client has the capacity to understand his or her situation is the first step in helping your client in the empowerment process. You must remember that it is the *client* who is in the situation; thus he or she is the expert in defining what may be causing feelings of powerlessness. By letting your client express his or her feelings first, you will gain a better understanding of how he or she views the situation (Hancock, 1997; Hasenfield, 1987; Pinderhughes, 1983; Sheafor & Horejsi, 2006).

Feeling Words.   Developing a written list of ***feeling words*** that your clients can refer to in order to identify, sort out, and express their feelings is suggested. Examples of feeling words to put on your list for your clients may include:

manipulated	abandoned	worthless
apprehensive	embarrassed	ashamed
desperate	vulnerable	guilty
self-pity	frustrated	resentful
fearful	hateful	concerned
relieved	courageous	serene
protected	excited	confident
tough	contented	nervous

(*Feeling words list sources:* Cournoyer & Stanley, 2002; Sheafor & Horejsi, 2006)

Independence.   Acknowledging that your client is a victim of oppression, but at the same time, believing your client has the ability to learn new skills to overcome the oppression, is critical in eliciting active participation in the "helping relationship." Client self-confidence and self-respect will increase as you promote client involvement in the problem-solving process. Supporting and encouraging your client to think of positive and relevant processes that will bring about change will instill in your client "a sense of independence" (Hancock, 1997; Hasenfield, 1987; Pinderhughes, 1983; Sheafor & Horejsi, 2006).

Encouraging Client Problem Solving

Identifying Problems.   Before you can assist your client in finding solutions to various issues, your client needs to identify the problem(s). Allow your client to define the problem(s) as he or she views them, and encourage your client to share personal thoughts on possible solutions. By doing so, the client–worker relationship becomes a partnership. Your knowledge, skills, and experience will thereby be more acceptable and useful to your client (Colby & Dziegielewski, 2001; Hancock, 1997; Sheafor & Horejsi, 2006). According to Sheafor and Horejsi (2006), the best way to form this relationship is to "view your helping role as primarily that of a teacher-trainer or consultant" (p. 423).

Educating the Client.   Once your client has identified the problem(s), assist him/her in understanding various factors that may be contributing to feelings of powerlessness.

As a social worker, you need to educate your client about power dynamics and the system in which he or she lives (Pinderhughes, 1983; Sheafor & Horejsi, 2006). As a team, you and your client can design an educational plan that will enhance your client's understanding of:

1. **Social system structure and functions (the macroculture in which client lives)**
   a. Family
   b. Religion
   c. Education
   d. Economics
   e. Health system
   f. Political system (government)
   g. Legal system
   h. Science and technology
   i. Military
   j. Mass media
2. **Societal factors that determine one's power and powerlessness in society**
   a. *Resources*—status, wealth, power
   b. *Socioeconomic* status (class)—income, occupation, education
3. **Subculture in which client has been socialized (the client's microculture of)**
   a. Nuclear family and family of procreation
   b. Personal family functioning (dynamics)
   c. Neighborhood and community where client resides
4. **Support system structure and functions**
   a. Family
   b. Friends/peers
   c. Religion
   d. Community services

(*Social structure and influences sources:* Henslin, 2005; Macionis, 2005; Pinderhughes, 1983)

Educating your client on societal systems and functions, as well as possible factors that cause feelings of oppression and powerlessness, is just the beginning of the empowerment process. As a social worker, you need to assist your client in understanding and successfully utilizing potential sources of power so that he or she can learn to problem-solve independently.

Empowerment Guidelines

As you work with and educate your client on the various aspects of oppression and powerlessness, you must assist your client in discovering and using potential sources of power needed to complete the empowerment process. Guidelines you should adhere to when using the empowerment approach to assist your client in developing individual and community power include the following.

1. View and conduct your working relationship with your client as a "team endeavor."
2. Assist your client in increasing his or her capacity to understand and improve the situation on an individual and a community level.
3. Assist your client in building self-esteem and self-respect by encouraging the learning of new skills and behaviors.
4. Teach your client leadership skills that will strengthen his or her ability to take action when facing problems on an individual and a community level.
5. Assist your client in understanding factors that are contributing to his or her feelings.
6. Help your client in expressing and understanding his or her feelings so that the client can take positive action to eliminate any feelings of bitterness.
7. Encourage your client to grow by seeing past mistreatment and injustice as a learning process.
8. Assist your client in making arrangements and attending various learning opportunities within agencies and community functions.
9. Encourage your client to interact with program administrators, politicians, and community leaders so that renewed hope for change can occur. Your client will also feel he or she has played an influential part in these changes.
10. Assist your client in developing a list of his or her personal strengths that are key components in the empowerment process.
11. Monitor and support your client's new feelings of power so that they are used in a planned and disciplined manner.
12. Make sure your client understands that change is slow and that certain existing factors limit change.

(*Empowerment Guidelines sources:* Compton & Galaway, 1999; Morales & Sheafor, 1998; Reamer, 2004; Sheafor & Horejsi, 2006)

Small-group Setting.   The small-group setting can also be an ideal environment when using the client empowerment approach. By using such a setting to empower your client, he or she will develop the following essential skills (Compton & Galaway, 1999; Morales & Sheafor, 1998; Sheafor & Horejsi, 2006):

1. Communication
2. Problem solving
3. Leadership
4. Critical thinking
5. Persuasion
6. Assertiveness
7. Negotiation
8. Mutual support

(*Empowerment skills source:* Compton & Galaway, 1999; Morales & Sheafor, 1998; Sheafor & Horejsi, 2006)

In a small-group setting, your client will also discover that he or she is not alone or different from others. Your client will come to the realization that many face the same

Applying what you have learned . . .

Understanding and Supporting Client Abilities

9.10 Why is it essential to believe in your client's abilities to view his or her situation and to develop solutions to solve the problem(s)?

9.11 Develop a personal list of feeling words (that are not listed in the chapter) that you believe would be appropriate for your client to use in expressing his or her feelings.

9.12 Develop an educational plan that will help your future clients understand:

   a. Social system structure and function (the macroculture the client lives in)

   b. Societal factors that determine one's power and powerlessness in society

   c. Subculture in which client has been socialized (the client's microculture)

   d. Support system structure and functions

9.13 Read through the Empowerment Guidelines. Develop a small-group setting plan that you believe would provide for successful client learning, problem solving, and empowerment.

struggles in life and that support systems are available to overcome these obstacles (Compton & Galaway, 1999; Morales & Sheafor, 1998; Sheafor & Horejsi, 2006).

When using the empowerment approach, encourage your client to make his or her own decisions and to follow through on the decisions. It is important that you respect your client's decisions and allow him or her to experience both positive and negative consequences. Your client will not learn how to make decisions and learn from the consequences if you do not allow the opportunity to do so. Self-determination needs to be integrated in all aspects of your involvement with your client in order for empowerment to be successful (Compton & Galaway, 1999; Morales & Sheafor, 1998; Sheafor & Horejsi, 2006).

Summary

Spirituality, or the striving to find a sense of meaning, purpose, values, and fulfillment in life, is a quality of "inner self" or soul. Through spirituality, we discover who we are and our meaning in life. Opportunities or deprivation in our social environment affect the way we see life overall, and this process pertains to your clients as well. Understanding and fostering your client's search for spirituality is a major part of being a social worker. Religion is defined as a set of beliefs, stories, traditions, and practices that nurture and support particular approaches to spiritual growth. Religion is, for the most part, community and group-based. With secularism, one's focus is on worldly affairs (such as helping the homeless) rather than on otherworldly issues (such as the afterlife).

As a social worker, you need to be clear and honest when you assess your personal spiritual or religious values and beliefs. This is an important step to understanding and respecting your client's differing values and belief systems. In so doing, you can avoid ethnocentric and judgmental thoughts that may become apparent to your client through your communication and collaboration.

Using a holistic approach that includes integrating spirituality with biological, psychological, and sociological dimensions of human behavior will help you gain a better understanding of your client. You should expect diversity with each client you work with, and remaining open-minded and accepting of these differences will enable you to develop a spiritually sensitive practice with your clients. A spiritually sensitive practice is a key component in the successful empowerment of clients.

It is important that you assess your personal values and moral standards and compare them to the NASW *Code of Ethics*. Remember, your conduct when working with clients will be influenced by both your elective personal code of ethics and the required NASW *Code of Ethics*. To be successful with clients, your personal code of ethics must be consistent with that of the NASW.

Empowerment, or the process by which one gains a sense of confidence or self-esteem, is the primary tool in fostering the strengths, resiliency, coping skills, and abilities that lie within your client. Your client will also be able to take control of his or her life through the empowerment process. Four key principles that will guide you in fostering client empowerment are believing that your client has the ability to acquire personal, interpersonal, and political power; knowing that every client has the capacity to understand his or her situation and can bring about desirable change; viewing your client as the "expert" in defining his or her situation and developing solutions; and believing that your client has the ability to learn new skills that will build self-confidence and self-respect.

As a social worker, you must be familiar with empowerment strategies. The key component in empowerment is understanding how the principle behind power and powerlessness works in society and how it influences human behavior. Believing in your client's abilities and encouraging your client to recognize his or her strengths is the first step in your client taking control of his or her life. You should let your client define his or her situation and express feelings related to the problems he or she is facing. Remember, if you want the empowerment process to be successful, your client has to see the client–worker relationship as a partnership.

KEY WORDS AND CONCEPTS

REFERENCES

Becvar, D.S. (1997). *Soul healing: A spiritual orientation in counseling and therapy.* New York: Basic Books.

Canda, E.R., & Furman, L.D. (1999). *Spiritual diversity in social work practice: The heart of helping.* New York: The Free Press.

Colby, I., & Dziegielewski, S. (2001). *Social work: The people's profession.* Chicago: Lyceum Books.

Compton, B.R., & Galaway, B. (1999). *Social work processes.* Pacific Grove, CA: Brooks/Cole Publishing Company.

Cournoyer, B.R., & Stanley, M.J. (2002). *The social work portfolio: Planning, assessing and documenting lifelong learning in a dynamic profession.* Pacific Grove, CA: Brooks/Cole Publishing Company.

Hancock, M.R. (1997). Empowerment: Helping people take control of their lives. In M.R. Hancock, *Principles of social work practice: A generic practice approach* (pp. 229–251). Binghamton, NY: Haworth Press.

Hasenfeld, Y. (1987). Power in social work practice. *Social Service Review, 61*(3), 469–483.

Henslin, J.M. (2005). *Sociology: A down-to-earth approach.* Boston, MA: Allyn & Bacon.

Macionis, J.J. (2005). *Sociology* (10th ed.). Upper Saddle Rever, NJ: Pearson Education.

Morales, A.T., & Sheafor, B.W. (1998). *Social work: A profession of many faces.* Needham Heights, MA: Allyn & Bacon.

National Association of Social Workers, Inc. (1997). *NASW Code of Ethics.* Washington, DC: NASW Press.

Pinderhughes, E.B. (1983). Empowerment for our clients and for ourselves. *Social Casework: The Journal of Contemporary Social Work, 64*(6), 331–338.

Reamer, F.G. (2004). *Ethical standards in social work: A review of the NASW Code of Ethics.* Washington, DC: NASW Press.

Roeder, K.R. (2002). Practicing with honorable spirit: The use and non-use of spirituality in social work practice. *The New Social Worker, 9*(4), 10–12.

Sermabeikian, P. (1994). Our clients, ourselves: The spiritual perspective and social work practice. *Social Work, 39*(2), 178–183.

Sheafor, B.W., & Horejsi, C.R. (2006). *Techniques and guidelines for social work practice.* Boston, MA: Pearson Education.

Sheridan, M.J. (2001). Defining spirituality sensitive social work practice: An essay review of spiritual diversity in social work practice: The heart of helping. *Social Work, 46*(1), 87–92.

Van Hook, M., Hugen, B., & Aguilar, M. (2001). *Spirituality within religious traditions in social work practice.* Pacific, Grove, CA: Brooks/Cole Publishing Company.

10 Communicating with Clients Using Professional Questioning Skills

Chapter 10 exposes you to the significance of using professional closed- and open-ended questions when interviewing clients. Diversity is an important consideration in the social work field, and you will learn the importance of examining cultural and gender aspects when developing client interview questions. The chapter includes examples of open- and closed-ended questions, and hands-on client interviewing exercises so that you can gain a thorough understanding of how social workers professionally communicate with their clients.

Section One: Defining Closed- and Open-ended Questions

Closed-ended Questions

Closed-ended questions are structured, and the response may be fixed in that you can choose from one of the categories provided. Closed-ended questions may also require simple answers such as a yes or no, age, and number of children (Neuman, 2003; Rubin & Babbie, 2001). Even though closed-ended questions limit your client's response, this type of question must be used to collect specific information needed before you begin working with your client. The information you collect with closed-ended questions, such as gender and ethnicity, will also help you understand your client's communication and behavior during a session (Compton & Galaway, 1999; Miley, O'Melia, & DuBois, 1998; Sheafor & Horejsi, 2006). Closed-ended questions on a form would be written similar to the following:

1. "What is your gender?"
2. "What is your race?"
3. "What is your ethnicity?"
4. "How old are you?"
5. "How many children do you have?"

When your client is confused or overwhelmed, closed-ended questions are appropriate for maintaining focus and direction (Compton & Galaway, 1999; Miley et al., 1998; Sheafor & Horejsi, 2006).

Open-ended Questions

Open-ended, or unstructured questions, like closed-ended questions, are used to obtain needed information; however, open-ended questions allow one the freedom to respond with any answer (Neuman, 2003; Rubin & Babbie, 2001). As a social worker, you will be using mainly open-ended questions that allow your client an opportunity to say whatever he or she thinks is significant (Compton & Galaway, 1999; Miley et al., 1998; Sheafor & Horejsi, 2006). Examples of open-ended questions include:

1. "Tell me about your husband."
2. "Tell me about your children."
3. "Tell me about your typical work day."

You can help your client focus on specific details by varying the amount of freedom you allow in your open-ended questions (Compton & Galaway, 1999; Miley et al., 1998; Sheafor & Horejsi, 2006). Such examples would be:

1. "What do you like about your husband?"
2. "What are your children's names?"
3. "What tasks do you do at work?"

Narrowing the Focus. ***Narrowing the focus*** (or funneling) is a useful tool to assist your client in maintaining focus when you are asking open-ended questions. Narrowing the focus consists of presenting a series of questions you can use to direct and assist your client in expressing concerns or explaining the situation with more specificity (Sheafer & Horejsi, 2006). An example would be:

CLIENT: "Things are a disaster at work."

WORKER: "I am not sure what you mean by disaster. What happened at work?"

CLIENT: "My supervisor is always changing my job tasks without helping me to learn the new process. I am so frustrated and angry, I just want to quit."

The use of open-ended questions provides valuable and endless information about your client's problem or situation. This type of question also encourages your client to communicate thoughts and feelings about various factors that may be influencing his or her behaviors and views (Compton & Galaway, 1999; Miley et al., 1998; Sheafor & Horejsi, 2006).

Applying what you learned . . .

Understanding Client Questioning

10.1 What are the differences and similarities between open- and closed-ended questions?

10.2 What is *narrowing the focus (funneling)*, and why would you use it during the client questioning process?

Section Two: Communication Cycle and Skill Building of Client Questioning

Communication Cycle of Client Questioning

Every contact you have with your client is considered a communication cycle. You and your client are continuously exchanging information through the question and answer process. You should be conscientious about selecting the appropriate words when asking or answering client questions. You must also be aware of the significance of nonverbal communication and behavior you and your client are displaying during the client questioning process (Beall, 2004; Brantley & Miller, 2002). (Refer to Part Three, Chapter 4: What Are Verbal and Nonverbal Communication Skills?)

Eye Contact.   Eye contact is an extremely powerful means of communication. Your client's eyes will reveal to you the emotion, sensitivity, and/or understanding of his or her situation. Your client's openness and willingness to answer your questions will be indicated by eye contact with you. Anxiety, intimidation, closed-mindedness, and/or dishonesty will be indicated through failure to make eye contact. Keep in mind that the amount of eye contact varies from culture to culture, and remember to never force eye contact from your client during the questioning process (Beall, 2004; *Journal of Behavior Development*, 2001; *Journal of Nursing*, 2002; Kirch, 1979; Krim, 1953; Porter, 1969; Sue & Sue, 2003). (Refer to Part Three, Chapter 4: What Are Verbal and Nonverbal Communication Skills?)

Body Language.   Body language is always a part of the communication process. Body language is less deliberate than verbal communication, and mostly unconscious; therefore, your client's body language becomes more meaningful than his or her statements when responding to your questions. As a social worker, it is imperative that you become knowledgeable about various body languages that are displayed during the communication process. Body language will vary according to gender, race, ethnicity, age, and many other factors. Becoming skilled in understanding what affects body language is relevant to successful client questioning (Beall, 2004; *Journal of Behavior Development*, 2001; *Journal of Nursing*, 2002; Kirch, 1979; Krim, 1953; Porter, 1969; Sue & Sue, 2003). (Refer to Part Three, Chapter 4: What Are Verbal and Nonverbal Communication Skills?)

Proximity.   Proximity is the distance between individuals, and the nearness of your client will indicate his or her feelings of interest and trust. Keep in mind that each client will have a different *comfort zone* in terms of how close he or she wants to be to you when answering your questions. Read your client's body language and adjust nearness accordingly because some clients may find that being too close to them is threatening. If your client is feeling threatened by your closeness, he or she may avoid answering your questions and the communication process will be damaged (Beall, 2004; *Journal of Behavior Development*, 2001; *Journal of Nursing*, 2002; Kirch, 1979; Krim, 1953; Porter, 1969; Sue & Sue, 2003). (Refer to Part Three, Chapter 4: What Are Verbal and Nonverbal Communication Skills?)

Active Listening and Verbal Following.   Listening to your client, and following his or her words intensely, will provide you with direction in your questioning. As a social worker, you must be skilled in understanding *paralanguage*, or vocal cues. Paralanguage includes loudness of voice, pauses, silences, hesitations, rate, and inflections (tone), and will communicate the feelings, intentions, and emotions of your client. By actively listening to your client's paralanguage and following his or her words, you will be able to decipher whether your client is feeling fear, sorrow, happiness, or anger. This valuable *feeling insight* gives you the ability to ask appropriate questions that will result in receiving the needed information from your client so that the helping process is successful (Ambady, Bernieri, & Richeson, 2000; Brantley & Miller, 2002; LaPlante & Ambady, 2003; Porter, 1969; Sue, & Sue, 2003). (Refer to Part Three, Chapter 4: What Are Verbal and Nonverbal Communication Skills? and Part Five, Chapter 9: Client Spirituality and Empowerment, Section One.)

Skill Building of Client Questioning

In order for you to develop expertise in client questioning, you must practice, practice, practice. Knowing the basic skills of communication is not enough, however; you must be unwavering in your goal to acquire the professional questioning skills needed for productive communication with your client. The best way to attain professional client questioning is to learn the different phases you will go through during the client questioning process.

Intake Phase.   A question that will inevitably be in your client's mind is, "What kind of worker will this person be?" (Shulman, 1993, p. 161). Your client may be worried that you will judge him or her and not be able to understand his or her feelings. Thus, it is important to introduce yourself and greet your client in a friendly and professional manner. In so doing, you can establish a respectful and professional relationship that will remain constant throughout the helping process with your client (Miley et al., 1998; Sheafor & Horejsi, 2006; Shulman, 1993). For example (Sheafor & Horejsi, 2006):

> **WORKER:**   Good morning. I am Suzanne and I am so glad you were able to meet with me today.

Once you have introduced yourself, you can carefully and professionally proceed with the engagement phase by providing an explanation as to why you and your client are meeting. The engagement phrase is also the time when confidentiality should be discussed with your client. (Refer to Part Four, Chapter 6: Communicating about Confidentiality.)

Engagement Phase.   Giving special attention to clarifying the purpose of the meeting, and your role as social worker, is pertinent during both the intake and engagement phases of each client session. ***Explaining the purpose***, or providing your client with a simple, nonjargonized statement about the meeting, is part of the helping skill process. Explaining purpose also defines expectations and reduces confusion and anxiety for your client. You must begin every client meeting by explaining the purpose in a clear and "straight to the point" manner. This approach will encourage productive communication, which in turn leads to a successful helping process (Miley et al., 1998; Sheafor & Horejsi, 2006; Shulman, 1993). For example (Sheafor & Horejsi, 2006):

Intake and Engagement Phase

> **WORKER:**   As you know, your probation officer contacted the office about two weeks ago. He expressed concern about your employment. I would like to hear about your thoughts concerning your job, and if you also believe there are problems at work.

Engagement Phase of a Client Session

> **WORKER:**   I need to talk with you about your job. You have had negative verbal and physical encounters with coworkers twice in the last week. This is a serious problem.

If the client has requested the meeting with you, it is important for you to encourage him or her to begin the conversation. Allow your client to describe the purpose of the interview. If your client is struggling in providing a clear explanation as to why he or she requested the interview, you can ask general questions that will assist him or her in eliminating this ambiguity (Miley et al., 1998; Sheafor & Horejsi, 2006; Shulman, 1981).

Encouragement of Client Feedback.   You should encourage your client to respond to your questions and provide feedback in reference to your explanations. By encouraging feedback, your client can ask questions that may clarify any confusion and misconceptions. It also gives your client the chance to voice his or her disagreement with a statement you may have made (Miley et al., 1998; Sheafor & Horejsi, 2006; Shulman, 1981). An example would be (Sheafor & Horejsi, 2006):

> **WORKER:**   What are your reactions or feelings to what I have said about the situation at work?

OR

> WORKER: It is possible that you and I have different thoughts about your situation at work. I wonder how you see the situation.

Description of the Social Worker Role and Method.   By describing your social work role and method (s), you provide your client with an idea of how you will help with the situation or problem (Miley et al., 1998; Sheafor & Horejsi, 2006; Shulman, 1981). For example (Sheafor & Horejsi, 2006):

> WORKER: As you prepare to return to work, it is important that you anticipate problems with coworkers and figure out how to deal with them. This is why I would like to meet with you two to three times a week. I will share my ideas with you, and you can share your ideas as well. Between the two of us, we should be able to come up with a plan that will hopefully minimize the problems with coworkers.

Request for Between-Session Data.   At the beginning of each session, ask the client to bring you up-to-date on his or her situation and to identify the key topics to be discussed (Sheafor & Horejsi, 2006; Shulman, 1981). Be flexible. Your client's situation may have changed since your last meeting, and it is important that you adhere to the principle of "starting where the client is" (Sheafor & Horejsi, 2006, p. 147).

Common Errors in Client Questioning

Table 10.1 lists common errors that social workers make during client questioning. You need to become skilled in client questioning so that these errors can be avoided.

TABLE 10.1   Client Questioning Errors and Effects

Client Questioning Errors	Effects of Errors
Overusing closed-ended questions	Limit the amount of client information needed Prevent client from expressing his or her thoughts and feelings
Stacking questions	Ask client more than one question at a time Confuse client
Asking leading questions	Intimidate and insult client Push or pull client toward a certain response May force client to lie
Too many "why" questions	Produce "defensiveness" Force client to justify behavior Lead client to guess or give socially acceptable answers due to not understanding his or her behavior

(*Table 10.1 content sources:* Miley et al., 1998; Sheafor & Horejsi, 2006)

Applying what you have learned . . .

Practicing the Phases of Client Questioning

10.3 Make a list of the various nonverbal communication and behaviors you should be paying close attention to during the client questioning process.

10.4 Define active listening, verbal following, and paralanguage. Why are these three concepts important to the client questioning process?

10.5 *Practicing the phases of client questioning.* You have a client who will be meeting with you for the first time. Your new client has recently separated from his or her spouse after 35 years and has lost his or her job due to alcohol use during work hours. Choose a partner and practice the following:

a. Intake phase
b. Engagement phase
c. Encouragement of client feedback
d. Description of the social work role and method
e. Request for between-session data

**Make sure both you and your partner have the opportunity to practice the social worker and client role.

Section Three: Multicultural and Gender Interviewing

As discussed in Chapter 4, several factors known as *social rhythms* influence the communication process. Social rhythms such as culture and gender can block productive client questioning and lead to problems between you and your client if you are not aware of the interaction between these social rhythms and verbal and nonverbal communication and behavior (Beall, 2004; Brantley & Miller, 2002; Porter, 1969; Sue & Sue, 2003).

Multicultural Interviewing Skills

Culture.   Your client's culture is an extremely strong influential factor that needs to be considered during the client questioning process. Culture is not limited to just language, beliefs, clothing, and various holidays; it also includes one's societal status, education, and occupation. All these cultural characteristics influence your client's communication and behavior during the questioning process. It is essential that you are familiar and comfortable with your client's cultural background before conducting the initial interview (Beall, 2004; Brantley & Miller, 2002; Henslin, 2005; Porter, 1969; Sue & Sue, 2003). Here are suggestions for enhancing your understanding of various client cultures, (Schmolling, Youkeles, & Burger, 1993):

1. Research various literature to gain knowledge of several cultures in which your clientele may be socialized.
2. Study the various similarities and differences among varying cultures.
3. Gain an understanding of personal values and morals among varying cultures, and how these affect one's views of events and life.

As you communicate with your client in the future, you must continuously research and consider his or her cultural background as you formulate and ask questions (Beall, 2004; Brantley & Miller, 2002; Henslin, 2005; Porter, 1969; Sue & Sue, 2003). (Refer to Part Three, Chapter 4 for cultural social rhythms.)

Gender Interviewing Skills

Gender is culturally created through society's behavioral and attitudinal expectations of the male and female (Henslin, 2005). The societal rearing process influences how males and females communicate both verbally and nonverbally, and will affect how your client answers your questions. You must consider the gender of your client as you continuously conduct the questioning interview (Compton & Galaway, 1999; Lips, 2003; Miley et al., 1998; Sheafor & Horejsi, 2006).

Males.   Because most males are socialized to be "in control," your initial contact and questioning of your male client will probably lack emotion. He may also feel guilt, embarrassment, or shame owing to the inability to control his problem or situation alone. He may also see his problem or situation as being simply a matter of right or wrong. Because males in a patriarchal society are assigned the masculine characteristics of rugged individualism and competition, cooperation, communication, and the forming of an interpersonal relationship with your male client will take time (Henslin, 2005; Lips, 2003; Miley et al., 1998; Sheafor & Horejsi, 2006).

Females.   Most likely, your female client has been socialized to be "compliant" and to base her success on relationships. Your female client will probably be concerned with loyalty to her family and loved ones, and the harm her problem or situation may cause them (Gilligan, 1982). Expect displays of emotion from your female client (Henslin, 2005; Lips, 2003; Miley et al., 1998; Sheafor & Horejsi, 2006). (Refer to Part Three, Chapter 4, for the gender socialization process differences of males and females.)

Summary

Social workers communicate with their clients professionally through the use of *open-* and *closed-ended questions*. Open-ended questions are most commonly used because they allow the client the freedom to respond with any answer. Through this process, you give

Applying what you have learned . . .

Practice Client Questioning

10.6 Refer to the client scenario in *Section Two, Exercise Three.* Consider the following:
   a. How would you conduct the phases and client questioning if your client is male? female?

   b. Develop a list of three or four cultures in which your client may have been socialized. Research various characteristics of each culture. How would you conduct the phases and client questioning according to these differing cultures?

your client the opportunity to explain what is significant to him or her. There will be times, however, when you will have to direct or assist your client in expressing concerns or explaining a situation with more specificity. You can do this through *narrowing the focus*, or *funneling*.

Keep in mind that every contact you have with your client is part of a communication cycle. Be aware of nonverbal communication and behavior such as eye contact, body language, and proximity that you and your client are displaying during the client questioning process. *Active listening* and *verbal following* are necessary when you are communicating with your client. By paying close attention, and following your client's words intensely, you will be provided with direction during client questioning. By being skilled in *paralanguage*, or vocal cues, you can decipher your client's feelings, intentions, and emotions.

The phases that you will go through with your client include the *intake* and *engagement phases*. During these phases, encourage client feedback. Also, describe your role and the method you will be using to help your client with his or her situation or problem. Be flexible when *reaching for between-session data* because your client's situation may have changed since the last meeting, and it is important to adhere to the principle of "starting where the client is."

Lastly, *social rhythms* such as culture and gender influence how one communicates. As a social worker, you must enhance your understanding of various client cultures by researching and studying various backgrounds of your clientele. Remember, males and females are socialized differently; thus, their communication process will differ.

KEY WORDS AND CONCEPTS

Section One
Closed-ended questions, p. 142
Open-ended questions, p. 143
  Narrowing the focus, p. 143

Section Two
Common errors in client
  questioning, p. 147
Communication cycle
  of client questioning,
  p. 144
  Active listening and verbal
    following, p. 145
  Paralanguage, p. 145

Body language, p. 144
Eye contact, p. 144
Proximity, p. 145
Skill building of client
  questioning, p. 145
Description of social
  worker role and
  method, p. 147
Encouragement of client
  feedback, p. 146
Engagement phase, p. 146
  Explaining the
    purpose, p. 146

Intake phase, p. 145
Request for between-session
  data, p. 147

Section Three
Gender interviewing
  skills, p. 149
  Females, p. 149
  Males, p. 149
Multicultural interviewing
  skills, p. 148
  Culture, p. 148
Social rhythms, p. 148

REFERENCES

Ambady, N., Bernieri, F. J., & Richeson, J. A. (2000). Toward a history of social behavior: Judgmental accuracy from think slices of the behavioral stream. *Advances in Experimental Social Psychology, 32*, 201–207.

Beall, A. E. (2004). Body language speaks: Reading and responding more effectively to hidden communication. *Communication World, 21*(2), 18.

Body Language. (2001). *Journal of Behavior Development, 25*(4), 344–353.

Body Language. (2002). *Journal of Nursing, 102*(1), 845.

Brantley, C. P., & Miller, M. G. (2002). *Effective communication for colleges.* Cincinnati, OH: South-Western Educational Publishing.

Compton, B. R., & Galaway, B. (1999). *Social work processes.* Pacific Grove, CA: Brooks/Cole Publishing Company.

Gilligan, C. (1982) *In a different voice: Psychological theory and women's development.* Cambridge, MA: Harvard University Press.

Henslin, J. M. (2005). *Sociology: A down-to-earth approach.* Boston, MA: Allyn & Bacon.

Kirch, M. S. (1979). Non-verbal communication across cultures. *Modern Language Journal, 63*(8), 416–423.

Krim, A. (1953). *A study in non-verbal communications: Expressive movements during interviews.* Northampton, MA: Smith College School for Social Work.

LaPlante, D., & Ambady, N. (2003). On how things are said: Voice tone, voice intensity, verbal content, and perceptions of politeness. *Journal of Language and Social Psychology, 22*, 434–440.

Lips, H. M. (2003). *A new psychology of women: Gender, culture and ethnicity.* New York: McGraw-Hill Companies.

Miley, K. K., O'Melia, M., & DuBois, B. L. (1998). *Generalist social work practice: An empowering approach.* Needham Heights, MA: Allyn & Bacon.

Neuman, W. L. (2003). *Social research methods: Qualitative and quantitative approaches.* Boston, MA: Pearson Education.

Porter, G.W. (1969). Non-verbal communications. *Training and Development Journal, 23*(7–8). 3–8.

Rubin, A., & Babbie, E. (2001). *Research methods for social work.* Belmont, CA: Wadsworth/Thomson Learning.

Schmolling, P., Jr., Youkeles, M., & Burger, W. R. (1993). *Human services in contemporary America.* Belmont, CA: Wadsworth.

Sheafor, B. W., & Horejsi, C. R. (2006). *Techniques and guidelines for social work practice.* Boston, MA: Pearson Education.

Shulman, L. (1981). *Identifying, measuring and teaching helping skills.* New York: CSWE.

Shulman, L. (1993). *Interactional supervision.* Washington, DC: NASW Press.

Sue, D.W., & Sue, D. (2003). *Counseling the culturally diverse: Theory and practice.* New York: John Wiley & Sons.

11 Client Reflection

Chapter 11 defines reflection and stresses that successful client reflection requires empathy, understanding, and professional verbal and nonverbal communication skills. Content, feeling, and thinking or meaning reflection are discussed, with each concept and application highlighted. You and your classmates will benefit from the individual and group reflection practices exercises at the end of the chapter. These exercises will aid you in properly using reflection, along with further developing your professional communication skills needed when working with your clients.

Section One: What Is Reflection?

Defining Reflection

Reflection is a communication technique social workers use to let clients know they are listening to them. Social workers reflect feelings back to a client. For example, if a client says, "I'm really upset," a reflective statement would be "You seem awfully mad." Reflection permits acknowledgment of events, thoughts, and feelings of the client and identification of proper strategies to assist the client in dealing with issues (Miley, O'Melia, & DuBois, 1998; Sheafor & Horejsi, 2006).

Reflection Skills

Before using reflection with your client, you need to learn several skills so that the reflection process will be successful.

Empathy and Understanding.   To be a successful social worker, and to aid your client in the best way possible, you must have empathy. Having *empathy*, or the ability to identify with and understand your client's feelings or difficulties, is required in the social work field. Responding to your client in a warm, accepting, respectful, and empathetic manner will initiate a supportive relationship with your client (Cournoyer & Stanley, 2002; Miley et al., 1998).

Empathy is significantly different from sympathy and pity. *Sympathy*, or the inclination to think or feel the same as your client, is counterproductive. Displaying sympathy rather than empathy for your client will lead you to display a sense of pity or sorrow for your client, which will inevitably lead to an increase in your client's sense of helplessness (Cournoyer & Stanley, 2002; Miley et al., 1998).

Active Listener. As an ***active listener***, you are sharing the responsibility of establishing successful communication with your client. The skills required to be an active listener include concentrating, relating to what you are hearing, and analyzing signals so that you can acquire a deeper understanding of what is being said (Brantley & Miller, 2002). You can use the following techniques to become an active listener:

1. ***Maintain an open mind.*** Analyze and set aside your biases so that you can listen in an objective manner. Do not be judgmental!
2. ***Concentrate.*** Active listening is an intense mental process that requires you to maintain concentration. Concentration "keeps your mind from wandering," and your focus can remain on what your client is saying.
3. ***Maintain eye contact.*** If you maintain eye contact, you are more likely to listen to what is being said. Providing positive nonverbal feedback, such as an occasional nod, will let your client know you are actively listening.
4. ***Show manners.*** Do not interrupt your client. Wait your turn!
5. ***Determine the explanation.*** By being an active listener, you can organize the information you are hearing and get a better understanding of what the client is trying to explain to you.
6. ***Focus on key words.*** Focus on the key words your client is saying. This will help you remember pertinent details, along with assisting you in formatting various statements or questions you want to present to your client.
7. ***Analyze the message*** In order to make sure you have enough information to assist your client, analyze what your client has told you. If needed, ask for additional information from your client.

(*Active Listener Skills source:* Brantley & Miller, 2002)

When using reflection, it is pertinent to be an active listener so that you can reflect back to your client what you heard. This assures your client that you are listening and that you accurately understand what he or she said. This process also tells your client that you are paying attention (Miley et al., 1998; Sheafor & Horejsi, 2006).

Communication Skills. It is extremely important that you are aware of the various verbal, nonverbal and behavioral communications that your client will display when meeting with you. Your client's communication style is influenced by such factors as gender, age, education, race, and culture. You must pay close attention to your client's verbal and nonverbal communication and behavior so that you obtain a better understanding of your client's feelings and views of the situation. Remember, you will also be displaying nonverbal and behavior communication that your client will notice.

(For a refresher on the types of communications, Refer to Part Three, Chapter 4: What Are Verbal and NonVerbal Communication Skills?)

Applying what you have learned . . .

Understanding Reflection

11.1   Define reflection and describe, in your own words, the importance of using reflection in social work.

11.2   Using a legal size piece of paper, make three columns.

a. *First column:*   Develop a list of skills (from the chapter) required for successful reflection.

b. *Second column:*   Using the list of required reflection skills from the first column, choose the skills that you believe you already have for using reflection with a client successfully.

c. *Third column:*   Using the list of required reflections skills from the first column, choose the skills that you believe you need to strengthen before you can successfully use reflection with a client.

Section Two: Understanding the Styles and Applications of Reflection

The types of reflection to consider when working with your client include reflection of content, reflection of feeling, and reflection of thinking or meaning. When applying reflection, you must use a number of techniques so that reflection is successful.

Reflection of Content

Reflection of content involves listening to your client's explanation of his or her situation, and communicating your understanding back to the client. Remember, your client is the expert in what is going on in his or her life, so encourage your client to describe the situation and problem(s) in his or her own words. Let your client finish the specific area of discussion before you reflect on what has been said (Compton & Gallaway, 1999; Miley et al., 1998; Sheafor & Horejsi, 2006).

Applying Reflection of Content.   Applying all types of reflection requires active listening. As you actively listen to your client, pay close attention to the verbal and nonverbal communication, and your client's behavior. These three factors of communication will provide an array of information about your client's perspective on the situation or problem.

Once your client has finished explaining his or her situation or problem, reflect back to your client your understanding of what has been said. When reflecting content back to your client, use a paraphrasing rather than a verbatim style (Compton & Galaway, 1999; Miley et al., 1998; Sheafor & Horejsi, 2006):

CLIENT: "The caseworker is nasty whenever she comes to my house."

WORKER: "I hear you saying that the caseworker does not treat you with respect when she comes to your house."

You can also use reflection of content in an empathetic manner, such as (Compton & Galaway, 1999):

CLIENT: "My son just packed his bags and left when I was not home. He called from his dad's house and says he likes it there better."

WORKER: "He left without telling you, and now he does not want to come back."

Reflection of Feeling

Reflection of feeling means that you can understand your client's verbal and nonverbal expressions of feelings about situations or problems. Reflection of feeling requires the ability to correctly communicate back to your client what has been expressed (Compton & Galaway, 1999; Miley et al., 1998; Sheafor & Horejsi, 2006).

Applying reflection of feeling.   When using reflection of feeling, restate your client's expression of feelings with feeling words that are equivalent to the words he or she used. This tells your client that you are human and that you can understand and relate to your client's situation or problem. It also lets the client know that you are focused and really listening. Reflection of feeling encourages the client to say more (Compton & Galaway, 1999). An example of a proper use of reflection of feeling would be:

CLIENT: "When the caseworker comes to the house, I feel stupid and feel like I am a bad mom."

WORKER: "It sounds like you feel foolish and terrible about yourself when the caseworker visits you."

Remember, do not use the same feeling words your client used. If you reflect back to your client using a verbatim style of language, you will sound emotionless about his or her situation. You need to have a *feelings vocabulary* so that you can avoid just mimicking back or parroting the client's word. Your client may also view you as a phony (Compton & Galaway, 1999). (Refer to Part Five, Chapter Nine: Client Spirituality and Empowerment for a list of feeling words.)

Reflection of Thinking or Meaning

The key to successful *reflection of thinking or meaning* is understanding your client's thoughts and meanings he or she is expressing about the situation or problem and correctly reflecting back to your client what you heard. Reflection of thinking or meaning also requires that you encourage your client to explore the thoughts he or she has about the experiences surrounding the problem (Compton & Galaway, 1999; Miley et al., 1998; Sheafor & Horejsi, 2006).

Applying Reflection of Thinking or Meaning. Let your client express his or her thinking surrounding the problem or situation. Encouraging your client to explore various thoughts and feelings pertaining to his or her experiences will help your client gain a better understanding of the situation or problem (Sheafor & Horejsi, 2006).

> **CLIENT:** "I feel like a failure as a parent, and this is probably why my son left. The caseworker treats me terrible, and I feel like there is nothing I can do about how she treats me. I don't have a college education and am confused by some of the words the caseworker uses. I feel stupid on days she comes to my house. I just don't know what to do."

> **WORKER:** "From what you have been saying, I am hearing a number of things. You are feeling inadequate as a parent and blame yourself for your son leaving home. The caseworker makes you feel bad about yourself, and you believe you are powerless to change this feeling. Because the caseworker uses words that you do not understand, you feel puzzled and frustrated when she visits your home. Feeling inadequate around the caseworker seems to be hindering your ability to handle the situation and to come up with solutions to the problem. What do you think about that?"

As you actively listen to your client with an open mind, you can gain a better understanding of what the experiences mean to your client. Again, it is important to pay close attention to your client's nonverbal communication and behavior as he or she expresses thoughts and feelings.

Applying what you have learned . . .

Practicing Reflection

11.3 Develop a fictitious client problem/situation scenario. Make sure you have a specific gender, age, race, and culture of your client in mind. Once you have developed your client scenario, choose a partner to work with. Your partner for this exercise should be someone you do not know well on a personal level.

 a. Give your partner in advance details only on the gender, age, race, and culture of your fictitious client.

 b. In your role as "client," meet with your partner, who is playing the role of a social worker, and begin telling him or her your problem or situation.

 c. Keep track of how well you believe your partner used reflection with you.

 d. Partner as "social worker." Use the three types of reflection discussed in the chapter: reflection of content, reflection of feeling, and reflection of thinking or meaning when working with your partner.

 e. Reverse roles with your partner and do steps a–d.

---

*Note: This exercise requires student preparation outside of the classroom.

Summary

Reflection is a communication technique social workers use to let clients know they are listening to them. Social workers reflect feelings back to a client. Reflection is a team effort between you and your client and requires that you feel empathy toward your client's situation. Having empathy will enable you to identify with and understand your client's feelings. *Empathy* is required in social work so that acceptance and respect are maintained and a supportive relationship can develop between you and your client.

Successful reflection requires that you become an active listener. As an *active listener*, you share the responsibility of establishing successful communication with your client. Maintaining an open mind and eye contact, concentrating, and following communication rules are just a few tools you can use to become an active listener. You must be attentive to what your client is saying so that you can accurately reflect back to your client what he or she has said. Active listening assures your client that you are listening and encourages the client to say more.

Reflection of content involves listening to your client's explanation of his or her situation and communicating your understanding back to the client. *Reflection of feeling* means that you can understand your client's verbal and nonverbal expressions of feelings about his or her situation or problem. *Reflection of thinking or meaning* requires you to understand your client's thoughts and meanings he or she is expressing about the situation or problem. All three types of reflection require you to be an active listener.

When using reflection, you need to pay close attention to the verbal and nonverbal communication and the behavior of your client. *Remember*, do not use the same words your client used. By paraphrasing what your client has said, you will be like a human being with emotions instead of a parrot who repeats words! Encourage your client to explore various thoughts and feelings pertaining to his or her experiences. This will help your client gain a better understanding of the situation or problem, and empowerment of your client can begin.

KEY WORDS AND CONCEPTS

Section One
Active listener, p. 153
Communication skills, p. 153
Empathy, p. 152

Reflection, p. 152
Sympathy, p. 152
Section Two
Reflection of content, p. 154

Reflection of feeling, p. 155
Reflection of thinking
    or meaning, p. 155

REFERENCES

Brantley, C.P., & Miller, M.G. (2002). *Effective communications for colleges.* Cincinnati: South-Western Thomson Learning.

Compton, B.R., & Galaway, B. (1999). *Social work processes.* Pacific Grove, CA: Brooks/Cole Publishing Company.

Cournoyer, B.R., & Stanley, M.J. (2002). *The social work portfolio: Planning, assessing and documenting lifelong learning in a dynamic profession.* Pacific Grove, CA: Brooks/Cole Publishing Company.

Miley, K. K., O'Melia, M., & DuBois, B.L. (1998). *Generalist social work practice: An empowering approach.* Needham Heights, MA: Allyn & Bacon.

Sheafor, B.W., & Horejsi, C.R. (2006). *Techniques and guidelines for social work practice.* Boston, MA: Pearson Education.

12

Communicating with Clients Using Positive Confrontation and Information-Giving

The social worker who has perfected the art of positive confrontation skills provides honest communication to his or her clients. By comparing the Do's and Don'ts of positive client confrontation, you are able to see both the positive and the negative consequences of this technique if it is not used properly with your client. When working with clients, it is also important to use information-giving so that professional services are provided to your client. Thus, Chapter 12 will help you increase your professional communication skills relating to both positive client confrontation and information-giving.

Section One: Defining and Building Positive Client Confrontation Skills

Defining Positive Confrontation

The word *confrontation* in social work needs to be seen as positive. *Confrontation* is a technique that social workers use in a tentative and nonjudgmental way to encourage a client to explore and become aware of his or her thoughts, feelings, and behaviors. Professional confrontation is done in a gentle and respectful manner so that a client recognizes if he or she is using self-defeating methods such as distortions, deceptions, denials, or manipulations that build barriers to desirable change. Confrontation also points out discrepancies between what a client says and does, and addresses unrecognized client strengths. Used properly, confrontation encourages client learning and provides stimulus for change (Compton & Galaway, 1999; Miley, O'Melia, & DuBois, 1998; Schmolling, Youkeles, & Burger, 1993; Sheafor & Horejsi, 2006).

Building Positive Client Confrontation Skills

By implementing proper confrontation skills, you can assist your clients in recognizing and eliminating a self-defeating attitude while fostering their strengths that are needed for change (Compton & Galaway, 1999; Miley et al., 1998; Schmolling et al., 1993; Sheafor & Horejsi, 2006). Here is an example of positive client confrontation:

> **CLIENT:** I should be more involved with my wife and children. They keep telling me I don't care about them, and am not home much. I feel bad about it, but I just started a new job that is demanding, and my father is ill, so I don't have the time.

> **WORKER:** I recall you saying this several times over the past few weeks that we have been meeting. You say that you want to spend more time with your wife and children, but it is obvious that you are not doing what you feel you should be doing. You say one thing but do another. I am aware that you want to spend more time with your father because he is ill, and that your job is demanding, however, I cannot help but feel deep down you have decided to give up your role as husband and father. What is your honest reaction to what I am saying?

> (*Positive Client Confrontation Example source*: Sheafor & Horejsi, 2006)

Before using the confrontation technique with your client, you must become familiar with the various skills you will need so that confrontation is both positive and successful. Let's take a look at the Do's and Don'ts of positive client confrontation:

The Do's of Positive Client Confrontation

1. Show genuine concern for your client; that is a necessity!
2. Make sure you have the time to work with and become more deeply involved with your client's thoughts, feelings, and behavior. Get to know your client.
3. Have respect for your client; in turn, your client must respect you.
4. Recognize and support client strengths in your message.
5. Provide a detailed description of the client's self-defeating behavior while remaining nonjudgmental.
6. Make sure you have observations or data on which your message is based.

> (*Do's of Positive Client Confrontation sources:* Compton & Galaway, 1999; Miley et al., 1998; Schmolling et al., 1993; Sheafor & Horejsi, 2006).

The Don'ts of Positive Client Confrontation

1. Do not engage in confrontation when you are feeling angry. It may be interpreted as frustration or the desire to punish your client for something you do not agree with.
2. Avoid using client confrontation if you do not intend to take the time and assume the responsibility of helping your client in understanding the message and the future choices he or she may have.
3. Avoid engaging in confrontation if your client does not like or respect you; otherwise confrontation will lack a positive and beneficial impact.
4. Avoid negative and judgmental statements that trigger anger.

Applying what you have learned . . .

Understanding Confrontation

12.1 Think of the word "confrontation." Make a list of words or phrases that come to mind when you hear this word. Once you have compiled your list of words or phrases, ask yourself the following:

a. How many negative words or phrases are on my list?

b. Do I have any positive words on my list?

c. Would my interpretation(s) of the word "confrontation" be damaging to the helping process with my client? If you answered yes, think of ways you can turn your interpretation of the word "confrontation" into a positive one that will benefit your client.

12.2 You have been working with a female client for several weeks now. She is a single mom with two children, and the father does not pay child support. She complains that she is financially struggling to pay monthly rent and utility bills. She also has made you aware that she likes to buy new clothes for herself every week, has her nails done once a month, and goes out with friends every Friday night.

a. Take a few minutes to think about the client issues in the scenario. How do you think you should confront your client about her issues? Once you have a general idea of the positive confrontation you want to use with your client, choose a partner.

b. You are the "social worker." Choose a classmate to play the role of this "female client." Let your partner begin by paraphrasing the above client scenario; then you can proceed with your positive client confrontation.

c. Reverse the "social worker" and "female client" roles with your partner. Repeat step 2.b.

---

5. Avoid using ambiguous statements and vague details when discussing your observations and the inferences drawn from these observations.

(*Don'ts of Positive Client Confrontation sources:* Compton & Galaway, 1999; Miley et al., 1998; Schmolling et al., 1993; Sheafor & Horejsi, 2006).

Section Two: Types of Information-Giving Responses

As a social worker, you should have a sound knowledge base in reference to the information your client may need. You should also have well-developed professional communication skills (refer to Chapter 4) when using information-giving responses. Keep in mind that information-giving is productive for the client only if given immediately and when necessary. Among several types of information-giving are an orienting statement, instructions or directions, feedback, reframing, and informational statement (Compton & Galaway, 1999; Miley et al., 1998; Schmolling et al., 1993; Sheafor & Horejsi, 2006).

Orienting Statement

An *orienting statement* provides your client with information about the interviewing process. You can use an orienting statement to introduce your client to the organization and to explain various steps in the helping process. Your role, the client's role, the costs and benefits, and the experiences associated with the helping process is done through the orienting statement. The type of information in the orienting statement is derived from various knowledge bases to include program guidelines, and procedure and policy manuals (Compton & Galaway, 1999; Miley et al., 1998; Schmolling et al., 1993; Sheafor & Horejsi, 2006).

> **WORKER:** "Before we begin, I'd like to share with you a bit of information about the agency and services that we provide. You and I will be working closely together in helping you deal with your current situation. My job is to listen to your concerns and help you identify ways to improve the problem that's bothering you. We need to be open and honest with each other. I hope that you'll be committed to attending our scheduled sessions and to working with me as a team. At our agency, confidentiality is very important, and I'd like to cover that next."

Instructions or Directions

Instructions or, *directions* provide your client with information about his or her role as you work together in the helping process. This type of information-giving also can be used to describe a proposed behavior, to show how to carry it out, and to identify the potential positive and negative consequences of the behavior (Compton & Galaway, 1999; Miley et al., 1998; Schmolling et al., 1993; Sheafor & Horejsi, 2006).

> **CLIENT:** "My boyfriend and I fight every so often. We both start yelling and end up not talking to each other for days."
>
> **WORKER:** "People in relationships will occasionally disagree. What would happen if the next time you and your boyfriend have an argument, you take a break from each other, think about what you were arguing about, then come back and talk calmly in about an hour or two?"

Feedback

By providing *feedback* to your client, you assist him or her in understanding various thoughts, feelings, and behaviors. Actually, feedback is the simplest way to help your client reflect on and change his or her behavior. When you use neutral feedback, your client is able to attach his or her personal evaluations to the information you provided (Compton & Galaway, 1999; Miley et al., 1998; Schmolling et al., 1993; Sheafor & Horejsi, 2006).

CLIENT: "I'm really mad. My husband's family is so demanding and we can't even plan our own vacations or holidays."

WORKER: "You seem awfully upset. Why do you think you and your husband are struggling with making your own vacation and holiday plans without his family's interference?"

Alternative Perspective (Reframe)

Alternate perspective, or *reframing*, reinterprets a behavior in a positive manner. By helping your client "look on the bright side," negative thoughts may be eliminated, and a positive outlook that energizes your client can develop. Reframing can also prevent problems from developing (Compton & Galaway, 1999; Miley et al., 1998; Schmolling et al., 1993; Sheafor & Horejsi, 2006). An example:

CLIENT: "My wife's brother is nosy. He calls two or three times a day, and interferes in all our weekend plans. We never seem to spend time alone anymore."

WORKER: "It sounds like your wife's brother cares deeply about his sister, and is concerned about her welfare. How would you prefer your brother-in-law show interest and concern for your wife?"

Informational Statement

An *informational statement* provides an overview of information your client may need in reference to resources, people, or alternatives. It is important that you match the information with your client's ability to benefit from it. Avoid overloading your client with too much information at one time. Break the information down into organized units that your client can integrate or use (Compton & Galaway, 1999; Miley et al., 1998; Schmolling et al., 1993; Sheafor & Horejsi, 2006).

Information-Giving Guidelines

1. Recognize your client's need for information.
2. Provide the information to your client when required. Timing is critical!
3. Match the information to your client's current needs and goals.
4. Provide information when your client is most receptive.
5. For effective information-giving, use professional attending skills, and focus on your client's expression of emotions and attitudes through:
   a. Eye contact
   b. Verbal communication
   c. Body language
6. Be sure your eye contact, voice tone, and body posture are all appropriate in order for your client to be receptive of your information.
7. Be direct, clear, concise, and concrete when giving information to your client.

8. Divide information into organized units that your client can integrate or use.
9. Do not overload your client with too much information at once.

   (*Information-Giving Guidelines sources:* Compton & Galaway, 1999; Miley et al., 1998; Schmolling et al., 1993; Sheafor & Horejsi, 2006)

Maximizing Client Information-Giving

In order to maximize the use of information you have given to your client, you must complete the information-giving cycle with a follow-up response. You can do this with a brief statement or request that checks the degree to which your client has attended to the information you provided (Compton & Galaway, 1999; Miley et al., 1998; Schmolling et al., 1993; Sheafor & Horejsi, 2006). Suggestions include:

1. Ask your client to repeat the information you provided.
2. Ask your client to act upon the information you provided.
3. Engage your client in a discussion about the information you provided.

   (*Brief statement or request sources*: Compton & Galaway, 1999; Miley et al., 1998; Schmolling et al., 1993; Sheafor & Horejsi, 2006)

Keep in mind that information-giving is not an easy task. However, your professional information-giving communication skills will increase as you continue to practice the process.

Applying what you have learned . . .

Practicing Information-Giving

12.3 Read through the following client scenario:

You have a new male client who has just entered your office. He is married, has three children, and has been laid-off from his job for two weeks. He is having a hard time finding temporary work, and he does not want a full-time job because he is waiting to be called back to his previous employment. He tells you that he and his wife are arguing all the time now due to financial troubles. He feels his children are misbehaving more than usual, and he is struggling to deal with them. He feels like a "failure" because he cannot properly provide for his family, nor can he control his children's behavior.

a. Take a few minutes to think about the client issues in the scenario. *Refer to Section Two: Types of Information-Giving Responses* and come up with a plan that includes:

1. Orienting statement
2. Instructions or directions
3. Feedback
4. Alternative perspective (reframing)
5. Informational statement
6. Maximizing your client's use of the information

b. Once you have a written information-giving response plan, choose a partner.
c. You are the "social worker," and your partner is the "male client." Do your orienting statement, then let your partner read the above client scenario.
d. Once your partner has finished reading the scenario, you can proceed with the information-giving steps in 12.3a.
e. Reverse the "social worker" and "male client" roles with your partner. Repeat steps a–d.

Summary

Perfecting the art of *positive confrontation* is critical when developing a professional and honest communication cycle with your client. As a social worker, you will be using confrontation as a tool to assist your client in exploring his or her thoughts, feelings, and behaviors. Professional confrontation requires that you respect your client and help him or her recognize self-defeating methods, such as distortions, deceptions, denial, or manipulations, that may be hindering the helping process. Genuine concern and taking the time to get to know your client will lead to positive and successful confrontation.

As a social worker, you must have a sound knowledge base and well-developed communication skills so that your *information-giving process* with your client is successful. Through the *orienting statement*, you introduce your client to the organization and helping process, and then proceed with *instructions* or *directions* that clarify you and your client's role. Providing *feedback* to your client during the information-giving process will help him or her reflect on, and change behaviors.

Providing your client with an *alternative perspective (reframing)* helps the client to see problems in a positive manner, while eliminating negative thoughts. Reframing also serves to prevent future problems from developing. As you move into the *informational statement* with your client, make sure to break the information you are providing into organized units so that you do not overwhelm your client. It is important that you provide information to your client at the appropriate time; otherwise the information will be useless in the helping process. Finally, *maximizing information-giving* requires you to issue a follow-up statement to make sure your client understands the information you have provided.

KEY WORDS AND CONCEPTS

Section One

Do's of positive client
    confrontation, p. 159
Don'ts of positive client
    confrontation, p. 159
Positive client
    confrontation, p. 158

Section Two

Information-giving
    guidelines, p. 162
Information-giving
    responses, p. 160
Alternate perspective
    (reframing), p. 162

Feedback, p. 161
Informational statement, p. 162
Instructions or directions, p. 161
Orienting statement, p. 161
Maximizing client
    information-giving, p. 163

REFERENCES

Compton, B.R., & Galaway, B. (1999). *Social work processes.* Pacific Grove, CA: Brooks/Cole Publishing Company.

Miley, K.K., O'Melia, M., & DuBois, B.L. (1998). *Generalist social work practice: An empowering approach.* Needham Heights, MA: Allyn & Bacon.

Schmolling, P., Jr., Youkeles, M., & Burger, W.R. (1993). *Human services in contemporary America.* Belmont, CA: Wadsworth.

Sheafor, B.W., & Horejsi, C.R. (2006). *Techniques and guidelines for social work practice.* Boston, MA: Pearson Education.

13 Communicating in a Rural Setting

Social work practice is increasing in rural areas, and it is important that you understand the cultural characteristics of the rural community. Being aware of these cultural characteristics will build your cultural competence. Cultural competence will ensure that you enter the rural social work practice with accurate information and a thorough understanding of your clients' lifestyles and behaviors. By having accurate information and facts, along with being familiar with ethical issues that exist in a rural community, you will be able to communicate with those you serve in a professional and successful manner.

Section One: What Is a Rural Community?

Before the 1920s, most of the United States was considered "rural." By this decade 50 percent of the population lived in cities. *Urbanization*, or the movement from rural to urban areas, has steadily continued since then. Today approximately 80 percent of the population in the United States live in urban areas or cities (Henslin, 2005; Pugh, 2000). Even though only 20 percent of the population live in rural areas, the need for social workers in these communities is growing (Martinez-Brawley, 1980).

Characteristics of the Rural Community

Before we discuss the characteristics of a rural community, let's define the rural social worker. According to Barker (2003), rural social workers are defined as those "whose predominant clientele and practice activities are in sparsely populated regions. The most successful workers in these regions are well-trained, creative professionals who can work in relative isolation with limited additional resources" (p. 377, as quoted by Sidell, Boughton, Hull, Ertz, Seeley, & Wieder, 2006, p. 28). According to the NASW (2006–2009), "rural social workers contribute to the mission of advocating for social justice and extending services for underserved populations (p. 321).

Rural Community. As discussed in Chapter 2, there is no objective and universally accepted definition of ***rural***, but there is consensus on the description of rural areas. ***Rural***

areas are described as sparsely populated country communities with fewer than 2,500 citizens. For the most part, rural is better understood and defined by those who live or work in a rural area (Henslin, 2005; Martinez-Brawley, 1980, 2000; Pugh, 2000; Sidell et al., 2006; U.S. Census Bureau, 2000). (See *Chapter Two, Section Two, Table 2.4,* for population data.)

Privacy.   Most people living in rural communities consider *privacy* to be an advantage. As a result of their geographical isolation, people find that living in rural areas provides separation from bureaucratic agencies and services. They can also find privacy from neighbors by staying in their homes and limiting their interaction with others in the community (Fitchen, 1981).

Community and Kinship Ties.   *Kinship* (or family ties) is strong in rural communities. Relationships with family members may be strained at times, but the sense of kinship bond and community ties still exist. The area where family and friends live is the area where people feel they belong. Social interaction and mutual assistance networks have been established. All these factors tend to keep people from migrating to urban areas (Fitchen, 1981; NASW, 2006–2009).

Economy.   Most people think "farming" or "outdoors life" when they hear the word "rural". Even though farming, gardening, and hunting are common activities in rural areas, mining operations, factories, and light industries are also found in many rural communities. Rural areas today represent a service economy. Various large businesses provide either an "economic boom" to rural communities or economic devastation when employers leave the area. Job loss and urban movement are continuous in various rural areas (Fitchen, 1981; Pugh, 2000; Stoesen, 2002).

Transportation.   Private car ownership rates are high in rural areas owing to the lack of public transportation. Geographically, most people residing in rural communities have lengthy commutes to work (50 plus miles). Shopping and doctor appointments may also require a long drive (Fitchen, 1981; Pugh, 2000; Stoesen, 2002).

It is important for you to conduct further research on the particular rural setting in which you are located. In this way, you can begin your social work career prepared to assist your clients in a professional manner.

Communication in a Rural Community

Generalist Approach.   When working as a social worker in a rural community, you should take the *generalist approach* and learn a little bit about every field. Specializing in one field, such as family or aging, limits your ability to communicate with the diverse rural population. Your limited knowledge and communication skills restrict the number of people you may be able to help in a rural community (Stoesen, 2002).

Applying what you have learned . . .

What Is a Rural Community?

13.1 In your own words, describe *rural*. Make a list of words that come to mind when you hear the word "rural."

13.2 Refer back to the section *Characteristics of the Rural Community*. Develop your own list of characteristics you believe describe a rural community.

13.3 Refer back to the section *Communication in a Rural Community*.
   a. Develop a list of at least 10 reasons why the social work generalist approach is more helpful if working in a rural community.
   b. Develop a list of at least 10 reasons why being forthright and consistent when communicating with clients in a rural community is important.

Be Forthright and Consistent. As a rural social worker, you must guard against putting on "airs" with your client. Also avoid being *voluble*, or too talkative. It is best to get straight to the point, limiting your use of the discipline's technical terms. To be a successful social worker in a rural community, you need to emphasize the virtues of self-sufficiency, personal responsibility and self-determination in both your profession and social life. Because people in smaller communities have more opportunities to view your behavior in both professional and personal situations, your nonverbal communication and behavior must be consistent in both settings (Pugh, 2000; Stoesen, 2002). (Refer to and review Part Three, Chapter Four: What Are Verbal and Nonverbal Communication Skills?)

Section Two: Ethical Issues in a Rural Community

Rural areas are geographically isolated and possess a strong sense of community ties. You therefore need to expect ethical and confidentiality issues to arise when practicing social work in rural communities. You can also expert to confront the issue of dual relationships.

Community Involvement and Gossip

Community Involvement. Rural communities are often small in both radius and population when compared to urban areas. People in rural communities know their neighbors and keep updated on various activities of those living in the community. As a social worker practicing in a rural community, you should expect to be visible to various clients every time you leave your home. Going shopping and attending various community and sports events may expose you to considerable outside social interaction with your clients (Fenby, 1987; Pugh, 2000; Stoesen, 2002).

   Social interaction with your clients is inevitable in small communities. When you meet a client on the street or in a restaurant, keep the conversation casual and maintain a friendly demeanor. Remember, confidentiality is important to the social work field, so ***do not discuss work-related issues outside of the office*** (Fenby, 1987; Pugh, 2000; Stoesen, 2002).

Dual Relationships.   According to the NASW *Code of Ethics* (1996), dual relationships occur when "social workers relate to clients in more than one relationship, whether professional, social or business" (Standard 1.06[c], as quoted by Ginsberg, 2005). Dual relationships can include seeing a client at the local store or community event. The dual relationship that indicates a clear boundary violation and is forbidden in the NASW *Code of Ethics* is a sexual relationship with a client (Ginsberg, 2005).

It is important that you control and maintain your personal life by setting boundaries with your client(s). Avoid inviting your client(s) to dinner or coffee at your home. This will put your family into a situation where they become bound by confidentiality (Fenby, 1987; Pugh, 2000; Stoesen, 2002). By allowing your client(s) into your home and personal life, you open yourself up to unwanted community involvement and gossip. These types of invitations may also put you and your family at risk of harassment and violence from a client. Having an unlisted telephone number is also suggested (Green, Gregory, & Mason, 2003).

Gossip.   Unfortunately, ***gossip***, or chatty talk that reveals personal or sensational information about another person(s) is a form of communication that often serves to unite a rural community. As a professional social worker, you should ignore gossip you may hear about rural community members, especially your clients. It is crucial that you avoid "feeding into, and/or adding to" the gossip. By ignoring gossip, you can maintain a professional helping relationship with your client while maintaining respect from your coworkers and other members in the community (Fenby, 1987; Pugh, 2000; Stoesen, 2002).

Confidentiality in Rural Communities

Client confidentiality can be more difficult to maintain in rural communities than in urban areas. Rural people tend to know one another and have more contact with their neighbors, family, and friends. All the same, client confidentiality can be maintained if you remain professional. The following suggestions can help maintain client confidentiality in a rural community (Fenby, 1987; Pugh, 2000; Stoesen, 2002):

1. Adhere to the NASW *Code of Ethics* in reference to client confidentiality.
2. Refrain from entering into conversations about clients in a social setting.
3. Avoid talking about the helping relationship with your client in a social setting.
4. Ignore gossip that is heard, and avoid adding your point of view to the conversation.
5. Avoid client introductions such as "This is Bob, my client."
6. Have a "native" on the agency's staff to manage client appointments. This will assist your office in avoiding former spouses and nonspeaking in-laws from having appointments scheduled at similar times and inevitably running into each other in the waiting area.

Applying what you have learned . . .

Ethical Issues in a Rural Community

13.4 You have just taken a social work position in a rural community with a population of 1,500. Housing is limited, and you and your family have to rent a small home in town. You have an established clientele and have been working for several weeks now. As you and your family become familiar with the community and the people, you start to participate in community activities and sporting events. How should you handle the following client situations so that *client confidentiality* can be maintained?

a. You and your family are at the local store. A client of yours comes up to you and wants to talk about his or her last session, and begins to fill you in on this week's problems.

b. One of your adolescent clients' has been invited to your son's birthday party. When he arrives at the party, he announces that you are his social worker.

13.5 Refer to the social worker situation in *Exercise 13.4*. How should you handle the following dual relationship situation with your client:

a. You have been working with a particular client for a week. Your client has disclosed to you his or her intimate feelings toward you.

Chapter Summary and Conclusion

About 20 percent of the population reside in rural America today. Even though the percentage is small, social work practice is increasing in the rural areas. Thus, it is important that you are aware of the cultural characteristics of the rural community. One very important characteristic of a rural community is privacy. Even though community and kinship ties are strong in rural communities, most do respect their privacy and consider it an advantage. Also, "rural" is not limited to farming and outdoors activities; mining operations, factories, and light industries can also be found in rural communities. Public transportation is rare, and most people residing in rural areas must travel great distances to work, shopping, and doctor appointments.

The generalist approach, or having knowledge about all the various fields of social work practice, is more advantageous to your clients than specializing in just one particular field. It is extremely important to be forthright and consistent when working with clients in a rural community. Your behavior, demeanor, and verbal communication must be consistent in both professional and personal situations because inevitably you will have contact with your client(s) in public settings. Remember the importance of limiting dual relationships with your clients. Do not forget to maintain your own personal life so that possible harassment and violence from a client can be avoided. As a social worker, you should avoid gossip so that you can maintain a professional working relationship with your client(s).

Even though people in rural communities tend to know one another and have more contact with neighbors, family, and friends than is true in urban areas, maintaining client confidentiality in rural areas is still possible. Remaining professional, adhering to the NASW *Code of Ethics*, and refraining from talking about clients in a public setting are all key elements to maintaining client confidentiality in a rural community. As a social worker, it is important that you do your homework on the area where you intend to practice so that you can assist your client(s) in a productive and professional manner.

KEY WORDS AND CONCEPTS

Section One
Characteristics of a rural
  community, p. 165
  Community and kinship
    ties, p. 166
  Economy, p. 166
  Privacy, p. 166
  Rural community, p. 165
    Rural, p. 165
    Rural areas, p. 165

Transportation, p. 166
Communication in a rural
  community, p. 167
  Be forthright and
    consistent, p. 167
  Voluble, p. 167
  Generalist approach, p. 166
Rural community, p. 165
  Urbanization, p. 165

Section Two
Community involvement and
  gossip, p. 167
  Community involvement, p. 167
  Dual relationships, p. 168
  Gossip, p. 168
Confidentiality in rural
  communities, p. 168

REFERENCES

Barker, R. (2003). *The social work dictionary*, 5th ed. Washington, DC: NASW Press.

Census 2000: Urban and Rural Classification. (2000). Retrieved March 10, 2006 from U.S. Census Bureau Web Site: www.ask.census.gov

Fenby, B.L. (1987). *Social work in a rural setting*. Washington, DC: National Association of Social Workers.

Fitchen, J. M. (1981). *Poverty in rural America: A case study*. Boulder, CO: Westview Press.

Ginsberg, L. H. (2005). *Social work in rural communities* (4th ed.). Alexandria: Council on Social Work Education.

Green, R., Gregory, R., & Mason, R. (2003). It's no picnic: Personal and family safety for rural social workers. *Australian Social Work, 56*(2), 94–106.

Henslin, J.M. (2005). *Sociology: A down-to-earth approach*. Boston, MA: Allyn & Bacon.

Martinez-Brawley, E.E. (1980). Identifying and describing the context of *rural* in social work. *Aretau, 6*(2), 21–32.

Martinez-Brawley, E.E. (2000). Identifying and describing the context of *rural* in social work. *Arete, 6*(2), 21–32.

NASW (2006–2009). *Social work speaks* (7th ed.). Washington, DC: NASW Press.

National Association of Social Workers (1996). *NASW Code of Ethics* Washington, DC: Author.

Pugh, R. (2000). *Rural social work*. Dorset: Russell House Publishing.

Sidell, N., Boughton, B., Hull, P., Ertz, R., Seeley, K., & Wieder, J. (2006). Country life: Joys, challenges and attitudes of rural social workers. *Rural Social Work and Community Practice, 10*(2), 28–35.

Stoesen, L. (2002). *Reconnecting to a historical foundation: Rural social workers embrace challenge.* Washington, DC: NASW News.

14 Putting It All Together

Chapter 14 ties all the components of Chapter 2 through Chapter 13 together in an easy-to-read, all-embracing manner. The chapter reiterates the need for you to have an impressive resumé so that you can launch a successful social work career. Various professional communication skills pertinent to the social work profession are briefly reviewed. Concepts and procedures pertaining to social work duties and responsibilities are once again highlighted.

Section One: A Professional Resumé and Cover Letter

Development of a Professional Resumé

Traditional Resumé. One of the exercises in Chapter 2, was developing a professional resumé. Let's revisit the main points of a professional resumé so that you can check to make sure your resumé meets the standards outlined earlier.

Developing a Professional Resumé

1. Be neat and use a professional format. Reverse chronological format is most acceptable to employers. A one-page resumé is preferred.
2. Be sure your resumé is completely free of errors.
3. Be brief, and provide clear and specific information when developing your resumé. Use powerful language!
4. Provide contact information, employment objective, education, employment history with dates, and skills.
5. Give one telephone number. Make sure it is a number you check often, on which you can have a calm and professional conversation. Be sure to return the call in a timely fashion.
6. Be generous with margins. You should have a one-inch margin on all sides.

7. Remember *symmetry* so that your resumé has a balanced appearance. Have adequate white space.
8. Review and critique. Remember to have an adviser or someone in your field review and critique your resumé.

Developing a Professional E-Resumé

1. Be neat and use a professional format. Reverse chronological format is most acceptable to employers. A one-page resumé is preferred.
2. Be sure your resumé is completely free of errors.
3. Be brief, and provide clear and specific information when developing your resumé. Use powerful language!
4. Provide contact information, employment objective, education, employment history with dates, and skills.
5. Leave a one-and-a-half inch margin on all sides.
6. Use capital letters for section headlines. Align all text of the e-resumé to the left margin.
7. Use asterisks or dashes to highlight specific features of your e-resumé.
8. Use font size of 12–14 points (10 min. and 14 max.).
9. Use as many key words as possible. Examples include subtitles, job titles, skills, accomplishments, and education.
10. Review and critique. Remember to have an adviser or someone in your field review and critique your resumé.

(*Developing a Professional Resumé and E-Resumé sources:* Barthel & Jones, 2005; Beale, 2004; Hultberg, 2002; Hunter College Reading/Writing Center, 1999; Mansfield University Office of Career development, 2005)

Development of a Professional Cover Letter

To prepare a cover letter that will accent your resumé and highlight your professionalism, check to make sure the following information is present in the cover letter you developed in Chapter 2.

Developing a Professional Cover Letter

1. Prepare, your cover letter in a professional and error-free manner just as your resumé. Always send the original.
2. Include your address, personal telephone number (not cell phone number), and e-mail address. It should be typed in this exact order and located at the top, left-hand corner (do not indent).
3. Give the full date (month, day, year) next (left-hand side).
4. Follow with the contact name and title, and full business address (left-hand side).
5. Begin by selecting the most appropriate salutation (Dear Mr.; Mrs.; Ms.; Dr.; Professor, etc.), then type the last name (left-hand side).

6. Use standard English grammar format for the body of your cover letter, giving complete sentences and correct paragraph structure. Use a professional, block-style format with no indentions.

(*Cover Letter Guidelines sources:* Hultberg, 2002; Mansfield University Office of Career Development, 2005; Oldaker & Olson, 2005)

Section Two: Professional Social Work Communication Components

Research in Social Work

As discussed in Chapter 3, current research is pertinent to the social work profession. Every social worker should have the ability and desire to do research on various areas in the social work field. Let's revisit the planning, preparing and submitting process of research.

Preparing to Conduct Research for a Peer Reviewed Journal

1. Find a faculty mentor to assist you in understanding the various steps to conducting research for publication.
2. Read various types of journal articles so that you become familiar with different formats that are used.
3. Decide on the topic you would like to research. Visit the college and/or public library to find the information you need to write your research paper. Follow all the *Writing Tips* presented in Chapter 3.

Planning the submission to a Peer Reviewed Journal

1. Search out the various journals that you believe will reach your intended audience. Narrow down your list and choose the most appropriate journal for your research. Refer to NASW's *An Author's Guide to Social Work Journals*.
2. Make sure you know the specific guidelines, structure, and writing format for the journal you choose. Follow these guidelines. Do not assume that APA format is always used!
3. Ask yourself the following questions about the research you have just completed:
   a. Is your data true? Do the findings support the conclusions?
   b. Will your research have an impact on a situation, issue, and so on?
   c. Is your information useful?
   d. Does your information add to the field?
4. Meet with your faculty mentor for the final "ok" for your research. Ask your faculty mentor questions you have in reference to your paper and journal submission.
5. Examine scientific journal ethics and protocol. Send your paper to only one journal at a time.

(*Preparation and Planning sources:* Linsley, 2002; NASW, 1997)

Verbal Communication

Effective verbal communication always includes clear message content. In addition, both the sender and receiver must display politeness and respect toward each other in order for the communication process to be successful (Brantley & Miller, 2002). Let's look again at the *Six C's* from Chapter 4.

The Six C's of Effective Verbal Communication

1. *Courtesy* Make sure you reflect your client's point of view and address the client's needs.
2. *Clarity* Use appropriate vocabulary, and consider your client's background when choosing words (education, culture, race, class, etc.).
3. *Conciseness* Eliminate unnecessary words, and remember that more is not always better.
4. *Concreteness* Use specific words so that your client can build mental pictures.
5. *Correctness* Verify the accuracy of information before discussing it with your client.
6. *Completeness* Be sure to include all necessary information for your client's needs.

(*The Six C's source:* Brantley & Miller, 2002. The authors stress that the Six C's are effective strategies for both written and verbal communication.)

Remember, civility is a required component when working with your client. Civility includes politeness and respect, which serve to promote and maintain the dignity and worth of your client. Be kind and compassionate to your client's needs, and be empathetic with your client's situation (Brantley & Miller, 2002).

Nonverbal Communication

As discussed in Chapter 4, the exchange of information is not limited to written and verbal communication. You do not have to write or speak to communicate, and you should be aware of the significance of the nonverbal communication you and your client are exchanging during contact. Several factors known as social rhythms influence nonverbal communications and can block productive communication between you and your client if you are not aware of the interaction between these social rhythms and nonverbal communication (Beale, 2004; Brantley & Miller, 2002; Porter, 1969; Sue & Sue, 2003).

The social rhythms you need to consider when communicating with your client include, but are not limited to (Porter, 1969; Sue & Sue, 2003):

1. Culture and race
2. Gender
3. Social class
4. Educational attainment

Body Language

Body language is always present when you communicate with your client. As a social worker, you must be keenly aware of your body language and become skilled in displaying proper body language when working with your client. Your body language should match your verbal communication so that your client perceives you as genuine and sincere (Beale, 2004; *Journal of Behavior Development*, 2001; *Journal of Nursing*, 2002; Kirch, 1979; Krim, 1953; Porter, 1969; Sue & Sue, 2003).

Displaying proper kinesics such as posture, gait, and body positioning when communicating with your client is relevant to the communication process. Your facial expressions and eye contact should communicate interest, attention, concern, and respect. Proxemics, or spatial distance, will vary from client to client. Being familiar with your client's situation and social background is important to understanding the spatial distance that is comfortable for your client. Respecting your client's "comfort zone" will help establish effective communication between you and your client (Beale, 2004; *Journal of Behavior Development*, 2001; *Journal of Nursing*, 2002; Kirch, 1979; Krim, 1953; Porter, 1969; Sue & Sue, 2003).

Attending is the process of nonverbally communicating to others that you are receptive, nonjudgmental, accepting of them as people, and concerned with what they have to say. The key to encouraging your client to express himself or herself freely and completely is to have proper attending skills. As your client becomes familiar with you, and trust and friendship develop, attending and spatial distance with your client may change. Your client's nonverbal behavior will direct you (Beale, 2004; *Journal of Behavior Development*, 2001; *Journal of Nursing*, 2002; Sheafor & Horejsi, 2006).

Now that we have reviewed the professional communication components, let's tie what you have learned into the social work practicum.

Section Three: Applying Professional Communication Skills to Social Work Internship

Communication in Supervision

When you enter the Human Services workforce, communication with others will occupy most of your day. This includes supervision. As discussed in Chapter 5, your supervision will play a central role in your social work internship and professional goals, and you will use the professional communication skills covered throughout this book. It is important for you to understand that your supervisor has various roles, including teacher, enabler, and administrator. This warrants your patience as you learn the various components of social work practice.

It is unrealistic for you to believe that you will "mesh" with every staff member; indeed, a personality conflict may even arise between you and your supervisor. Conflict can be resolved in a professional manner by using the following communication resolution techniques:

1. Maintain a sense of humor.
2. Be courteous and use positive words when communicating with others.
3. Be empathetic so that you can identify with, and understand the ideas, feelings, and thoughts of coworkers.
4. Be flexible and willing to make reasonable compromises.

(*Communication Resolution Techniques sources:* Brantley & Miller, 2002; Schmolling et al., 1993; Sheafor & Horejsi, 2006)

Communication in the Helping Role

Confidentiality.   As learned from Chapter 6, your primary mission as a social worker is to enhance human well-being and help meet the basic needs of all people in a community. To reach this goal, you need to first establish a feeling of trust with clients and the community you are serving. In order to build trust and establish positive communication with your clients and the community, you must maintain client confidentiality. This can be accomplished by:

1. Keeping client file cabinets locked and limiting access to files by need-to-know professionals.
2. Taking the time to review various forms with your client before he or she signs, especially the *Consent for Release of Information* form. Your client must fully understand the *what, who,* and *why* of the information that is being released.
3. Holding client-related conversations in privacy.
4. Avoiding discussions with or about clients in public settings.

(*Confidentiality sources:* Morales & Sheafor, 1998; NASW *Code of Ethics,* 1996; Reamer, 1998; Roberts & Greene, 2002; Sheafor & Horejsi, 2006)

Casework Documentation.   As you will remember, Chapter 7 discussed direct services to clients and casework documentation. When you provide direct services, your interactions with your clients will be recorded using casework documentation. It is important to remember that documentation should be completed each time you have contact with a client. This process provides organization, reflection, and a guarantee of proper, continuous client care in your absence (Darowski, 2005).

Using proper casework documentation is critical in correctly assessing and understanding your client's situation. Proper casework documentation serves three functions: assessment and planning, service delivery, and continuity and coordination of services. It is also critical that your case note documentation is accurate. Characteristics and results of accurate case note documentation are as follows:

1. *Clear and comprehensive documentation*—Correct client assessment and understanding, solid foundation to design and deliver high-quality services
2. *Careful and thoughtful information collection*—Adequate basis for professional reasoning and intervention plans
3. *Continuity and coordination*—Ensures up-to-date client information and continuation of appropriate services
4. *Strong recordkeeping practices*—Maintains integrity of programs offered to clients

(*Characteristics and Results of Accurate Case Note Documentation sources:* Compton & Galaway, 1999; Miley, O'Melia, & DuBois, 1998; Reamer, 2004; Schmolling, Youkeles, & Burger, 1993; Sheafor & Horesjsi, 2006; Wilson, 1976)

Types and Content of Case Note Recordings. Chapter 7 discussed various types of case note recordings used in social work. The types discussed included Narrative (process) Recording, Problem-Oriented recording (POR), and the SOAP Format (Sheafor & Horejsi, 2006; Wilson, 1976).

1. ***Narrative Recording***—a type of comprehensive process recording in which everything that takes place in the interview with the client and social worker must be written down. The process and in-depth details required when using the narrative recording is beneficial to you when you are developing your first case note documentation. Enhancing self-awareness, improving assessment skills, and assisting you in learning to work effectively with clients are some of the benefits you can expect from using narrative recording (Miley et al., 1998; Sheafor & Horejsi, 2006; Wilson, 1976). (Refer to Chapter 7, Section Two, for more information on narrative recording.)
2. ***Problem-Oriented Recording (POR)***—a method of recordkeeping that consists of four components: client database; list of specific problems, each assigned an identifying number; action development for each problem; and plan implementation (Reamer, 2004; Sheafor & Horejsi, 2006; Wilson, 1976). (Refer to Chapter 7, Section Two, for more information on problem-oriented recording.)
3. ***SOAP Format***—the proposed action and rationale for the action when using the Problem-Oriented Recording (POR). The SOAP acronym represents subjective information, objective information assessment, and plan (Reamer, 2004; Sheafor & Horejsi, 2006; Wilson, 1976). (Refer to Chapter 7, Section Two, for more information on the SOAP format.)

Risk-management Guidelines. Detailed risk-management guidelines to increase delivery of services to clients have been developed. The guidelines have also been created to protect social workers in the event of ethics complaints and lawsuits contending professional negligence. The risk-management guidelines relating to case recording documentation fall into four individual categories: documentation content, language and terminology, credibility, and record and documentation (Reamer, 2004).

Case note documentation content guidelines include the following:

1. Serve and protect your client by providing sufficient details when doing case note documentation. This ensures that your client receives proper services and will also protect you in the event of an ethics complaint or lawsuit.
2. "Strike a balance." Striking a balance results in properly assessing clients' needs, accountability to clients, various providers, the courts, and utilization review bodies.
3. Avoid overdocumentation in a client crisis.
4. Use caution with personal notes because this information can quickly become the property of the courts if subpoenaed by a lawyer. The information contained in personal notes could be a risk to you and your client.
5. Keep separate records for sensitive information when providing services to families and couples so that you can protect each client in the event of a dispute.

6. Never put details and personal opinions of agency and/or staff programs and competencies in clients' files. This information should be in administrative files only!

(*Documentation Content source:* Reamer, 2004)

Language and Terminology.   Appropriate language and terminology should be used in case note documentation because you always have an audience (client, supervisor, agency, or court)! The guidelines for appropriate language and terminology include:

1. Be clear, precise, and specific in your wording.
2. Always provide supporting details when drawing conclusions.
3. Protect yourself against yourself by avoiding committing *libel* (written) or *slander* (spoken), the two forms of defamation of character.
4. Be thorough and professional in your writing.

(*Language and Terminology Guidelines source:* Reamer, 2004)

Credibility.   Maintaining accurate records provides essential evidence of your credibility. The following guidelines help maintain credibility (Reamer, 2004):

1. Complete your client documentation of decisions and actions in a timely manner.
2. Do not record planned interventions and events until they happen. Prematurely recorded notes can lead to inaccurate reflection and undermines your credibility.
3. Write or print legibly, using proper grammar and spelling. Illegible entries and grammar and spelling errors can destroy your credibility as a professional.
4. Always acknowledge your errors. Make sure you clear up any confusion with a new entry acknowledging and correcting the error by drawing a line through the error, initialing, dating, and labeling it "error." This should be done as soon as the error is discovered. Changing, hiding, losing or destroying records, and using Wite-Out® to change errors will destroy your credibility quickly!

(*Credibility source:* Reamer, 2004)

Accessing Records and Documentation.   One hundred percent confidentiality of case records does not exist. Thus, it is beneficial for you to be familiar with the laws and rules that surround the disclosure of confidential documents, and security risks in the age of technology. In order to protect yourself and your clients, you should (Reamer, 2004):

1. Acquire legal know-how. There is a difference between subpoenas to appear with documents and a court order to disclose the document's contents.
2. Know relevant federal and state statutes and regulations pertaining to the handling of confidential information and records. Resources include the Federal Health Insurance Portability and Accountability Act (HIPAA), Family Education Rights and Privacy Act (FERPA), and Confidentiality of Alcohol and Drug Abuse Patient Records (42 C.F.R. Part 2).

3. Secure records and exercise caution at all times. Client records should be stored in secure locations to prevent unauthorized access. Be careful when using computer data entry systems, and take precautions so that information cannot be accessed by unauthorized personnel.

4. When records are destroyed or disposed of, still, endeavor to protect client's confidentiality.

(*Protection source*: Reamer, 2004)

Multicultural Competence. Chapter 8 mentioned two challenges you must face if you expect to become multiculturally competent and gain the ability to professionally communicate with diverse clients: be accepting of "difference" and relate to and understand these differences. Understanding social diversity and gaining cultural competence are dependent on your gaining an understanding and acceptance of *your* cultural beliefs, values, and behaviors. Let's revisit the key concepts in Chapter 8:

1. ***Enlightened consciousness*** Having a sound, open-minded understanding and acceptance of facts surrounding your own beliefs, values, and behaviors will free you of ignorance, prejudice, or superstition toward your own culture and the culture of others (Fong, 2001; Galambos, 2003; Henslin, 2005; Mama, 2001; Miley et al., 1998; Seaton, 2003).

2. ***"Conscious use of self"*** (Garvin, 1997, p. 90, as quoted by Seaton, 2003, p. 54) This concept requires you to have an "open mind and heart" (Okayama, Furuto, & Edmondson, 2001, p. 89). The steps to "self" include:
   a. Acknowledging and accepting your personal strengths and weaknesses
   b. Becoming aware of your behaviors, habits, and customs
   c. Demonstrating a willingness to increase your awareness of your own culture and cultural identity
   d. Developing an appreciation of your own cultural heritage and identity

   (*Multicultural Competences sources*: Fong, 2001; Okayama et al., 2001; Sue & Sue, 2003)

3. ***Cultural relativism*** The ability to understand another's culture within its context without prejudice is essential. By understanding your clients' cultural characteristics, you will be able to build a trusting and communicative relationship with them. Relating to your clients' values, norms, and behaviors in a positive manner will lead to a productive social worker–client relationship (Fong, 2001; Galambos, 2003; Henslin, 2005; Mama, 2001; Miley et al., 1998; Seaton, 2003; Sheafor & Horejsi, 2006).

4. ***Client individualism*** This concept is important, as you work with clients from various cultural and racial backgrounds. Being aware of human diversity is necessary so that you can individualize each client and avoid stereotyping values, beliefs, and behaviors in relation to your client's physical features, ethnic identity, and socioeconomic status. In order to individualize each client, you must become culturally sensitive (Henslin, 2005; Hyde, 2004; Morales & Sheafor, 1998; Sheafor & Horejsi, 2006).

5. *Cultural sensitivity*   Culturally sensitive social workers acknowledge and understand that prejudicial feelings and stereotyping affect interactions between people. The willingness to learn about another's culture and to respect existing differences is a necessity in reaching cultural sensitivity (Fong, 2001; Okayama et al., 2001). You must continuously research various client cultures and develop professional communication skills in order to successfully engage with a culturally diverse client population (Galambos, 2003).

6. *Grounded knowledge base*   Continuously gaining knowledge about your various clients' cultures and subcultures will assist you in accumulating multicultural competence and skills. Do your "homework" and gather information on the following client characteristics:

   a. Gender, age, and race
   b. Socioeconomic status—income, occupation, and education
   c. Religious beliefs
   d. Family structure and behavioral patterns
   e. Residence location
   f. Support network
   g. Any other details that will provide you with insight into your client's culture/subculture

   (*Client Characteristics sources:* Houston, 2002; Morales & Sheafor, 1998)

By collecting in-depth client information, appreciating differences and gaining sensitivity toward your client's culture become possible. You will be able to connect your client's behaviors to the possible effects of his or her social environment, and you may discover that your client's behavior is actually meeting the social expectations (norms) within his or her subculture (Fong, 2001; Galambos, 2003; Henslin, 2005; Okayama et al., 2001; Seaton, 2003).

Spirituality, or striving to find a sense of meaning, purpose, values, and fulfillment in life, was discussed in Chapter 9. Through spirituality, we become conscious of who we are and our meaning and purpose in life. Our individual views of right and wrong are defined through spirituality. Understanding and fostering your client's search for spirituality is an important part of being a social worker. To refresh your memory about the individual characteristics and factors that influence your client's sense of "inner self" and spirituality, see Chapter 9, Table 9.1 (Compton & Galaway, 1999; Henslin, 2005; Sheafor & Horejsi, 2006; Van Hook, Hugan, & Aguilar, 2001).

Spirituality is considered a life-long, dynamic journey, and it is important that you assist and support your clients in their spiritual excursion (Sheafor & Horejsi, 2006). You can develop a spiritually sensitive social work practice by:

1. Being clear and honest when assessing your personal spiritual or religious values and belief systems. You need to realize that your values and belief systems will filter into your social work profession so that you can be aware of personal influences on your client. Respecting religious or spiritual diversity will lead to sensitive and competent personal growth for both you and your client (Canda & Furman, 1999; Sheridan, 2001).

2. Using a holistic approach that includes integrating spirituality with biological, psychological, and sociological dimensions of human experience to produce a better understanding and acceptance of human behavior. Gaining knowledge and skills in all these areas will help you create a spiritually sensitive social work practice.
3. Understanding and accepting that your clientele will be diverse in most aspects, and being aware of various successful techniques utilized in social work, are relevant to the success of your relationship with your clients (Becvar, 1997; Canda & Furman, 1999; Sheridan, 2001).
4. Focusing on the reasons why your client has sought help. As you and your client interact and build a relationship of trust and respect, spirituality will inevitably begin to filter into your future communication and collaboration (Becvar, 1997).
5. Making pure that both your personal ethics and the NASW *Code of Ethics* are consistent so that you will service your clients in a positive and successful way (Canda & Furman, 1999; NASW *Code of Ethics*, 1997; Reamer, 1998). (Refer to Chapter 9, Section Two, for information regarding NASW *Code of Ethics* and controversial issues of spirituality in social work.)

Client empowerment. Chapter 9 discussed client empowerment as the central theme in professional social work. Empowerment emphasizes the client's strengths, resiliency, coping style, and ability to succeed. The client self-determination and involvement model includes the client in the helping process so that the client can gain independence and empowerment (Hancock, 1997). As a social worker, you can emphasize your client's strengths and abilities through the empowerment process, so that ultimately, the client takes control over his or her life (Colby & Dziegielewski, 2001; Hancock, 1997; Hasenfeld, 1987; Sheafor & Horejsi, 2006). Let's again take a look at the primary principles of empowerment covered in Chapter 9:

The key principles of empowerment include:

1. Client power
2. Firm conviction
3. Client as the "expert"
4. Self-confidence and self-respect

(*Principles of Empowerment sources*: Colby & Dziegielewski, 2001; Hancock, 1997; Hasenfeld, 1987; Pinderhughes, 1983; Sheafor & Horejsi, 2006)

Strategies for fostering client empowerment include:

1. Understanding power and powerlessness
2. Believing in client abilities
3. Developing a list of feeling words
4. Striving for independence

(*Fostering Client Empowerment sources*: Colby & Dziegielewski, 2001; Cournoyer & Stanley, 2002; Hancock, 1997; Hasenfeld, 1987; Pinderhughes, 1983; Sheafor & Horejsi, 2006)

Strategies of encouraging client problem-solving include:

1. Assisting your client in identifying his or her problems, as the first step in helping your client find solutions. Remember, allow your client to define the problem(s) as he or she views them, and encourage your client to share personal thoughts on possible solutions (Colby & Dziegielewski, 2001; Hancock, 1997; Sheafor & Horejsi, 2006).
2. Educating your client about power dynamics and the system in which he or she lives. This strategy is fundamental to the empowerment process (Pinderhughes, 1983). As a team, you and your client can design an education plan that will enhance your client's understanding of (Henslin, 2005; Macionis 2005; Pinder-hughes, 1983):
   a. social structure and functions
   b. societal factors that determine one's power and powerlessness in society
   c. subculture in which your client has been socialized
   d. support system structure and functions

Empowerment guidelines you should adhere to include the following:

1. View and conduct your working relationship with your client as a "team endeavor."
2. Assist your client in increasing his or her capacity to understand and improve the situation on an individual and community level.
3. Assist your client in building self-esteem and self-respect by encouraging him or her to learn new skills and behaviors.
4. Teach your client leadership skills that will strengthen his or her ability to take action when facing problems on an individual and community level.
5. Assist your client in understanding factors that are contributing to his or her feelings.
6. Help your client in expressing and understanding his or her feelings so that he or she can take positive action to eliminate any feelings of bitterness.
7. Encourage your client to grow by seeing past mistreatment and injustice as a learning process.
8. Assist your client in making arrangements and attending various learning opportunities within agencies and community functions.
9. Encourage your client to interact with program administrators, politicians, and community leaders so that renewed hope for change can occur. Your client will also feel that he or she has played an influential part in these changes.
10. Assist your client in developing a list of his or her personal strengths that are key components in the empowerment process.
11. Monitor and support your client's new feelings of power so that it is used in a planned and disciplined manner.
12. Make sure your client understands that change takes time and that certain factors may limit change.

(*Empowerment Guidelines sources*: Compton & Galaway, 1999; Morales & Sheafor, 1998; Reamer, 2004; Sheafor & Horejsi, 2006)

Remember, a small-group setting, individual, and family are all ideal environments in which to use the empowerment approach. Your client will be able to develop essential skills in:

Communication	Problem solving
Leadership	Critical thinking
Persuasion	Assertiveness
Negotiation	Mutual support

(*Empowerment Skills sources*: Compton & Galaway, 1999; Morales & Sheafor, 1998; Sheafor & Horejsi, 2006)

Client Questioning.   As discussed in Chapter 10, open-ended questions are mostly used in social work in order to obtain needed information about your client. By narrowing the focus, or funneling, you can help your client in maintaining concentration and expressing concerns when asking open-ended questions. Narrowing the focus also assists your client in explaining his or her situation with more specificity (Compton & Galaway, 1999; Miley et al., 1998; Neuman, 2003; Rubin & Babbie, 2001; Sheafor & Horejsi, 2006).

Skill Building of Client Questioning

1. Be conscientious about selecting the appropriate words when asking or answering client questions. Be aware of the significance of the nonverbal communication and behavior you and your client are displaying during the client questioning process.
2. Maintain eye contact because it is an extremely powerful means of communication. Your client's eyes will reveal to you emotion, sensitivity, and/or understanding of his or her situation. Your client's openness and willingness to answer your questions will be indicated by eye contact with you. Anxiety, intimidation, closed-mindedness, and/or dishonesty will be indicated through the absence of eye contact. Keep in mind that the amount of eye contact varies from culture to culture, and remember to never force eye contact from your client during the questioning process.
3. Be aware that body language is always present in the communication process. Body language is less deliberate and mostly unconscious; therefore, your client's body language becomes more meaningful than his or her statements when responding to your questions. Body language will vary according to gender, race, ethnicity, age, and the like. Becoming skilled in understanding the factors that affect body language is relevant to successful client questioning.
4. Keep in mind that proximity is the distance between individuals and that the nearness of your client may indicate his or her feelings of interest and trust. Each client will have a different comfort zone in terms of how close he or she wants to be to you when answering questions, so you must read your client's body language and adjust nearness accordingly. The client who feels threatened by the counselor's closeness may avoid answering questions and the communication process will be damaged.
5. Adopt habits of active listening and verbal following to give you direction in your questioning. As a social worker, you must be skilled in understanding paralanguage or vocal cues that will communicate to you the feelings, intentions, and emotions of

your client. By actively listening to your client's paralanguage and following his or her words, you will be able to decipher whether your client is feeling fear, sorrow, happiness, or anger. This valuable *feeling insight* gives you the ability to ask appropriate questions that will result in giving you the information you need from your client.

6. Encourage client feedback. In so doing, your client will have the opportunity to ask questions that will serve to clarify any confusion and misconceptions. It will also give your client the chance to voice his or her disagreement with a statement you have made.

7. Describe the social worker role and method so that your client will have an idea of how you will help him or her with the situation or problem.

8. Reach for between-session data at the beginning of each session: this will bring you up-to-date on your client's situation. It also will identify the key topics that need to be discussed. Be flexible because your client's situation may have changed since your last meeting, and it is important that you adhere to the principle of "starting where the client is" (Sheafor & Horejsi, 2006, p. 147). (Refer to Chapter 10, Section Three, for multicultural and gender interviewing.)

(*Skill-building of Client Questioning sources:* Ambady, Bernieri, & Richeson, 2000; Beale, 2004; Brantley & Miller, 2002; *Journal of Behavior Development*, 2001; *Journal of Nursing*, 2002; Kirch, 1979; Krim, 1953; LaPlante & Ambady, 2003; Miley et al., 1998; Porter, 1969; Sheafor & Horejsi, 2006; Shulman, 1981; Sue & Sue, 2003)

Reflection.   Reflection is a team effort involving both you and your client. Events, thoughts, and feelings of the clients are acknowledged through reflection, and the proper strategies to assist each client in dealing with issues are identified (Miley et al., 1998; Sheafor & Horejsi, 2006). Let's again take a look at the reflection skills, types, and application covered in Chapter 11.

Reflection Skills

1. Empathy and understanding
2. Active listening, which requires that you:
   a. Maintain an open mind.
   b. Concentrate.
   c. Maintain eye contact.
   d. Have manners.
   e. Determine client explanation—organize information you are hearing.
   f. Use key words—help you to remember pertinent details.
   g. Analyze your client's message.
3. Communication skills—(Refer to Part Three, Chapter 4, What Are Verbal and Nonverbal Communication Skills?)

(*Reflection and Active Listener Skills sources*: Cournoyer & Stanley, 2002; Brantley & Miller, 2002; Miley et al., 1998)

Reflection Type and Application

1. **Reflection of Content.** Your client explains his or her situation or problem, and you then reflect back to your client your understanding of what has been said. Remember, to use paraphrasing style when reflecting content back to your client.
2. **Reflection of Feeling.** Reflection of feeling means that you can understand your client's verbal and nonverbal expressions of feelings about his or her situation or problem. Reflection of feeling also requires the ability to correctly communicate back to your client what has been expressed. Restate your client's expression of emotions with feeling words that are equivalent to the words he or she used. Do not use verbatim style when reflecting because you will sound emotionless about your client's situation, and your client may also view you as a phony.
3. **Reflection of Thinking or Meaning.** Reflection of thinking or meaning requires that you understand your client's thoughts and the meanings he or she is expressing about the situation or problem, and can correctly reflect back to your client what you heard. Reflection of thinking or meaning also requires that you encourage your client to explore the thoughts he or she has about the experiences surrounding the problem. Let your client express his or her thinking surrounding the problem or situation. Encouraging your client to explore various thoughts and feelings pertaining to his or her experiences will help your client gain a better understanding of the situation or problem.

(*Reflection Types and Applications sources:* Compton & Galaway, 1999; Miley et al., 1998; Sheafor & Horejsi, 2006)

Positive Confrontation and Information-giving.   As we noted in Chapter 12, the social worker who has perfected the art of positive confrontation skills provides honest communication to his or her clients. Remember, confrontation in social work needs to be seen as positive because it is a technique that social workers use in a tentative and nonjudgmental way to encourage a client to become aware of his or her thoughts, feelings, and behaviors.

Positive client confrontation is done in a gentle and respectful manner so that it:

1. Points out discrepancies between what your client says and does.
2. Addresses the unrecognized strengths of your client.
3. Fosters your client's strengths that are needed for change.
4. Encourages your client's learning and provides stimulus for change.
5. Assists your client in recognizing and eliminating a self-defeating attitude.

(*Positive Client Confrontation sources*: Compton & Galaway, 1999; Miley et al., 1998; Schmolling et al., 1993; Sheafor & Horejsi, 2006)

Remember, in order for client confrontation to be successful:

1. Show genuine concern for your client!
2. Make sure you have the time to work with and become more deeply involved with your client's thoughts, feelings, and behavior. Get to know your client.

3. Have respect for your client; your client must also respect you.
4. Recognize and support client strengths in your message.
5. Provide a detailed description of the client's self-defeating behavior while remaining nonjudgmental.
6. Make sure you have observations or data on which your message is based.

(*Successful Client Confrontation sources*: Compton & Galaway, 1999; Miley et al., 1998; Schmolling et al., 1993; Sheafor & Horejsi, 2006)

Types of Information-giving Responses.   The types of information-giving responses discussed in Chapter 12 included:

1. ***Orienting Statement,*** which provides your client with information about the interviewing process. The orienting statement:
   a. Introduces your client to the organization.
   b. Explains various steps in the helping process.
   c. Explains your role and the client's role.
   d. Explains the costs and benefits, as well as experiences, associated with the helping process.
2. ***Instructions or Directions,*** which provide your client with information about his or her role as you work together in the helping process. Instructions or directions also:
   a. Describe a proposed behavior and how to carry out the behavior.
   b. Point out the potential positive and negative consequences of the behavior.
3. ***Feedback,*** which assists your client in understanding various thoughts, feelings, and behaviors. Feedback also:
   a. Helps your client reflect on and change his or her behavior.
   b. Enables your client to attach his or her personal evaluations to the information you provided.
4. ***Alternative perspective (reframing),*** which reinterprets a behavior in a positive manner. Reframing:
   a. Helps your client to "look on the bright side."
   b. Potentially eliminates negative thoughts.
   c. Energizes your client by developing a positive outlook.
   d. Prevents problems from developing.
5. ***Informational statement,*** which provides an overview of information your client may need in reference to resources, people, or alternatives. When using informational statements:
   a. Match the information with your client's ability to benefit from it.
   b. Avoid overloading your client with too much information at one time.
   c. Break the information down into organized units.

(*Information-Giving Responses sources:* Compton & Galaway, 1999; Miley et al., 1998; Schmolling et al., 1993; Sheafor & Horejsi, 2006)

Information-Giving Guidelines

1. Recognize your client's need for information.
2. Provide the information to your client when required. Timing is critical!
3. Match the information to your client's current needs and goals.
4. Provide information when your client is most receptive.
5. Use professional attending skills and focus on your client's expressions of emotions and attitudes.
6. Maintain appropriate eye contact, voice tone, and body posture in order for your client to be receptive of your information.
7. Be direct, clear, concise and concrete when giving information to your client.
8. Divide information into organized units that your client can integrate or use.
9. Do not overload your client with too much information at once.
10. Maximize client information-giving by providing a follow-up response such as a brief statement or request.

(*Information-Giving Guidelines sources:* Compton & Galaway, 1999; Miley et al., 1998; Schmolling et al., 1993; Sheafor & Horejsi, 2006)

Communicating in a Rural Setting.   As noted in Chapter 13, social work practice is increasing in rural areas, and it is important that you understand the cultural characteristics of the rural community. Being aware of these cultural characteristics is the first step in building the cultural competence needed to enter the rural social work practice with accurate information and a thorough understanding of your clients' lifestyle and behaviors. Again, having accurate information and facts, along with being familiar with ethical issues that exist in a rural community, will enable you to communicate with those you serve in a professional and successful manner. Let's revisit the main components of the rural community that were discussed in Chapter 13.

Main Characteristics of a Rural Community

1. Rural areas are sparsely populated country communities with less than 2,500 citizens.
2. Privacy is considered an advantage to most people living in rural communities.
3. Community and kinship ties are strong in rural communities.
4. The economy in a rural area also includes mining operations, factories, and light industries.
5. Transportation is mostly through private car ownership owing to the lack of public transportation.
6. There are endless cultural characteristics in a rural community. Do your homework on the geographic area in which you plan to practice social work.

(*Rural Community Characteristics sources:* Fitchen, 1981; Henslin, 2005; Martinez-Brawley, 1980; Martinez-Brawley, 1980; Pugh, 2000; Sidell et al., 2006; Stoesen, 2002; U.S. Census Bureau, 2000)

Generalist Approach.   If you plan to practice social work in a rural community, it is best to take the generalist approach and learn a little bit about every field (Stoesen, 2002). Also, when practicing social work in a rural community, remember to:

1. Be forthright and consistent.
2. Expect to be visible to various clients every time you leave your home.
3. Expect to be exposed to social interaction with your clients.
4. Maintain a personal life and limit or avoid dual relationships with clients.

(*Generalist Approach and Practice sources:* Fenby, 1987; Ginsberg, 2005; Green, Gregory & Mason, 2003; NASW *Code of Ethics*, 1996; Pugh, 2000; Stoesen, 2002)

Congratulations! You are on your way to a bright and promising career in social work, having been exposed to basic communication skills necessary for success. Do not stop learning, growing, and applying these skills as you progress in your career.

REFERENCES

Ambady, N., Bernieri, F.J., & Richeson, J.A. (2000). Toward a history of social behavior: Judgmental accuracy from think slices of the behavioral stream. *Advance in Experimental Social Psychology, 32,* 201–207.

An author's guide to social work journals. (1997) National Association of Social Workers. Washington, DC: NASW Press.

Barthel, B., & Goldrick-Jones, A. (n.d.). *Resumés.* Retrieved October 18, 2005, from The Writing Center at Rensselaer Web Site: http://www.wecc.rpt.edu/

Beale, A.V. (2004). Body language speaks: Reading and responding more effectively to hidden communication. *Communication World, 21*(2), 18.

Beale, A.V. (2004). Tips for writing winning resumes: Answers to students' most frequently asked questions. *Techniques, 79*(5), 22–25.

Becvar, D. S. (1997). *Soul healing: A spiritual orientation in counseling and therapy.* New York: Basic Books.

Body Language. (2001). *Journal of Behavior Development, 25*(4), 344–353.

Body Language. (2002). *Journal of Nursing, 102*(1), 845.

Brantley, C.P., & Miller, MG. (2002). *Effective communication for colleges.* Cincinnati, OH: South-Western Educational Publishing.

Canda, E.R., & Furman, L.D. (1999). *Spiritual diversity in social work practice: The heart of helping.* New York: The Free Press.

Census 2000: Urban and Rural Classification. (2000). Retrieved March 10, 2006 from U.S. Census Bureau Web site: www.ask.census.gov

Colby, I., & Dziegielewski, S. (2001). *Social work: The people's profession.* Chicago: Lyceum Books.

Compton, B.R., & Galaway, B. (1999). *Social work processes.* Pacific Grove, CA: Brooks/Cole Publishing Company.

Cournoyer, B.R., & Stanley, M. J. (2002). *The social work portfolio: Planning, assessing and documenting lifelong learning in a dynamic profession.* Pacific Grove, CA: Brooks/Cole Publishing Company.

Darowski, W.A. (2005). *In the field: A real life survival guide for the social work internship.* Boston, MA: Allyn & Bacon.

Fenby, B.L. (1987). *Social work in a rural setting.* Washington, DC: National Association of Social Workers.

Fitchen, J.M., (1981). *Poverty in rural America: A case study.* Boulder, CO: Westview Press.

Fong, R. (2001). *Culturally competent social work practice: Past and present.* Boston, MA: Allyn & Bacon.

Galambos, C.M. (2003). Moving cultural diversity toward cultural competence in health care. *Health & Social Work, 28*(1), 3–4.

Garvin, C. (1997). *Interpersonal practice in social work: Promoting competence and social justice* (2nd ed.). Boston, MA: Allyn & Bacon.

Ginsberg, L. H. (2005). *Social work in rural communities,* 4th ed. Alexandria, VA: Council on Social Work Education.

Green, R., Gregory, R., & Mason, R. (2003). It's no picnic: Personal and family safety for rural social workers. *Australian Social Work, 56*(2), 94–106.

Hancock, M.R. (1997). Empowerment: Helping people take control of their lives. In M.R. Hancock, *Principles of social work practice: A generic practice approach* (pp. 229–251). Binghamton, NY: Haworth Press.

Hasenfeld, Y. (1987). Power in social work practice. *Social Service Review, 61*(3), 469–483.

Henslin, J.M. (2005). *Sociology: A down-to-earth approach.* Boston, MA: Allyn & Bacon.

Houston, S. (2002). *Reflections on habitus, field and capital: Towards a culturally sensitive social work.* London: Sage Publications.

How-to help on resumés (2003). Retrieved October 18, 2005 from the Mansfield University Office of Career Development Web Site: www.mansfield.edu/~careserv

Hultberg, R. (2002). Job search tips for social workers. *The New Social Worker, 9*(3)7.

Hyde, C.A. (2004). Multicultural development in human services agencies: Challenges and solutions. *Social Work, 49*(1), 7–10.

Kirch, M.S. (1979). Non-verbal communication across cultures. *Modern Language Journal, 63*(8), 416–423.

Krim, A. (1953). *A study in non-verbal communications: Expressive movements during interviews.* Northampton, MA: Smith College School for Social Work.

LaPlante, D., & Ambady, N. (2003). On how things are said: Voice tone, voice intensity, verbal content, and perceptions of politeness. *Journal of Language and Social Psychology, 22,* 434–440.

Linsley, J. (2002). Put it in writing: Tips on writing for professional publication. *The New Social Worker, 9*(4), 7–9.

Macionis, J.J. (2005). *Sociology.* Upper Saddle River, NJ: Pearson Education.

Mama, R.S. (2001). Preparing social work students to work in culturally diverse settings. *Social Work Education, 20*(3), 373–383.

Martinez-Brawley, E.E. (1980). Identifying and describing the context of *rural* in social work. *Aretau, 6*(2), 21–32.

Miley, K.K., O'Melia, M., & DuBois, B. (1998). *Generalist social work practice: An empowering approach.* Needham Heights, MA: Allyn & Bacon.

Morales, A.T., & Sheafor, B. W. (1998). *Social work: A profession of many faces.* Needham Heights, MA: Allyn & Bacon.

National Association of Social Workers. (1996). NASW *Code of Ethics.* Washington, DC: Author.

National Association of Social Workers. (1997). *NASW Code of Ethics.* Washington, DC: NASW Press.

Neuman, W.L. (2003). *Social research methods: Qualitative and quantitative approaches.* Boston, MA: Pearson Education.

Okayama, C.M., Furuto, S.B.C.L., & Edmondson, J. (2001). Components of cultural competence: Attitudes, knowledge, and skills. In R. Fong, *Culturally competent social work practice: Past and present* (pp. 89–99). Boston, MA: Allyn & Bacon.

Oldaker, A., & Olson, A. (2005). *Cover letters: Preparing to write a cover letter.* Retrieved October 26, 2005 from The Writing Lab & OWL Purdue University Web Site: http://owl.english.purdue.edu/

Pinderhughes, E.B. (1983). Empowerment for our clients and for ourselves. *Social Casework: The Journal of Contemporary Social Work, 64*(6), 331–338.

Porter, G.W. (1969). Non-verbal communications. *Training and Development Journal, 23,* 7–8.

Pugh, R. (2000). *Rural social work.* Dorset: Russell House Publishing.

Reamer, F.G. (1998). *Ethical standards in social work: A review of the NASW Code of Ethics*. Washington, DC: NASW Press.

Reamer, F.G. (2004). *Ethical standards in social work*. Washington, DC: NASW Press.

Roberts, A.R., & Greene, G.J. (2002). *Social workers' desk reference*. New York: Oxford University Press.

Rubin, A., & Babbie, E. (2001). *Research methods for social work*. Belmont, CA: Wadsworth/Thomson Learning.

Schmolling, P., Youkeles, M., & Burger, W.R. (1993). *Human Services in Contemporary America*. Pacific Grove, CA: Brooks/Cole Publishing Company.

Seaton, C. (2003). Empowered use of self in social work: Understanding personal narrative through guided autobiography. *Social Work & Christianity, 31*(1), 51–77.

Sheafor, B.W., & Horejsi, C.R. (2006). *Techniques and guidelines for social work practice*. Boston, MA: Pearson Education.

Sheridan, M.J. (2001). Defining spirituality sensitive social work practice: An essay review of spiritual diversity in social work practice: The heart of helping. *Social Work, 46*(1), 87–92.

Shulman, L. (1981). *Identifying, measuring and teaching helping skills*. New York: CSWE.

Shulman, L. (1993). *Interactional supervision*. Washington, DC: NASW Press.

Sidell, N., Boughton, B., Hull, P., Ertz, R., Seeley, K., & Wieder, J. (2006). Country life: Joys, challenges and attitudes of rural social workers. *Rural Social Work and Community Practice, 10*(2), 28–35.

Sue, D.W., & Sue, D. (2003). *Counseling the culturally diverse: Theory and Practice*. New York: John Wiley & Sons.

Stoesen, L. (2002). Reconnecting to a historical foundation: Rural social workers embrace challenge. *NASW News*.

Wilson, S.J. (1976). *Recording: Guidelines for social workers*. New York: The Free Press.

Writing the resumé. (1999). Retrieved October 18, 2005 from Hunter College Reading/Writing Center Web Site: http://rwc.hunter.cuny.edu

INDEX